# PUNISHMENT

*James A. McCafferty*

Aldine • Atherton
*Chicago & New York*

FOR JANE

The comments in this reader reflect the views of the the editor and the contributors and not necessarily those of the Federal judiciary or those of the Administrative Office of the U.S. Courts.

*Capital Punishment*
edited by James A. McCafferty



First published 1972 by
Aldine • Atherton, Inc.
529 South Wabash Avenue
Chicago, Illinois 60605

Library of Congress Catalog Number 74-169503
ISBN 0-202-30238-5, cloth; 0-202-30239-3, paper

Printed in the United States of America
DESIGNED BY LORETTA LI

CAPITAL PUNISHMENT

*Consulting Editor*

GILBERT GEIS
*California State College, Los Angeles*
SOCIAL PROBLEMS

## *The Editor*

JAMES A. McCAFFERTY is Assistant Chief of Operations, Division of Information Systems, Administrative Office of the United States Courts. He served as a criminologist with the United States Bureau of Prisons for 12 years prior to his present position. His M.A. thesis, *Capital Punishment in the United States, 1930–1952,* is a comprehensive study of the subject. He has written several articles on capital punishment, including a research study published as part of a Maryland Legislative Council report on Capital Punishment (1962). He has also written several articles on Judicial statistics. Mr. McCafferty received his B.S. and M.A. at The Ohio State University. He has done advanced graduate work and taught at American University, Washington, D. C.

# CAPITAL

EDITED BY

# Preface

The most challenging contributions to the capital punishment controversy of the twentieth century were made during the 1960s. The 1970s promise a resolution of what has been an endless and arduous debate.

Most of the research and independent studies on the subject of capital punishment were produced during the last decade. Therefore, it was a demanding task to select articles that represent an evenhanded discussion of the controversy and include a meaningful dialogue between the proponents and opponents of the death penalty. The major effort was to provide readers with recent writings that tend to illustrate selected points. The material herein represents only a fraction of the recent literature on capital punishment.

Capital punishment has been debated since the founding of this country both in small groups and in the halls of the state legislatures and the Congress of the United States. Emotions often run counter to reasonable discussion. Capital punishment advocates conjure up crime victims who have met horrible deaths by shooting, poisoning, strangling, butchery and other horrors. Capital punishment opponents describe the whine of the electric generator as it surges a charge of electricity through the condemned's body, his gasp for air in the gaseous asphyxiation chamber, or the snap of the rope and the death rattle of the body at the end of the hangman's noose. Instead of attending to such material, this book is dedicated to a nonemotional, rational study of capital punishment.

This book is prepared for those students of human behavior who seek relevant information about what is happening in a crucial area of the criminal justice system. Sir Winston Churchill noted that "the mood and temper of the people with regard to the treatment of crime and criminals is one of the unfailing tests of the civilization of any country." Those who speak of rehabilitation of offenders on the one hand and, on the other hand, signify their acceptance of capital punishment are faced with a difficult "mind bending" situation. Herein lies a possible credibility gap between our effort to maintain life and the complete destruction of the lives of condemned persons. It is the responsibility of today's students, who will be future leaders, to determine what protections are needed from the wanton killer who seemingly cannot be deterred except by the ultimate penalty.

Unlike many social issues there is no real middle ground in the capital punishment controversy. Both sides of the controversy will be told here. It will be the responsibility of the reader to determine which set of arguments best supports his position. Whether the choice is to oppose or to defend the death penalty, the decision will be reinforced or eroded by day-to-day events.

A word on style: instead of a complete presentation in the Introduction, I have used the beginning of each chapter to develop the overall exposition. Collectively, the introductory statements should provide a thorough picture of the capital punishment controversy.

I am indebted to my friends who permitted me to republish their contributions. Because of space limitations, fully one-half of the material for which permission for publication was obtained had to be set aside. Special acknowledgements go to Dr. Gilbert Geis, who suggested this controversy, to Dr. Walter C. Reckless, who advised me on my thesis on capital punishment at The Ohio State University and to Victor Evjen, who as editor of *Federal Probation* asked me to write on this subject some years ago. Thanks to my wife and children, Cindy, Stanley and Bridget for permitting me to put aside household chores so that I could devote time to preparation of this material. Nancy Hunt and Mrs. Sally Howley assisted in the preparation of the manuscript and David Martin helped with the bibliography.

Finally, my thanks to you the reader as you study this subject. Look to this volume and to the many other writings on capital punishment with special reference to the selected bibliography. The use or disuse of capital punishment indicates society's response to questions going directly to the issues bearing on the preservation of civilization.

# *Contents*

*Preface* vii

*Introduction* 1
JAMES A. MCCAFFERTY

**Part I Facts and Figures** 5

1 : *General Introduction* 7
HUGO A. BEDAU

2 : *The Use of the Death Penalty: A Factual Statement* 38
WALTER C. RECKLESS

**Part II The Issues** 63

3 : *The Capital Punishment Controversy* 65
WILLIAM O. HOCHKAMMER, JR.

**Part III Proponents of Capital Punishment** 85

4 : *In Favor of Capital Punishment* 89
JACQUES BARZUN

5 : *On Deterrence and the Death Penalty* 102
ERNEST VAN DEN HAAG

6 : *Capital Punishment: Your Protection and Mine* 117
EDWARD J. ALLEN

7 : *A Prosecutor Looks at Capital Punishment* 129
RICHARD E. GERSTEIN

8 : *The Death Penalty* 140
JAMES V. BENNETT

**Part IV Opponents of Capital Punishment** 157

9 : *Capital Punishment as Seen by a Correctional Administrator* 161
RICHARD A. MCGEE

10 : *To Abolish the Death Penalty* 176
RAMSEY CLARK

11 : *Capital Punishment: The Challenge of Crime in a Free Society* 181
PRESIDENT'S COMMISSION ON LAW ENFORCEMENT AND ADMINISTRATION OF JUSTICE

12 : *Thou Shalt Not Kill* 185
JUDICATURE

13 : *For Whom the Chair Waits* 187
SARA R. EHRMANN

14 : *Let's Abolish Capital Punishment* 218
VICTOR H. EVJEN

**Part V Attack on the Death Penalty** 225

15 : *Varieties of Attack on the Death Penalty* 231
JACK GREENBERG and JACK HIMMELSTEIN

16 : *The Supreme Court, Cruel and Unusual Punishment, and the Death Penalty* 245
SOL RUBIN

*For Further Reading* 262

*Index* 267

# CAPITAL PUNISHMENT

# *Introduction*

JAMES A. McCAFFERTY

During the 1960s sentences of death and the actual imposition of such sentences grew increasingly further apart. During the early part of the decade, an average of 100 persons were sentenced to death each year. About 15 of these were ultimately executed. In the final four years of the sixties, the number of persons sentenced to death remained the same, but only three persons were executed.

To some extent, the decrease in executions has been the result of automatic appeals and executive reprieves, both of which result in further delay. Outright commutation to life imprisonment, such as was announced in 1971 by Governor Winthrop Rockefeller for 15 men in Arkansas's death row, brought to a finality the moratorium on executions in that state. Signaling his long opposition to the death penalty, the Governor was the first state executive to commute all death sentences. He announced that the individual records of the nine men convicted of murder and the six sentenced for rape were not relevant to his decision.

Why has capital punishment become a national concern? The reason appears to be that for the first time in American jurisprudence, appeals have been taken into both State and Federal courts on behalf of capital offenders. This effort has been organized by groups of citizens who are unalterably opposed to the death sentence. Pending the disposition of such appeals, the use of capital punishment has been held in abeyance.

As we move through the seventies, it appears that the imposition of the death sentence may become more infrequent. This may indicate that, generally, American society is disowning the death sentence as a practice, though maintaining it as a visible control on the statute books.

Our ambivalence regarding the death sentence, that is, our willingness to sentence a person to death but our unwillingness to have this sentence carried out, has created a serious problem for American criminal justice processes. A growing number of persons wait in the "death rows" of the various states. At the beginning of the sixties the number of individuals held under death sentences stood at 189. In 1970, there were 623 persons (including three women) on "death rows" across the United States.

For those who were convicted and sentenced to be executed, hope rests in continuous appeals and reprieves. What alchemy of events prevents executions? What brings about reprieves, reversals of sentences, mental breakdowns resulting in transfers to mental hospitals, or outright commutation by executive order, removing the possibility of "walking the last mile"? In the 1960s about one out of ten persons sentenced to death was executed. Can capital punishment be regarded as equitable when the death sentence is not applied to nine out of ten persons sentenced to death? Or have we built in such protections that only the most heinous offenders are executed? Does the one execution out of ten represent more than a random imposition of the death sentence?

The articles presented here provide an overview for a serious study of capital punishment. The burden of proof has been on those persons who seek the repeal of capital punishment statutes. Those who support capital punishment can continue to do so merely by remaining silent. The proponents recognize that it is difficult to overturn a practice that has historically been a part of man's control over man.

# I Facts and Figures

An understanding of the death penalty needs to be based on some fundamental facts and figures. Therefore, it is appropriate to begin this controversy with a statement about the origins of capital punishment. The first article is taken from Hugo Adam Bedau's vigorous anthology, *The Death Penalty in America.* Bedau has compressed into a few pages a description of capital punishment as it existed under English criminal law, with its monstrous list of capital offenses, in the sixteenth century. Conviction for any of these offenses called for a death sentence; in those rare instances when the sentence was not imposed, lands and property, together with all right of inheritance, were forfeited.

Bedau's background article explains the derivation of the death penalty laws in the American colonies and the effort by the colonists to move away from this English heritage through a redefinition of the crime of murder. It details the development of new methods of execution and provisions for private execution. Courts were given the option to sentence defendants to death or to life imprisonment at this time, a procedure offering the first opportunity in Anglo-Saxon history to recognize differences in culpability.

The second article included in this section is by Walter C. Reckless. It brings together the legal status of capital punishment in the world and in the United States as well as the available factual insights into the deterrent effect. Reckless's article reviews data and research that shed light on the effect of abolition and the restricted use of the death penalty on homicide and crimes of violence. Reckless uses the official United States government executions reports as well as studies by Clarence H. Patrick and James A. McCafferty to build a statistical base for his article. He shows that there is no evidence that capital punishment provides deterrence. Using studies of homicide rates in contiguous states, Reckless notes that the evidence shows no discernible effect of capital punishment. Nor do homicide rates appear to change in periods before, during or after abolition. In those states which impose capital punishment, according to Reckless, there is no significant increase in murders before or after an execution.

The Reckless article offers a beginning point from which the reader can determine if there has been a major change in policy toward the death penalty.

# 1 *General Introduction*

## HUGO A. BEDAU

American criminal law was not created out of nothing by the original colonists and the Founding Fathers. Rather, it took its shape directly from English criminal law of the sixteenth, seventeenth and eighteenth centuries. In order to appreciate the structure that this tradition imparted to the American law of capital punishment, it is necessary to review, if only briefly, the experience in England with the death penalty during our nation's formative years. Accordingly, in the following paragraphs, we shall examine the main features of the capital laws of England as a foundation for a study of the pattern of capital laws in colonial America. With this background of English and early American law in mind, we will then be in a position to appreciate the major American innovations in capital punishment developed during the past century and a half (privacy of executions, redefinition of the crime of murder, new methods of execution, and optional death penalties), innovations that give distinctive shape to this mode of punishment as it now exists in our country.

## Capital Punishment in England and America: "The Bloody Code"

By the end of the fifteenth century, English law recognized eight major capital crimes: treason (including attempts and conspiracies), petty treason (killing of a husband by his wife), murder (killing a person with "malice"), larceny, robbery, burglary, rape and arson.[1] Under the Tudors and Stuarts, many more crimes entered this category. By 1688 there were nearly fifty. During the reign of George II, nearly three dozen more were added, and under George III the total was increased by sixty. The highpoint was reached shortly after 1800. One estimate put the number of capital crimes at 223 as late as 1819. It is impossible to detail here the incredible variety of offenses involved. Crimes of every description against the state, against the person, against property, against the public peace were made punishable by death. Even with fairly lax enforcement after 1800, between 2,000 and 3,000 persons were sentenced to death each year from 1805 to 1810.[2]

Conviction of a capital offense, whether or not sentence was executed, resulted in attainder: forfeiture of all lands and property, and denial of all right of inheritance ("corruption of blood"). Although appeal of the death sentence itself to a higher tribunal was all but impossible, the descendants of an executed criminal occasionally succeeded in appealing the attainder.

The usual mode of execution was hanging, though there were several crimes for which this was deemed insufficient. The bodies of pirates were hung in chains from specially built gibbet irons along the wharves of London. Throughout England, the rotting corpses of executed criminals dotted the countryside, a grim warning to other malefactors. Executions were always conducted in public and often became the scene of drunken revels. Thackeray's vivid description is famous; he wrote in part:

> I must confess . . . that the sight has left on my mind an extraordinary feeling of terror and shame. It seems to me that I have been abetting an act of frightful wickedness and violence, performed by a set of men against one of their fellows; and I pray God that it may soon be out of the power of any man in England to witness such a hideous and degrading sight. Forty thousand persons (say the Sheriffs), of all ranks and degrees—mechanics, gentlemen, pickpockets, members of both Houses of Parliament, street-walkers, newspaper-writers, gather together before Newgate at a very early hour: the most part of them give up their natural quiet night's rest, in order to partake of this hideous debauchery, which is more exciting than sleep, or than wine, or the last new ballet, or any other amusement they can have. . . .[3]

Traitors, whether guilty of petty or high treason, were subject to especially aggravated forms of execution. Burning to death was the fate of many a woman convicted of killing her husband. As late as 1786, a crowd of thousands watched as one Phoebe Harris was burned at the stake. But the worst punishment was reserved for criminals guilty of high treason. When Sir Walter Raleigh touched the headsman's sword, he is supposed to have quipped, " 'Tis a sharp medicine." Beheading was the least of it. The standard practice, according to the great authority on English law, Sir William Blackstone, consisted of drawing, hanging, disemboweling, and then beheading, followed by quartering.[4] In 1812, this death sentence was pronounced in England on seven men convicted of high treason:

> That you and each of you, be taken to the place from whence you came, and from thence be drawn on a hurdle to the place of execution, where you shall be hanged by the neck, not till you are dead; that you be severally taken down, while yet alive, and your bowels be taken out and burnt before your faces—that your heads be then cut off, and your bodies cut into four quarters, to be at the King's disposal. And God have mercy on your souls.[5]

This "bloody code," as Arthur Koestler has called it, with its scores of capital offenses and almost daily public executions, was considerably mitigated by benefit of clergy and the Royal prerogative of mercy. Benefit of clergy arose from the struggle between church and state in England, and it originally provided that priests, monks and other clerics were to be remanded from secular to ecclesiastical jurisdiction for trial on indictment of felony. In later centuries, this privilege was applied in ordinary criminal courts to more and more persons and for an ever larger number of felonies. Eventually, all persons accused of capital crimes were spared a death sentence if the crime was a first felony offense and if it was clergyable, provided only the criminal could recite the "Neck verse" (the opening lines of Psalm LI), this being construed by the court as proof of his literate (and thus clerical) status. Benefit of clergy became in effect the fictional device whereby first offenders were given a lesser punishment.[6]

A far different practice having a comparable effect was the trial court's frequent recommendation to the Crown that mercy be granted. Such recommendations were natural enough, since the judge had no alternative upon the conviction of an accused but to sentence him to death; all felonies carried a mandatory death penalty. Because the court's plea for mercy was usually granted (even during the years when Parliament was increasing the number of capital crimes!), hundreds of persons convicted and sentenced to death were not executed. Instead, they were transported to the colonies. During the last decade of the eighteenth century, in London and Middlesex alone, more than two-thirds of all death sentences were reversed through the Royal prerogative of mercy. Although death sentences issued annually throughout England sometimes ran in the thousands, by the 1800's executions apparently never exceeded seventy.[7]

Near the end of his *Commentaries,* Blackstone paused to reflect on the system of criminal justice whose workings he had so thoroughly described (and which has been only summarily outlined above). He said, speaking particularly of the methods of execution,

> Disgusting as this catalogue may seem, it will afford pleasure to an English reader and do honor to the English law, to compare it with that shocking apparatus of death and torment to be met with in the criminal codes of almost every other nation in Europe.[8]

It would never have occurred to Blackstone to measure England's criminal law by that prescribed in her colonies across the Atlantic. But were he to have made the comparison, he would have found it somewhat less than flattering to the mother country.

The American colonies had no uniform criminal law. The range of variation during the seventeenth and eighteenth centuries, so far as capital punishment is concerned, was considerable. It may be gauged from the differences in the penal codes of Massachusetts, Pennsylvania, and North Carolina. The earliest recorded set of capital statutes on these shores are those of the Massachusetts Bay Colony, dating from 1636. This early codification, titled "The Capitall Lawes of New-England," lists in order the following crimes: idolatry, witchcraft, blasphemy, murder ("manslaughter, committed upon premeditate malice, hatred, or cruelty, not in a man's necessary and just defense, nor by mere casualtie, against his will"), assault in sudden anger, sodomy, buggery, adultery, statutory rape, rape (punishment of death optional), man-stealing, perjury in a capital trial, and rebellion (including attempts and conspiracies).[9] Each of these crimes was accompanied in the statute with an Old Testament text as its authority. How rigorously these laws were enforced is not known, nor is it known why the rest of the nearly three dozen capital laws in the Mosaic Code were not also adopted in the Bay Colony.

In later decades, this theocratic criminal code gave way in all but a few respects to purely secular needs. Before 1700, arson and treason, as well as the third offense of theft of goods valued at over forty shillings, were made capital, despite the absence of any biblical justification. By 1785, the Commonwealth of Massachusetts recognized nine capital crimes, and they bore only slight resemblance to the thirteen "Capitall Lawes" of the Bay Colony: treason, piracy, murder, sodomy, buggery, rape, robbery, arson and burglary.[10]

Far milder than the Massachusetts laws were those adopted in South Jersey and Pennsylvania by the original Quaker colonists. The Royal charter for South Jersey in 1646 did not prescribe the death penalty for any crime, and there was no execution in this colony until 1691.[11] In Pennsylvania, William Penn's Great Act of 1682 specifically confined the death penalty to the crimes of treason and murder. These ambitious efforts to reduce the number of capital crimes were defeated early in the eighteenth century when the colonies were required to adopt, at the direction of the Crown, a far harsher penal code. By the time of the War of Independence, many of the colonies had roughly comparable capital statutes. Murder, treason, piracy, arson, rape, robbery, burglary, sodomy, and, from time to time, counterfeiting, horse-theft, and slave rebellion—all were usually punishable by death. Benefit of clergy was never widely permitted,[12] and hanging was the usual method of inflicting the death penalty.

Some states, however, preserved a severer code. As late as 1837, North Carolina required death for all the following crimes: murder, rape, statutory rape, arson, castration, burglary, highway robbery, stealing bank notes, slave-stealing, "the crime against nature" (buggery, sodomy, bestiality), duelling if death ensues, burning a public building, assault with intent to kill, breaking out of jail if under a capital indictment, concealing a slave with intent to free him, taking a free Negro or mulatto out of the state with intent to sell him into slavery; the second offense of forgery, mayhem, inciting slaves to insurrection, or of circulating seditious literature among slaves; being an accessory to murder, robbery, burglary, arson, or mayhem. Highway robbery and bigamy, both capitally punishable, were also clergyable.[13] This harsh code persisted so long in North Carolina partly because the state had no penitentiary and thus had no suitable alternative to the death penalty.

## The Movement for Reform

In England, the first of hundreds of capital statutes to be repealed early in the last century was a law enacted in 1565 which made picking pockets a capital offense; it was abolished in 1810 "without opposition or comment."[14] Penal reform in America dates from about the same period,[15] and was inspired by the same continental thinkers who stimulated reform in England. In May 1787, Dr. Benjamin Rush (1745–1813) gave a lecture in Benjamin Franklin's house in Philadelphia to a group of friends, recommending the construction of a "House of Reform," a penitentiary, so that criminals could be taken off the streets and detained until purged of their antisocial habits. A little over a year later, Rush followed this lecture with an essay, entitled "Inquiry into the Justice and Policy of Punishing Murder by Death." He argued its impolicy and injustice. This essay, published a few years later, became the first of several memorable pamphlets originating in this country to urge the cause of abolition, and Dr. Rush is usually credited with being the father of the movement to abolish capital punishment in the United States.

Rush's argument was based on the analysis originating with the Italian jurist, Cesare Beccaria, whose book, *On Crimes and Punishments,* had been published a generation earlier and had stirred all European intellectuals. The main points of Rush's argument were simple enough: scriptural support for the death penalty was spurious; the threat of hanging does not deter but increases crime; when a government puts one of its citizens to death, it exceeds the powers entrusted to it. In the years immediately following the publication of Rush's essay, several other prominent citizens in Philadelphia, notably Franklin and the Attorney General, William Bradford, gave their support to reform of the capital laws. In 1794, they achieved the repeal of the death penalty for all crimes in Pennsylvania except for the crime of "first degree" murder.

These reforms in Pennsylvania had few immediate influences in other states. Whereas in England, Samuel Romilly began to make a Pariliamentary career for himself in the service of penal reform, in the United States no major public figures emerged as leaders in this movement until several decades later. The most distinguished American lawyer in this group was Edward Livingston (1764–1836). Under commission from the Louisiana legislature, and inspired by the radical approach to crime and punishment being preached with such persuasiveness in France and England, Livingston prepared a revolutionary penal code for Louisiana. At the center of his proposals, he insisted, was "the total abolition of capital punishment."[16] The legislature was not convinced, and it rejected most of his recommendations, including this one. Livingston did not live long enough to learn that during the next half-century, the leading piece of anti-capital punishment propaganda in the United States was a thirty-page excerpt from his model Louisiana code.[17]

Not until the 1830's did the literary efforts of Rush and Livingston begin to bear fruit. By this time, the legislatures in several states (notably Maine, Massachusetts, Ohio, New Jersey, New York and Pennsylvania) were besieged each year with petitions on behalf of abolition from their constituents. Special legislative committees were formed to receive these messages, hold hearings, and submit recommendations. Anti-gallows societies came into being in every state along the eastern seaboard, and in 1845 an American Society for the Abolition of Capital Punishment was organized.[18] With the forces arrayed against slavery and saloons, the anti-gallows societies were among the most prominent groups struggling for social reform in America.

The highwater mark was reached in the later 1840's, when Horace Greeley, the editor and founder of the *New York Tribune,* became one of the nation's leading critics of the death penalty. In New York, Massachusetts and Pennsylvania, abolition bills were constantly before the legislature. Then, in 1846, the

Territory of Michigan voted to abolish hanging and to replace it with life imprisonment for all crimes save treason. This law took effect on March 1, 1847, and Michigan became the first English-speaking jurisdiction in the world to abolish the death penalty, for all practical purposes.[19] In 1852, Rhode Island abolished the gallows for all crimes, including treason; the next year Wisconsin did likewise. In several other states, capital punishment for many lesser crimes was replaced by life imprisonment, and other reforms affecting the administration of the death penalty were adopted. By the middle of the last century in most of the northern and eastern states, only treason and murder universally remained as capitally punishable crimes. Few states outside the South had more than one or two additional capital offenses. The anti-gallows movement rapidly lost its momentum, however, as the moral and political energies of the nation became increasingly absorbed in the struggle over slavery.

After the Civil War and the Reconstruction Era, both Iowa and Maine abolished the death penalty, only to restore it promptly. In 1887, Maine again abolished it, thereby becoming the first American jurisdiction which has twice voted to end the death penalty. During this period, the federal government, after extensive debate in Congress, did reduce its dozens of capital crimes to three: murder, treason and rape (and for none was death mandatory). Colorado abolished the death penalty for a few years, but reinstated it in the face of what at the time seemed the threat of mob rule. In that state, public dissatisfaction with mere imprisonment twice resulted in lynchings during the abolition years.

Between the peak of the Progressive Era and the years when women got the vote and whiskey got the gate, no less than eight states—Kansas, Minnesota, Washington, Oregon, North and South Dakota, Tennessee, and Arizona—abolished the death penalty for murder and for most other crimes. In only a few states did the reform last, however. By 1921, Tennessee, Arizona, Washington, Oregon and Missouri had reinstated it. During the Prohibition Era, when law enforcement often verged on total collapse, the abolitionists were nearly routed in several states.

Had it not been for the persuasive voices of Clarence Darrow, the great "attorney for the damned," and of Lewis E. Lawes, the renowned warden of Sing Sing Prison, and the organization in 1927 of the American League to Abolish Capital Punishment, the lawless era of the twenties might have seen the death penalty reintroduced in every state in the Union.

Throughout this period in England, the abolition movement remained somewhat more popular. Primarily through the dedicated efforts of Roy Calvert, a Select Committee of the House of Commons studied the issue and published a scholarly report in 1931. Although they recommended an experimental period of five years without the death penalty,[20] no action was taken by the government. Immediately after the end of World War II, while the Labor Party controlled the government, several Labor M.P.s struggled to have their Party vote out the death penalty, as abolition was one of the social reforms that labor and socialist parties in many countries had promised for decades. Even so, the government was not receptive. In 1949 it created a Royal Commission on Capital Punishment and suspended all executions. But the Commission was expressly forbidden to consider whether the death penalty should be abolished. Nevertheless, it was these investigations, stretching over four years, which set off the current wave of agitation against the death penalty in the Commonwealth countries and in the United States.

It was quite clear that the Royal Commissioners favored complete abolition as the best solution to the complex legal and penal problems they were forced to face, even though their explicit recommendations (eventually embodied in an unrecognizable form in the Homicide Act of 1957) were required to fall short of this radical position. No sooner was their report published than the Canadian Parliament established its own inquiry into capital punishment, and several United States experts gave testimony at these hearings. Concurrently, debates at the United Nations often touched on the compatibility of the state's right to kill and the individual's right to live.[21] Many of the delegates, especially the Scandinavian, Benelux, and Latin American representatives, were from nations that had long abandoned recourse to the executioner in peace time. Thus it was that several American organizations, notably the Society of Friends and the American League to Abolish Capital Punishment, were encouraged to restimulate public interest against the death penalty in the United States as well.

By the later 1950's, abolition groups were once again active and moderately well organized in nearly two dozen death penalty states in this country. Public hearings on abolition bills were again echoing in legislative chambers, reminiscent of the 1840's and 1910's. Except for Delaware, where the death penalty was abolished in 1958, abolitionists were able to obtain no more than a few legislative committee reports in their favor. Suddenly, in November 1964, all capital penalities in Oregon were voted out by a large majority, and the log jam was broken. Within six months, New York and three other states followed suit.

The checkered pattern of experiment with abolition in the United States from 1846 to date [to 1965, Ed.] is summarized in Table 1.1.

## Major Trends in Capital Punishment

The focus of the abolition movement in America has always been on reform of the punishment for murder, as most death sentences and executions have been for this crime. Not many observers have noticed that in recent years capital punishment for certain other crimes has been quietly removed from the statute books, even though the death penalty for murder has remained unaltered. For instance, in 1961, Nevada dropped trainwrecking from its list of capital crimes, and Illinois repealed the death penalty for dynamiting. On the whole, however, many more capital statutes have been added during this century than have been removed, and considerable publicity has surrounded these additions. The best known example is the crime of kidnapping, which, in one form or another (usually kidnapping for ransom, or kidnapping where the victim is not released unharmed), was elevated to capital status in over two dozen states during the 1930's, after the death of the kidnapped Lindbergh baby in

1932. Revenge and deterrence seem to be about equally powerful motives in the minds of most of those who favored making this crime a capital offense.

There have been other occasions when particularly shocking crimes have provoked this response. After President William McKinley was assassinated in 1901, Connecticut and New Jersey

TABLE 1.1: *Abolition of Death Penalties in the United States*

| *Jurisdiction* | *Date of Abolition* | *Date of Restoration* | *Date of Reabolition* |
|---|---|---|---|
| Michigan | 1846[a] | — | — |
| Rhode Island | 1852[b] | — | — |
| Wisconsin | 1853 | — | — |
| Iowa | 1872 | 1878 | 1965 |
| Maine | 1876[c] | 1883 | 1887 |
| Colorado | 1897 | 1901 | — |
| Kansas | 1907[d] | 1935 | — |
| Minnesota | 1911 | — | — |
| Washington | 1913 | 1919 | — |
| Oregon | 1914 | 1920 | 1964 |
| North Dakota | 1915[e] | — | — |
| South Dakota | 1915 | 1917 | — |
| Tennessee | 1915[f] | 1917 | — |
| Arizona | 1916 | 1918 | — |
| Missouri | 1917 | 1919 | — |
| Puerto Rico | 1917 | 1919 | 1929 |
| Alaska | 1957 | — | — |
| Hawaii | 1957 | — | — |
| Virgin Islands | 1957 | — | — |
| Delaware | 1958 | 1961 | — |
| West Virginia | 1965 | — | — |
| Vermont | 1965[g] | — | — |
| New York | 1965[h] | — | — |

[a] Death penalty retained for treason until 1963.

[b] Death penalty restored in 1882 for any life term convict who commits murder.

[c] In 1837 a law was passed to provide that no condemned person could be executed until one year after his sentencing and then only upon a warrant from the Governor.

[d] In 1872 a law was passed similar to the 1837 Maine statute (see note c above).

[e] Death penalty retained for murder by a prisoner serving a life term for murder.

[f] Death penalty retained for rape.

[g] Death penalty retained for murder of a police officer on duty or guard or by a prisoner guilty of a prior murder, kidnapping for ransom, and killing or destruction of vital property by a group during wartime.

[h] Death penalty retained for murder of a police officer on duty, or of anyone by a prisoner under life sentence.

made murder or attempted murder of a high public official a capital crime. Airplane bombings in 1958–59, air piracy in 1960–61, and the assassination of President Kennedy in November 1963, led Congress to make such offenses punishable by death under Federal law. Most capital statutes added during the past generation cannot be traced to any such spectacular causes; e.g., providing narcotics to a minor (1946, Federal law), espionage violations of the Atomic Energy Act (1946, Federal law), assault by a life term prisoner (1939, Pennsylvania; 1941, California), armed robbery (1955, Tennessee; 1957, Georgia), third offense of a capital crime after having received mercy at the prior convictions (1955, South Carolina). Very few death sentences have issued from these novel laws, and even fewer executions. Yet their number and variety is undeniable evidence that the death penalty is still believed in many quarters to be an effective deterrent and an appropriate punishment for several different kinds of crime.

The ostensible failure of the abolition movement in this country, after a century and a half of effort, may be in part attributable to the weakness of the arguments and the fickleness of the sentiments on which they are based. It may also be because only a few Americans in each generation bother to inform themselves on the facts surrounding the actual use of the death penalty and on the merits of the abolitionist's position. Furthermore, support for the death penalty may rest on attitudes that are nearly universal, unconscious and impervious to rational persuasion. But it is far more likely that the very reforms in the administration of capital punishment, the hard-won results of the struggle for abolition during the last century, have paradoxically become the major obstacles to further statutory repeal. They have mitigated the rigidity and brutality of this form of punishment to a point where the average citizen no longer regards it as an affront to his moral sensibilities. As a consequence, he has no strong motive to press for further reduction, much less complete abolition, of the death penalty. The reforms referred to here are several, but four of them are particularly important: the disappearance of violent and repulsive modes of carrying out the sentence; the protection of the general public from exposure to executions; the limitation of the death penalty to the highest degree of murder; and the extension of authority to the trial jury in capital cases to grant imprisonment rather than death as the punishment.[22] As all these reforms originated in the United States, and as each is an integral part of our present system of capital punishment in every jurisdiction, they deserve the closest attention.

## *Methods of Execution*

The variety of ways in which men have put one another to death under the law is appalling. History records such exotic practices (fortunately, largely unknown in the Anglo-American tradition) as flaying and impaling, boiling in oil, crucifixion, pulling asunder, breaking on the wheel, burying alive, and sawing in half. But not so many generations ago, in both England and America, criminals were occasionally pressed to death, drawn and quartered, and burned at the stake. Had any of these punishments survived the eighteenth century, there is little doubt that public reaction would have forced an end to capital punishment long ago.

Originally, the purpose of *peine forte et dure* (pressing to death) was to force an accused person to plead to an indictment. Such tactics became necessary because anyone who refused to plead to a felony indictment (that is, refused to plead either guilty or innocent) could avoid forfeiture even if he was later found guilty. The effect of pressing on an uncooperative accused was, and was intended to be, fatal. As early as 1426, pressing was used in England, though it never seems to have enjoyed wide popularity with the courts. Its sole recorded use in this country seems to have been during the notorious Salem witchcraft trials, in 1692, when one Giles Cory was pressed to death for refusal to plead to the charge of witchcraft.[23]

Burning at the stake is intimately connected with the punishment of witchcraft and heresy, having been endorsed for these crimes by several medieval Christian theologians. In civilized countries, such as England, if we may believe Blackstone, it was the practice to strangle the condemned person before the flames reached him. There are records showing that in New York and New Jersey, and probably elsewhere in the American colonies, rebellious Negro slaves were burned at the stake during the early and middle eighteenth century. Except for these occasional excesses, however, burning at the stake seems to have played no part among standard methods of execution actually practiced on these shores.

It is somewhat curious that any of these barbarous and inhumane methods of execution survived as long as they did, for the English Bill of Rights of 1689 proscribed "cruel and unusual punishments." This phrase worked its way through several of the early American state constitutions into the federal Bill of Rights (in the Eighth Amendment) of 1789. Supreme Court opinions interpreting this clause have been few, but they agree in declaring that the intent of the Framers of the Constitution was to rule out, once and for all, the aggravations attendant on execution, e.g., drawing and quartering, pressing, or burning.[24] These practices had all but totally disappeared by 1789 and they had never taken firm root here, anyway; but their express exclusion by Jefferson, Madison and the other authors of the Bill of Rights was a service to the interests of a free and humane people. Except when executing spies, traitors and deserters, who could be shot under martial law, the sole acceptable mode of execution in the United States for a century after the adoption of the Eighth Amendment was hanging.

In the 1880's, as one story has it, in order to fight the growing success of the Westinghouse Company, which was pressing for nationwide electrification with alternating current, the advocates of direct current staged public demonstrations to show how dangerous their competitor's product really was: if it could kill animals—and awed spectators saw that, indeed, it could—it could kill human beings as well. Within a few years, this somber warning was turned completely around, and in 1888, the New York legislature approved the dismantling of its gallows and the construction of an "electric chair," on the theory that in all respects, scientific and humane, executing a condemned man by electrocution was superior to executing him by hanging.[25] On August 6, 1890, after his lawyer had unsuccessfully argued the unconstitutionality of this "unusual" method of execution, one William Kemmler became the first criminal to be put to death by electricity. Although the execution was little short of torture for Kemmler (the apparatus was makeshift and the executioner clumsy), the fad had started. Authorities on electricity, such as Thomas Edison and Niccola Tesla, continued to debate whether electrocution was so horrible that it never should have been invented. The late Robert G. Elliot, electrocutioner of 387 men and women, assured the public in his memoirs that the condemned man loses consciousness immediately with the first jolt of current.[26] The matter remains controversial to this day. Despite the record of bungled executions,[27] the unavoidable absence of first-hand testimony, and the invariable odor of burning flesh that accompanies every electrocution, most official observers favor the electric chair. However ironical it may be, it is a fact that electrocution was originally adopted and is still employed in two dozen states on the grounds of its superiority to hanging as a civilized method of killing criminals.

Not satisfied with shooting, hanging or electrocution, the Nevada legislature passed a bill in 1921 to provide that a condemned person should be executed in his cell, while asleep and without any warning, with a dose of lethal gas. Governor Emmet Boyle, an avowed opponent of capital punishment, signed the bill, confident that it would be declared unconstitutional on the grounds of "cruel and unusual punishment." Nothing much was done one way or the other until one Gee Jon was found guilty of murder and sentenced to death. When the Nevada Supreme Court upheld the constitutionality of lethal gas, a chamber was hurriedly constructed after practical obstacles were discovered in the original plan for holding the execution in the prisoner's cell. On February 8, 1924, Jon became the first person to be legally executed with a lethal dose of cyanide gas. A Nevada newspaper editorial hailed the event: "It brings us one step further from the savage state where we seek vengeance and retaliatory pain infliction."[28]

It is doubtful whether any serious scientific inquiry has ever substantiated the claims advanced on behalf of either electrocution or gassing. According to a 1953 Gallup Poll, the American public strongly favored electrocution over lethal gas, while hanging and shooting had very few supporters (twelve per cent registered no opinion, or recommended "drugs" or "any of them, but let the prisoner choose"). Also during 1953, though few Americans knew it, the British Royal Commission on Capital Punishment stated:

> . . . we cannot recommend that either electrocution or the gas chamber should replace hanging as the method of judicial execution in this country. In the attributes we have called "humanity" [rapidity with which unconsciousness is induced] and "certainty" [simplicity of the apparatus] the advantage lies, on balance, with hanging; and though in one aspect of what we have called "decency" [decorum with which executions can be conducted, and absence of mutilation to the body of the condemned man] the other methods are preferable, we cannot regard this as enough to turn the scale.[29]

When representatives of the British Medical Association were cautiously sounded out on the question whether they would be willing to endorse and administer death sentences by lethal injections, they made it quite clear to the Royal Commissioners that they wanted nothing to do with it, no matter how humane, certain and decent it might be.

In this country, voices are occasionally still heard, protesting the risks, indignities and mutilations incident on hangings, shootings, electrocutions and gassings. "Contemporary methods of execution," it has been said, "are unnecessarily cruel"; they are "archaic, inefficient, degrading for everyone involved."[30] Novelties, such as allowing the condemned man to choose the method of his execution, or even to administer it to himself, or to become the subject of medical experiments until he dies of a fatal one, have lately been suggested.[31] But these objections and suggestions seem to go almost entirely unheeded. Retentionists —those who favor keeping, adopting or extending the death penalty—usually have no curiosity about the regrettable details of actual executions, and abolitionists, being totally out of sympathy with the whole business, have no interest in finding a more humane way to do what they disapprove of on principle.

## *Private Executions*

The strongest argument in favor of public executions and of cruel methods of inflicting the death penalty was that such procedures greatly increased the deterrent effect. Hence, the desirability of having children and the criminal fringe of society witness these spectacles. Also, the notion of executions hidden from public view suggested to many the unsavory aspects of secret Star Chamber proceedings. Thackeray's reaction (quoted in part above), however, seems to have been the judgment of most sensitive witnesses: "I feel myself ashamed and degraded at the brutal curiosity which took me to that brutal sight." It was probable, too, that the deterrent effect of attending an execution was considerably overrated. A classic tale has it that when pick-pocketing was a capital crime in England, pick-pockets plied their trade at the foot of the gallows while the other spectators watched a pick-pocket being hanged! The story is probably apocryphal[32] (as is another oft-told tale, that in England during Henry VIII's reign, over 72,000 persons were hanged[33]), but it illustrates the point. Somewhat more reliable may be the observation of the chaplain at Bristol Prison, England, who reported that all but three of the 167 men sentenced to death whom he had interviewed had, at one time or another, witnessed a hanging.[34] Nor could terror and hatred of the criminal increase if he took his punishment like a man. As the New York Legislative Commission on Capital Punishment observed,

> . . . the very boldness with which he [the condemned man] marched from the cell to the scaffold is extolled as an act of heroism and as evidence of courage and valor. "He was game to the last" has been many a ruffian's eulogy.[35]

But public executions continued well into the last century. Dr. Benjamin Rush, in his address of 1787 delivered in Franklin's house, attacked "The Effects of Public Punishments Upon Criminals and Upon Society." In response to his arguments and the support they aroused, the Walnut Street Jail was built in Philadelphia three years later. From this primitive beginning sprang the whole penitentiary system, and a realistic alternative to hangings at last was available. But nothing was done about public executions until New York, in 1830, imposed some control on the county sheriffs, requiring them (but only at their discretion!) to hold executions away from public view. Not until 1835 did New York increase the stringency of this law so as to prohibit public executions. Within the next few years, several other states followed suit, and this reform—at most, merely a sop to abolitionists—was underway.

The reform was by no means universal or thorough-going, however. Pennsylvania and New Jersey, for instance, stipulated only that executions should take place within the walls or buildings of the county jail. Since in most cases the gallows was erected out of doors in the jail yard, it was a simple enough matter for any interested spectator to watch the entire proceedings from a vantage point well outside the walls. Not until nearly the end of the last century were such abuses prohibited. Even so, flagrantly public executions continued in some states until quite recently. The last such event in the United States is said to have been the hanging of a Negro in Owensboro, Kentucky in August 1936. A news service photograph taken moments after the "drop" shows some 20,000 people packed around the gallows, with the dead man dangling at the end of his rope. Several spectators are atop a nearby utility pole, and others are leaning out of windows a block away. The platform is jammed with official witnesses.[36] Two years later, Kentucky passed a statute prohibiting all but official witnesses from attending future executions.

Even today, however, most states allow considerable discretion to the warden in charge of an execution as to how many persons shall qualify as official guests and witnesses. Wardens and executioners have often told how the announcement of an execution (required by law) brings a flood of requests for permission to attend. Such requests, they say, are never granted. But if the condemned man is enough of a celebrity, the mass news media will send their representatives, and these, plus the officials directly and indirectly involved, often swell the total to several dozen, as in the execution of Julius and Ethel Rosenberg at Sing Sing in 1953 and of Caryl Chessman at San Quentin in 1960.

The relative privacy of executions nowadays (even photographs of the condemned man dying are almost invariably strictly prohibited) means that the average American literally does not know what is being done when the government, in his name and presumably on his behalf, executes a criminal. Lately, it has been suggested, though with what seriousness it is hard to gauge, that executions should be televised for public viewing.[37] More than one abolitionist has wistfully recalled the days when all executions were holiday occasions, confident that if this were to happen today, the whole practice of killing criminals would be rapidly outlawed. The adage, "out of sight, out of mind," goes some distance toward explaining why even the opponents of the death penalty today are not as evangelical as were the reformers in the last century.

Actually, the relative loss of ardor and persistency among today's abolitionists probably has its main explanation elsewhere. Capital punishment today is not thought to be the dreadful evil it once was, partly because the number of persons executed has been drastically reduced. Whereas there is now about one execution a week in the nation, with a population of 180 million people, in 1900, with a population half that size, executions were held on an average three times as often. Reliable statistics on the annual number of executions prior to 1930 are unavailable, but there is no doubt that the number was steadily decreased during the last generation. Although executions seem to be fewer and fewer, the number of death sentences shows a slower decline. Hence, an increasing number of men each year are awaiting execution under sentence of death. This circumstance tends to veil the fact that for a century and a half, the ratio of death sentences to convictions for capital crimes has itself been steadily decreasing. When we add to this the widespread belief that only the worst murderers and other felons are even sentenced to death, thanks to the American innovations of degrees of murder and jury discretion in sentencing, it is not difficult to understand why the abolition movement has achieved so few successes during the past decade.

## *Degrees of Murder*

Since time immemorial, death has been regarded as the supremely suitable manner of punishing murderers. The Bible, somewhat cryptically, tells us, "Whoso sheddeth man's blood, by man shall his blood be shed" (Genesis IX:6). But what is the crime of murder, as distinct from the fact of homicide? Blackstone, speaking for the English tradition, declared:

> . . . all homicide is malicious, and . . . amounts to murder unless where *justified* by the command or permission of the law; *excused* on account of accident or self-preservation; or *alleviated* into manslaughter, by being either the involuntary consequence of some act not statutorily lawful, or (if voluntary) occasioned by some sudden and sufficiently violent provocation.[38]

The effect of this definition, which became a standard interpretation of the law of murder in this country, was to make into "murder," and thus punishable by death, all homicide not involuntary, provoked, justified or excused.

With the intention of giving the trial jury an opportunity to exclude from the punishment of death all murderers whose crime was not of the gravest nature, William Bradford, the Attorney General in Pennsylvania and a friend of Dr. Rush's, proposed the following now classic division of murder into "degrees":

> . . . all murder, which shall be perpetrated by means of poison, or by lying in wait, or by any other kinds of wilful, deliberate and premeditated killing, or which shall be committed in the perpetration or attempt to perpetrate any arson, rape, robbery, or

> burglary, shall be deemed murder of the first degree; and all other kinds of murder shall be deemed murder in the second degree; and the jury, before whom any person indicted for murder shall be tried, shall, if they find such person guilty thereof, ascertain in their verdict, whether it be murder of the first or second degree. . . .[39]

To this was added the stipulation, "That no crime whatsoever hereafter committed (except murder of the first degree) shall be punished with death in the State of Pennsylvania." The legislature adopted this statute in 1794. With certain minor modifications, the distinction of degrees of murder, with the death penalty limited to first degree murder, was quickly adopted in Virginia (1796), somewhat later in Ohio (1815), and during the next generation in most other states, until today all but a few states use it.

The distinction of murder into degrees has often been disputed as an improvement over the common law notion of murder. It is arguable whether the common law concept of "malice" is really clarified by the equally shadowy notions of wilfulness, deliberateness and premeditation.[40] But it was an effective compromise of the policy that murderers shall be punished with death, since it left for the jury to decide in each case whether the accused, though he may be guilty, had committed his crime with sufficient conscious calculation to deserve the maximum punishment. One of the main objections to the doctrine of degrees of murder is that it can often have just the opposite of the intended effect. For example, a mean, impulsive and violently brutal person who kills suddenly and without a weapon nor in the course of another felony (and thus kills in absence of wilfulness, deliberation or premeditation) may be as great (or even greater) a menace to society than is another person who carefully plans the death of some one victim, e.g., a doctor who decides to put a hopelessly incurable patient out of his misery. Indeed, in the latter case, a jury might wish to mete out light, or even no, punishment. But it could do so only by flouting the letter of the law, since the doctor's crime is clearly first degree murder.

After weighing the merits of the doctrine of degrees of murder for more than a century, the English have concluded that it is a clumsy tool for demarking the class of murderers meriting execution. The Report of the Royal Commission trenchantly observes:

> There are strong reasons for believing that it must inevitably be found impracticable to define a class of murders in which alone the infliction of the death penalty is appropriate. The crux of the matter is that any legal definition must be expressed in terms of objective characteristics of the offense, whereas the choice of the appropriate penalty must be based on a much wider range of considerations, which cannot be defined but are essentially a matter for the exercise of discretion.[41]

Besides the difficulties surrounding the distinction of degrees of murder, another equally disastrous tendency originated in the same 1794 Pennsylvania statute and has spread throughout American criminal law. Under the common law of England, all homicides not excusable or justifiable were murder and punishable by death. In the sixteenth century, manslaughter was made non-capital on the ground that such homicide lacked the required *mens rea,* or criminal intent, to deserve such severe punishment. But according to the Pennsylvania statute, first degree murder includes not only willful, deliberate and premeditated homicide; it includes also all "homicides in or in the attempt to perpetrate arson, rape, robbery or burglary." This notion that killings in the course of a felony (other than the felony of murder itself) are on a par with willful, deliberate and premeditated killing seems a complete throwback to the primitive theory that a person is to be punished not for what he intends to do (e.g., rob a store) but for what results from his action (e.g., the death, however unintended, of the store keeper). The most remarkable feature of the concept of felony murder is the way it has grown in several states so as to encompass homicides done in the course of *any* felony (where "felony" is defined as any crime punishable by death or by more than a year in prison), and to allow a felon to be punished as a first degree murderer for a homicide committed by a co-felon or even by a *police officer!*[42] Considerable experience with this doctrine has shown not only that it has thoroughly defeated any hope its originators may have had to mitigate the severity and inequity of capital punishment—rather, its effect has been exactly the opposite—but also that it makes for bad law, so much so that the American Law Institute has recently advocated abandoning the entire doctrine.[43]

## *Jury Discretion*

The early reformers may have dimly sensed what was to come, and while they deserve the credit for inventing the distinction of degrees of murder, they also deserve the blame for expanding the concept of felony murder. They and their successors must have seen the need for a better solution to the problem of making the punishment fit the crime and of limiting the severity of punishment, whenever possible, something less than death.

The solution seems obvious enough now, though only quite recently has it been universally adopted: make the punishment fit both the crime and the criminal by abolishing all mandatory death penalties, and instead authorize the jury in capital trials to sentence a guilty person either to death or to life imprisonment. The democracy of the idea was one source of its appeal. To give discretion to the jury meant that the Governor's arbitrary power to extend clemency would be considerably curbed, if not by law at least by force of public opinion, and thus this vestige of the old Royal privilege would be curtailed in favor of popular expression of the community's will.[44]

But by far the most pronounced argument in favor of ending mandatory death penalties, echoed on every side, was the extreme difficulty of obtaining convictions in cases where a conviction is tantamount to a death sentence. Because this difficulty was one of the strongest complaints against capital punishment, retentionists may have recognized that they could cut the ground from under the abolitionists by adopting the simple expedient of discretionary death sentences. Abolitionists may well have looked with some dismay on this development, as they could hardly fail to appreciate how much more difficult this reform would make achievement of their ultimate aim, while at the same time they could not deny that it was a step in the right direction.

A history of the principle of jury discretion in capital trials has yet to be written,[45] and the suggestions in the above paragraphs are largely speculations. We do not in fact know whether the idea of jury discretion was invented by abolitionists, retentionists, or some third party seeking a middle way. Nor do we know where or when the idea originated (it should be noticed that it apparently was a feature of the Massachusetts "Capitall Lawes" of 1636 for the crime of rape), nor when it was first applied to the punishment for murder. We do know that in Maryland, where the jury had the power to fix degrees of murder, the death penalty became optional in 1809 for treason, rape and arson, but not for homicide;[46] that Louisiana in 1846 may have been the first state to make all its capital crimes optionally punishable by life imprisonment;[47] and that jury discretion was introduced specifically for the punishment of murder in California in 1873, in Illinois the next year, and in Georgia the following year. According to one report, some thirty-two states had given either the judge or the jury discretion as to the punishment in capital cases by the year 1926.[48] Between 1949 and 1958, five more states (Massachusetts, Connecticut, North Carolina, New Mexico and Vermont) introduced this procedure.[49]

At present, twenty-two jurisdictions—just half the total—have made all their capital crimes optionally punishable by death or by imprisonment. It is interesting to note that many of those states which were the first to accept the doctrine of degrees of murder were among the last to add the doctrine of jury discretion for this crime. Ohio did not accept it until 1898, New Jersey until 1916, Pennsylvania until 1925. When the District of Columbia abolished the mandatory death sentence for murder in March 1962,[50] New York remained the last stronghold of this practice in the United States. After considerable pressure, including pleas from the District Attorney of New York County, the Legislature abolished this restriction in April 1963, and Governor Nelson Rockefeller signed it into law, to take effect the following July.

It often used to be maintained by abolitionists that if the death penalty were abolished, convictions would increase.[51] There seems to be little or no evidence that this is so.[52] Had the practice of jury discretion, however, not been introduced in most death penalty states over fifty years ago, there might have been considerable evidence to support this claim. There is some slight evidence in this direction, in favor of the view that the change from a mandatory to an optional death sentence for murder has resulted in significantly more convictions of first degree murder. In Philadelphia, for instance, in the last year of mandatory death penalties (1924), there were 118 indictments for first degree murder, but only six convictions were sustained by the courts after appeals. Some twenty years later (1947), out of 102 such indictments, twenty-six convictions were obtained and in twelve of these the jury had granted mercy, i.e., life imprisonment.[53] On the other hand, far more cases went to trial in 1947 than in 1924. Under the mandatory law, twenty-one first degree murder indictments were not opposed by the accused, giving full sentencing discretion to the judge; whereas in 1947, under the law that gave sentencing discretion to the jury, only seven defendants were willing to leave their fate in the hands of the judge. Presumably, they thought they would have a better chance of mercy from the jury. But no nationwide statistics are available against which we can place these data; they may or they may not be representative.

Whereas Americans seem to have their doubts about complete abolition of the death penalty for the crime of murder (since only twenty-one states have ever abolished it, and half of these later reintroduced it), the optional death penalty has been thoroughly accepted. There seems to be but one case of backsliding. Vermont adopted jury discretion in 1911, and a veritable crime wave of twenty murders occurred the next year. Although it subsided noticeably after one Elroy Kent was sentenced to death (with the jury exercising its discretion in favor of the death penalty), the legislature voted overwhelmingly to return to the mandatory death penalty for murder in 1913.[54] More than forty years were to pass before Vermont reabolished this mandatory law. Today there is no jurisdiction in the United States in which the jury is denied sentencing discretion for the crime of murder.

## Conclusion

It would be premature at this juncture to attempt to estimate either the merits or the probability of complete abolition of the death penalty in this country. Supporters of abolition in the past have been noticeably sanguine in their predictions. Thirty-five years ago, Raymond Bye, one of the sociologists to pioneer in the study of this subject, remarked, "There is reason to believe that in the course of the present century the use of the death penalty will finally pass away."[55] A decade ago, another observer said that "the over-all, international trend is toward the progressive abolition of capital punishment."[56] It is difficult to believe these predictions, if that is what they are. As these lines are being written, the Soviet Union has announced execution under *ex post facto* laws for currency speculation,[57] the French government is in an uproar over the failure of a special tribunal to issue a death sentence to renegade Army generals, the Union of South Africa has decided to impose the death penalty on its colored population for a host of crimes, South Korea has executed six soldiers for embezzlement of military funds, and Israel has announced that the notorious Adolf Eichmann has been hanged. The political executions in Cuba, Algeria, and the Congo are too infamous to need comment.

Yet it is true that in the United States, as the next chapter will show, nearly half the states now use the death penalty so sparingly that it plays almost no part in their program of law enforcement and criminal treatment. Of all the persons today in state and federal prisons, only about one in a thousand is under sentence of death.[58] The obvious inference is that the death penalty in our country is an anachronism, a vestigial survivor of an earlier era when the possibilities of an incarcerative and rehabilitative penology were hardly imagined. Although killing persons in the name of the law for racial, political, and military crimes remains one of the familiar social phenomena elsewhere in the modern world, yet the infrequency with which ordinary peacetime criminal offenses against persons and property are punished with death outside the United States[59] focuses attention on the persistence of this ancient practice in our own land. It is for the rest of this book to describe in detail the surroundings and the consequences of this practice, and to weigh the results as they bear on the justification of capital punishment in the present and for the future.

## NOTES

1. Theodore Plucknett, *A Concise History of the Common Law* (5th ed., 1956), pp. 424–454.
2. Leon Radzinowicz, *A History of English Criminal Law* (1948), I, pp. 3–5, 153.
3. William Thackeray, "Going to see a Man Hanged," *Fraser's Magazine* (August 1840), p. 156.
4. William Blackstone, *Commentaries on the Law of England* (1769), IV, p. 92.
5. Quoted in G. Ryley Scott, *The History of Capital Punishment* (1950), p. 179.
6. Thus, the phrase, "without benefit of clergy," which came to be attached to capital statutes during the nineteenth century in England and in America, meant not that a condemned man must go to his grave without the consolations of a spiritual advisor during his last moments, but that his conviction for a capital crime was not subject to a reduction in sentence on the ground that it was a first offense.
7. Radzinowicz, *op. cit.*, pp. 151, 153.
8. Blackstone, *op. cit.*, p. 377.
9. George Haskins, " 'The Capitall Lawes of New-England'," *Harvard Law School Bulletin* (February 1956), pp. 10–11. A brief survey of the development of capital laws in Massachusetts after 1636 is available in Massachusetts, *Report on the Death Penalty* (1958), pp. 98–103.
10. "Capital Punishment in the United States," *Law Reporter* (March 1846), p. 487.
11. This case is of unusual interest, for it involved the attempt to detect the murderer by means of "the right of bier," the superstition that if a murderer is brought near his victim's corpse, it will bleed ("blood

will out") and thus identify him. See Joseph Sickler (ed.), Rex et Regina v. Lutherland (1948).

12. For a full study of this subject, as well as for much else of value on the history of capital punishment in England and America, see George Dalzell, *Benefit of Clergy in America* (1955).
13. *Revised Statutes of North Carolina* (1837), chapter 34. Virginia laws of a slightly earlier date punished Negro slaves with death for any of seventy crimes, though for whites only five crimes were capital. See Charles Spear, *Essays on the Punishment of Death* (1844), pp. 227–231.
14. Radzinowicz, *op. cit.*, pp. 498–500.
15. On the subject in general, see Louis Filler, "Movements to Abolish the Death Penalty in the United States," *The Annals* (November 1952), and David Davis, "The Movement to Abolish Capital Punishment in America, 1787–1861," *American Historical Review* (October 1957). The next few paragraphs are based almost entirely on these articles.
16. *The Complete Works of Edward Livingston* (1873), II, p. 224.
17. *Ibid.*, pp. 192–224. It was taken from Livingston's "Introductory Report to the System of Penal Law Prepared for the State of Louisiana," completed in 1824 but not published until 1833.
18. Albert Post, "Early Efforts to Abolish Capital Punishment in Pennsylvania," *Pennsylvania Magazine of History and Biography* (January 1944), p. 49.
19. See Louis Burbey, "History of Execution in What is Now the State of Michigan," *Michigan History Magazine* (Autumn 1938).
20. Great Britain, *Select Committee Report on Capital Punishment* (1931), p. c, §475. In general, see Elizabeth Tuttle, *The Crusade Against Capital Punishment in Great Britain* (1961).
21. See James Avery Joyce, "Capital Punishment at UN," *Contemporary Review* (March 1962), and "The United Nations and the Issue of Capital Punishment," *U. N. Monthly Chronicle* (1966).
22. Reform has also moved with a comparable effect in three other directions (not discussed below): toward a statutory minimum age of sixteen, below which a capital indictment may not issue (this is usually accomplished by restricting jurisdiction over juveniles to special courts); toward a statutory requirement of an automatic writ of error to issue upon a death sentence, with an accompanying stay of execution, ordering a review of the case by a higher court; and toward a two-stage trial, in which the jury first determines the question of guilt and then, if it decides on a conviction and after hearing further testimony relevant to the sentence, whether the punishment shall be death or a term of imprisonment. Some states, e.g., California, have all three provisions.
23. Some details of the case (which figures in Arthur Miller's play, *The Crucible)* are available in Dalzell, *op. cit.*, pp. 182–185.
24. See Wilkerson v. Utah, 99 U. S. 130 (1878) at p. 135, and subsequent decisions. In this opinion, the Court held that there was nothing "cruel and unusual" in Utah's practice of allowing a condemned man to choose either the firing squad or the hangman for his executioner.
25. See the *Report* of the New York Legislative Commission on Capital Punishment (1888), pp. 52–92.
26. Robert Elliot, *Agent of Death* (1940).

27. Several were cited by the defense in the remarkable case of Louisiana *ex rel.* Francis v. Resweber, 329 U. S. 459 (1947); some are mentioned in Barrett Prettyman, Jr., *Death and the Supreme Court* (1961), pp. 105 ff.
28. A.P. dispatch from Carson City, Nevada; see e.g. *Newark News* of April 8, 1960.
29. Great Britain, Royal Commission on Capital Punishment, *Report* (1953), p. 256.
30. Respectively, Clarence Farrer, in *American Journal of Psychiatry* (1958), p. 567, and Rufus King, "Some Reflections on Do-It-Yourself Capital Punishment," *American Bar Association Journal* (July 1961), p. 669.
31. King, *op. cit.,* and Jack Kevorkian, "Capital Punishment or Capital Gain?" *Journal of Criminal Law, Criminology and Police Science* (May–June 1959).
32. See Radzinowicz, *op. cit.,* p. 498. The story may have started from a chance remark in the testimony given before the first Royal Commission on Capital Punishment; see its *Report* (1886), p. 302 (#2294).
33. Thorsten Sellin, "Two Myths in the History of Capital Punishment," *Journal of Criminal Law, Criminology and Police Science* (July–August 1959); and Radzinowicz, *op. cit.*, p. 139.
34. Spear, *op. cit.*, p. 53.
35. New York, *op. cit.*, p. 93.
36. The photo is reproduced in Negley Teeters, "Public Executions in Pennsylvania, 1682 to 1834," *Journal of the Lancaster County Historical Society* (Spring 1960), p. 117.
37. Vigorous opposition to this idea was expressed by convicts in *The San Quentin News* (March 5, 1959), p. 2. Their former warden, however, seems to support it, though only in order to educate and shock the public and thereby to secure greater support for abolition; see Clinton Duffy, *88 Men and 2 Women* (1962), p. 21.
38. Blackstone, *op. cit.*, p. 201.
39. Quoted in Edwin Keedy, "History of the Pennsylvania Statute Creating Degrees of Murder," *University of Pennsylvania Law Review* (May 1949), pp. 772–773.
40. The classic criticism of the doctrine is by Benjamin Cardozo, in his essay, "What Medicine Can Do for Law" (1928), reprinted in his *Selected Writings* (1947), pp. 382–384.
41. Royal Commission, *op. cit.,* p. 173. How little effect the Commission's advice had may be seen from the fact that the Homicide Act passed by Parliament in 1957 attempted to draw this distinction in the very way the Commission declared to be impossible. See, on this and other points, Sidney Prevezer, "The English Homicide Act," *Columbia Law Review* (May 1957).
42. See especially Norval Morris, "The Felon's Responsibility for the Lethal Acts of Others," *University of Pennsylvania Law Review* (November 1956), and Note, "Felony Murder As a First Degree Offense," *Yale Law Review* (January 1957).
43. See American Law Institute, *Model Penal Code Tentative Draft No. 9* (1959), pp. 33–39, 115–120, especially pp. 65–70; and the *Proceedings* of the Institute's Thirty-sixth Annual Meeting (1959), pp. 123–133.

44. On this subject, see Christen Jensen, *The Pardoning Power in the American States* (1922).
45. The leading article is by Robert Knowlton, "Problems of Jury Discretion in Capital Cases," *University of Pennsylvania Law Review* (June 1953). For current American Law in this area, see American Law Institute, *op. cit.*, pp. 121–126.
46. *Dorsey's Maryland Laws* (1809), pp. 573 ff.; cf. "Capital Punishment in the United States," *Law Reporter* (March 1846), p. 484.
47. Act of June 1, 1846, cited in State v. Lewis (1848), 3 *Louisiana Annotated Reports* 398.
48. Raymond Bye, "Recent History and Present Status of Capital Punishment in the United States," *Journal of Criminal Law, Criminology and Police Science* (August 1926), p. 239.
49. Sara Ehrmann, "Capital Punishment Today—Why?" in Herbert Bloch (ed.), *Crime in America* (1961), pp. 81, 91.
50. For an instructive public debate over the mandatory death penalty, see the *Congressional Record,* March 14, 1962, pp. 3771–3801.
51. See, e.g., Maynard Shipley, "Does Capital Punishment Prevent Convictions?" *American Law Review* (May–June 1909), and the remark of the Governor of Minnesota, that in the three years after abolition (1911–1913), convictions for murder increased "approximately fifty per cent," cited in Lamar Beman (ed.), *Selected Articles on Capital Punishment* (1925), p. 355.
52. Raymond Bye, *Capital Punishment in the United States* (1919), pp. 50–55.
53. Thomas White, "Punishment for Murder in the First Degree," *The Shingle* (March 1948), p. 62.
54. Reported in Beman (ed.), *op. cit.,* p. 8.
55. Bye, *op. cit.* note 48 *supra,* p. 245.
56. Frank Hartung, "Trends in the Use of Capital Punishment," *The Annals* (November 1952), p. 19.
57. See particularly "The Death Penalty and the USSR," *Bulletin of the International Commission of Jurists* (November 1961), pp. 55–62.
58. James McCafferty, "Major Trends in the Use of Capital Punishment," *Federal Probation* (September 1961), p. 21.
59. Until recently no reliable survey of the status of capital punishment in foreign countries existed; cf. Sara Ehrmann, *op. cit.*, p. 92, James Avery Joyce, *Capital Punishment* (1961), p. 261, and *Bulletin of the International Commission of Jurists* (November 1961), p. 63. Now, however, the reader should consult Marc Ancel, *The Death Penalty in European Countries* (1962), published by the Council of Europe, and his comprehensive worldwide report released under auspices of the United Nations, *Capital Punishment* (1962).

# 2 The Use of the Death Penalty: A Factual Statement

WALTER C. RECKLESS

Undoubtedly the most important trend in capital punishment has been the dramatic reduction in the number of offenses statutorily punishable by the death penalty. About two hundred years ago England had over two hundred offenses calling for the death penalty; it now has four. Some countries have abolished capital punishment completely; a few retain it for unusual offenses only. The trend throughout the world, even in the great number of countries that retain the death penalty, is definitely toward a *de facto,* not a *de jure,* form of abolition. In the United States, where the death penalty is possible in three-fourths of the states, the number of executions has declined from 199 in 1935 to an average of less than three in the last four years. This change is related to public sentiment against the use

From *Crime and Delinquency,* Vol. 15, No. 1, January 1969, National Council on Crime and Delinquency, pp. 43–56.

of the death penalty and even more directly to the unwillingness of juries and courts to impose a first-degree sentence. The increasing willingness of governors to commute a death sentence and of courts to hear appeals also contributes to this decline. A review of the evidence indicates that use of the death penalty has no discernible effect on the commission of capital offenses (especially murder).

Capital punishment has a rich catalogue of literature passionately critical of its use. But, except for the recording of certain dramatic historical events, the factual information about the subject has been sparse.

Two outstanding studies, one by Clarence H. Patrick and the other by James A. McCafferty, have attempted to supply systematized data on the world-wide legal status of capital punishment and the legal provision for its use in the United States. In addition, for almost a generation the U.S. Bureau of Prisons has collected statistical information on the yearly number of executions in the states, the District of Columbia, and the federal jurisdiction.

This paper will attempt to bring together the facts regarding the legal status of capital punishment in the world and in the United States as well as the available factual insights into its deterrent effect, and it will review the data and research, particularly Thorsten Sellin's, which shed light on the effect of abolition or restricted use of the death penalty on homicide and crimes of violence.

## De Jure vs. de Facto, Internationally

Patrick circulated a questionnaire through embassy sources and received replies from 128 out of 146 countries.[1] He discovered that it was unrealistic to divide countries into those which have and those which do not have the death penalty, because some countries are abolitionist *de jure* and others are abolitionist *de facto.*[2] In 1962, *de jure* abolition was found (see Table 2.1) in eighteen countries, the federal government of Mexico and twenty-five of its states, one state in Australia (Queensland), and five states in the United States (Alaska, Hawaii, Maine, Minnesota, and Wisconsin).[3]

Thirty-six of eighty-nine countries with capital punishment reported that they had no executions during the five-year period 1958–62.[4] This is certainly abolition *de facto*. The tiny country of Liechtenstein, while retaining capital punishment on the

TABLE 2.1: *Countries Without the Death Penalty (de Jure) in 1962*[a]

| *Country* | *Date of Abolition* |
|---|---|
| Bolivia | 1962 |
| Colombia | 1910 |
| Costa Rica | 1870 |
| Dominican Republic | 1924 |
| Ecuador | 1907 |
| Germany (Federal Republic) | 1949 |
| Greenland | 1954 |
| Honduras | 1957 |
| Iceland | 1928 |
| Italy | 1944 |
| Monaco | 1962 |
| Mozambique | 1867 |
| Panama[b] | |
| Portugal | 1867 |
| Puerto Rico | 1929 |
| San Marino | 1865 |
| Uruguay | 1905 |
| Venezuela | 1848 |
| Australia (Queensland only) | 1922 |
| Mexico: Federal Government and 25 of 29 states | 1931 |
| United States of America[c]: | |
| Alaska | 1957 |
| Hawaii | 1957 |
| Maine | 1887 |
| Minnesota | 1911 |
| Wisconsin | 1853 |

[a] Source: Patrick, *supra* note 1, p. 408.
[b] Never provided for.
[c] The death penalty was completely abolished in Michigan in 1963.

books, has not had an execution since 1798. In Belgium, the rarely pronounced death sentence is almost customarily commuted to life imprisonment; between 1867 and 1962, only one person was executed.[5]

Actually, *de facto* status is not easy to interpret. If a country retains capital punishment on the books because its power structure believes that this law has a deterrent effect, does commutation after imposition of the death sentence constitute *de facto* abolition?

Somewhere between *de jure* abolition and *de facto* abolition fall the countries and states within a country which have legally limited application of the death penalty. In these instances, the

TABLE 2.2: *Countries Limiting the Death Penalty to Unusual Crimes Under Unusual Circumstances, 1962*[a]

| *Country* | *Crimes or Circumstances* |
|---|---|
| Argentina | Under military code only |
| Austria | By court martial only |
| Brazil | For treason and espionage only |
| Denmark | During occupation and wartime only |
| Finland | Under martial law only |
| Indonesia | Treason, espionage, and attack on the life of the head of the government |
| Israel | Treason, espionage, Nazi crimes, genocide |
| Nepal | Murder or attempted murder of chief of state or member of the royal family |
| Netherlands | In time of war only |
| New Zealand | Treason |
| Norway | Under military code only |
| Sweden | In time of war only |
| Switzerland | For military offenses in time of war only |
| United States (3 states): | |
| Michigan[b] | Treason |
| North Dakota | Treason; first-degree murder by a prisoner already serving a life sentence for first-degree murder. |
| Rhode Island | Murder by a prisoner under a sentence of life in prison |

[a] Source: Patrick, *supra* note 1, p. 408.
[b] Michigan abolished the death penalty for treason in 1963 and thus became completely abolitionist.

penalty is provided for unusual crimes only, such as treason, espionage, murder of a chief of state, etc. Thirteen countries and two states in the United States belonged in this category in 1962 (see Table 2.2); some of them in past discussions have been mistakenly cited as abolitionist.

*De facto* abolition has a long history, evidenced in earlier times by substitute measures such as "benefit of clergy" and banishment to a penal colony. The movement to reduce the number of penal code offenses punishable by death has developed since the late eighteenth century. At that time, it is estimated, England's penal law listed over two hundred crimes calling for capital punishment. It now has four.[6]

## *Decline in Number of Executions*

Patrick analyzed the 1958–62 data from eighty-nine countries that have capital punishment (see Table 2.3) and found that, for the entire group, the annual average number of executions was 535.3, or 6 per country per annum. While six of the countries executed more than fifty persons a year during the five-year period, thirty-six countries executed none at all. Without comparable data on the prevailing value system of each country, the operation of the police and court systems, population trends, urbanization, crime reports, etc., interpretation of these figures on

TABLE 2.3: *Average Number of Executions Annually, 89 Countries with Capital Punishment (1958–62)*[a]

| *Number of Countries* | *Average Number of Executions per Year* |
|---|---|
| 36 | 0.0 |
| 13 | 0.1 to 1.0 |
| 24 | 1.1 to 5.0 |
| 3 | 5.1 to 10.0 |
| 5 | 10.1 to 25.0 |
| 2 | 25.1 to 50.0 |
| 6 | 50.1 to 100.0 |

[a] Source: Patrick, *supra* note, 1 p. 409.

execution is almost impossible, other than the fact that six executions per year for countries having the death penalty is not very many. Patrick contends that in historical perspective this average of 535.3 represents a "phenomenal decline."[7]

## *Methods of Execution*

Execution styles have always occupied an important niche in discussions of capital punishment, undoubtedly because the reform movement has stimulated a search for methods presumably more humane than the older ones. Patrick tabulated seven methods of execution in use in 1962—hanging (fifty-four countries), shooting (thirty-five), beheading (eight), electrocution (the Philippines and parts of the United States), asphyxiation (parts of the United States), strangulation (Spain), and stoning (Saudi Arabia). Most countries have only one method for cases tried in regular courts and often have a second method for cases handled by military courts. While it is hard to agree that hanging, beheading, and shooting are humane methods, they are certainly less painful than burning at the stake, crucifixion, torture on the rack or wheel, stoning, and strangulation. The most humane and painless method of execution is anesthetization before electrocution, granted by request of the condemned person in the Philippines.[8]

## *Public Execution; Minimum Age*

In 1962, only nine countries permitted public executions: Cambodia, Cameroun, Central African Republic, Ethiopia, Haiti, Iran, Laos, Nicaragua, and Paraguay.[9] In nine other countries Patrick found that the authorities may order an execution to be open to the public. In about 82 per cent of the countries reporting, executions are closed to the public. These figures represent a radical change from the recent past, when most executions were attended by thousands of men, women, and children. (One of the reasons for removing executions from public view was the adverse effect of the occasion on the multitude. Drunkenness, fighting, vulgarities, disorder, pickpocketing, etc., almost always occurred.)

Sixty death-penalty countries observe a minimum age of eighteen—that is, an offender younger than that at the time the crime was committed cannot be executed. In two countries, the minimum age is twenty-one; in one, it is twenty-two.[10] The trend has definitely been in the direction of eighteen as the minimum age, but the movement to raise this minimum will probably grow. In the U.S., where the age of jurisdiction of the juvenile court usually extends to the eighteenth birthday, several states have concurrent jurisdiction clauses that permit transfer of juvenile capital cases to the criminal court. Some juveniles under eighteen have received the death penalty.

## Legal Status of Capital Punishment in the U.S.

McCafferty performed the monumental task of analyzing the legal provisions for application of the death penalty in the laws of every state of the United States, the federal government, and the District of Columbia.[11] In 1952, six states out of the forty-eight were listed as abolitionist: Maine, Michigan (except for treason), Minnesota, North Dakota (except for treason and for murder in the first degree by a prisoner serving a life term for first-degree murder), Rhode Island (except for murder by a prisoner sentenced for life), and Wisconsin. Actually, to be rigorous about the matter, only three states—Maine, Minnesota, and Wisconsin—had complete abolition on their law books in 1952.

The McCafferty survey indicated that forty-four capital-punishment jurisdictions varied greatly in their coverage of various capital crimes and also in regard to whether the law defining a crime as a capital offense made the death penalty mandatory or permissive. (See Table 2.4.) Specific findings are as follows:

TABLE 2.4: *Number of Jurisdictions in the United States in 1952 in Which the Death Penalty is Mandatory or Permissive, by Type of Offense*[a]

| *Offense* | *Total Jurisdictions* | *Mandatory* | *Permissive* |
|---|---|---|---|
| Murder | 44 | 2 | 42 |
| Kidnaping | 35 | — | 35 |
| Treason | 26 | 15 | 11 |
| Rape | 20 | 1 | 19 |
| Dueling | 18 | 1 | 17 |
| Train wrecking | 15 | — | 15 |
| Lynching | 10 | — | 10 |
| Perjury in a capital trial | 10 | 5 | 5 |
| Dynamiting | 7 | — | 7 |
| Armed robbery | 7 | — | 7 |
| Arson | 6 | — | 6 |
| Train robbery | 5 | 1 | 4 |
| Burglary | 4 | — | 4 |
| Killing a woman by abortion | 4 | — | 4 |
| Aggravated assault by a life prisoner | 2 | 1 | 1 |
| Other offenses | 16 | 1 | 15 |

[a] Source: McCafferty, *op. cit. supra* note 11, p. 26.

1. Of the forty-four jurisdictions authorizing the death penalty for murder, only the District of Columbia and Vermont made it mandatory.
2. The nine jurisdictions which authorized the death penalty for murder but not for kidnaping were the District of Columbia, Kansas, Maryland, Massachusetts, Mississippi, North Carolina, New Hampshire, Oregon, and Pennsylvania.
3. There is little likelihood of a charge of—to say nothing of a conviction for—"treason against the state." Nevertheless, twenty-six states make treason punishable by death, and, in fifteen of them, the death penalty on conviction for this crime is mandatory.
4. Most of the twenty jurisdictions which authorize the death sentence for rape are in the South
5. In the ten states where capital punishment is authorized for lynching—Alabama, Arkansas, Georgia, Indiana, Kansas, Kentucky, Pennsylvania, South Carolina, Virginia, and West Virginia—the death penalty is not mandatory.

6. Though perjury in a capital trial is practically unknown, five of the ten states authorizing capital punishment for this offense make the death penalty mandatory.
7. The seven jurisdictions that make dynamiting a capital crime are Alabama, Georgia, Illinois, Iowa, Missouri, Mississippi, and Montana.
8. Armed robbery is punishable by death in Alabama, Kentucky, Missouri, Mississippi, Texas, and Virginia, and in the federal jurisdiction.
9. Alabama, Arkansas, Georgia, North Carolina, Vermont, and Virginia can punish arson by the death penalty; in Arkansas the death penalty is mandatory if the arsonist is a prisoner and the structure he burns is a prison.
10. Train robbery is a capital offense in Alabama, Arizona, Nebraska, Nevada, and New Mexico. (In New Mexico the death sentence is mandatory.)
11. In four states—Alabama, Kentucky, North Carolina, and Virginia—burglary is a capital crime.[12]

McCafferty compiled the number of jurisdictions in the United States that listed the death penalty for one or more offenses. (See Table 2.5.) One state (Georgia) applied the death penalty to fourteen offenses; another (Arkansas) applied it to eleven. One state (New Hampshire) specified only one crime (murder) subject to the death penalty; another (Massachusetts) specified two (murder and dueling).[13] Of the forty-four jurisdictions in the United States retaining capital punishment in 1952, twenty-two listed from one to four capital offenses; the remainder listed from five to fourteen capital offenses. (See Table 2.5.)

## *Special Provisions for Execution*

Of the forty-four jurisdictions that provided for capital punishment in 1952, twenty-five used electrocution; nine, lethal gas; eight, hanging; and one, shooting or hanging. The federal government used whatever mode was in effect in the state facility where the federal prisoner was kept.[14]

McCafferty's survey included legal provisions dealing with (a) the warrant, (b) regulations governing confinement, (c) the place of execution, (d) the time of execution, (e) the executioner, (f) the type of execution, and (g) witnesses of the execution. Some of the most interesting provisions are as follows:

> A warrant (including the date for execution, which has been set by the court) is issued by the clerk of the court and is given to the sheriff, who, in turn, delivers the prisoner and the accompanying warrant to the warden of the state prison designated as the place for the execution.
>
> In 1952, thirty-eight jurisdictions carried out executions under state auspices at a state-operated prison; four did so under local auspices.
>
> In two-thirds of the jurisdictions the warden of the state prison or his deputy is specified as the executioner or as the official who directs the execution.[15]

There were other special provisions for (a) condemned prisoners who become insane after being admitted to prison, (b) condemned female prisoners who are pregnant, (c) condemned prisoners who escape, (d) return of the warrant to the commit-

TABLE 2.5: *Number of Capital Offenses Covered by the Laws in Forty-four Jurisdictions of the United States in 1952*[a]

| *Number of Capital Offenses* | | *Jurisdictions* |
|---|---|---|
| 1 | | 1 |
| 2 | | 1 |
| 3 | | 9 |
| 4 | | 11 |
| 5 | | 7 |
| 6 | | 5 |
| 7 | | 4 |
| 8 | | 1 |
| 9 | | 1 |
| 10 | | 2 |
| 11 | | 1 |
| 12 | | — |
| 13 | | — |
| 14 | | 1 |
| | Total | 44 |

[a] Source: McCafferty, *op. cit. supra* note 11, p. 29. Based on Table A1, p. 74.

TABLE 2.6: *Abolition of the Death Penalty in the United States. 1846–1970*
(States are listed according to year most recent action was taken)

| State | Year of partial abolition | Year of complete abolition | Year of restoration | Year of reabolition |
|---|---|---|---|---|
| New Mexico | 1969 [a] | – | – | – |
| New York | 1965 [b] | – | – | – |
| Vermont | 1965 [c] | – | – | – |
| West Virginia | – | 1965 | – | – |
| Iowa | – | 1872 | 1878 | 1965 |
| Oregon | – | 1914 | 1920 | 1964 |
| Michigan | 1847 [d] | 1963 | – | – |
| Delaware | – | 1958 | 1961 | – |
| Alaska | – | 1957 | – | – |
| Hawaii | – | 1957 | – | – |
| South Dakota | – | 1915 | 1939 | – |
| Kansas | – | 1907 | 1935 | – |
| Missouri | – | 1917 | 1919 | – |
| Tennessee | 1915 [e] | – | 1919 | – |
| Washington | – | 1913 | 1919 | – |
| Arizona | 1916 [f] | – | 1918 | – |
| North Dakota | 1915 [g] | – | – | – |

| | | | | |
|---|---|---|---|---|
| Minnesota | – | 1911 | – | – |
| Colorado | – | 1897 | 1901 | – |
| Maine | – | 1876 | 1883 | 1887 |
| Wisconsin | – | 1853 | – | – |
| Rhode Island | 1852[h] | – | – | – |

[a] Death penalty retained for the crime of killing a police officer or prison or jail guard while in the performance of his duties, and in cases where the jury recommends the death penalty and the defendant commits a second capital felony after time for due deliberation following commission of first capital felony.

[b] Death penalty retained for persons found guilty of killing a peace officer who is acting in line of duty, and for prisoners under a Life sentence who murder a guard or inmate while in confinement or while escaping from confinement.

[c] Death penalty retained for persons convicted of first-degree murder who commit a second "unrelated" murder, and for the first-degree murder of any law enforcement officer or prison employee who is in the performance of the duties of his office.

[d] Death penalty retained for treason. Partial abolition was voted in 1846, but was not put into effect until 1847.

[e] Death penalty retained for rape.

[f] Death penalty retained for treason.

[g] Death penalty retained for treason, and for first-degree murder committed by a prisoner who is serving Life sentence for first-degree murder.

[h] Death penalty retained for persons convicted of committing murder while serving a Life for any offense.

Source: Information in the files of the National Prisoner Statistics program., U.S. Bureau of Prisons. This is an updated Table supplied by the Editor.

ting court after the execution, (e) disposition of the body after execution, (f) restrictions of publication of details (four states at the time prohibited publication of any statement other than that the prisoner was executed according to law), and (g) compensation to the executioner (in ten states $25 or $50; in one state, $100).[16]

## THE TREND

Since the McCafferty survey in 1952, several states have gone into the abolitionist column. Table 2.6 is an up-to-date summary.

Alaska and Hawaii abolished the death penalty in 1957, before statehood; in 1964–65, they were joined by Iowa, New York, Oregon, Vermont, and West Virginia. Six states—Maine, Michigan, Minnesota, North Dakota, Rhode Island, and Wisconsin—had abolished the death penalty between 1846 and 1915. In October 1968, the count stood at thirteen states that do not have the death penalty; of fifty-two jurisdictions in the United States (including the federal government and the District of Columbia), thirty-nine retain capital punishment.

Eight states (Arizona, Colorado, Delaware, Kansas, Missouri, South Dakota, Tennessee, and Washington) restored the death penalty after having abolished it. On the other hand, three states (Iowa, Maine, and Oregon) which had restored capital punishment abolished it once again.

Table 2.7 presents the yearly count of the number of executions in the United States since 1930, showing a marked downward trend since 1936. Several increases over the previous year's figure occurred throughout the overall period of decline. Why these spurts took place is not clear; accumulation of delayed cases may perhaps account for them.

The dramatic decline in the number of executions—to alr the vanishing point[17]—does not mean a drastic reduction of the crime rate. Crimes against the person and especially crimes against property have increased more than the increase in popu-

TABLE 2.7: *Number of Executions in the United States, by Year, 1930–70*[a]

| *Year* | *No.* | *Year* | *No.* |
|---|---|---|---|
| 1930 | 155 | 1951 | 105 |
| 1931 | 153 | 1952 | 83 |
| 1932 | 140 | 1953 | 62 |
| 1933 | 160 | 1954 | 81 |
| 1934 | 168 | 1955 | 76 |
| 1935 | 199 | 1956 | 65 |
| 1936 | 195 | 1957 | 65 |
| 1937 | 147 | 1958 | 49 |
| 1938 | 190 | 1959 | 49 |
| 1939 | 160 | 1960 | 56 |
| 1940 | 124 | 1961 | 42 |
| 1941 | 123 | 1962 | 47 |
| 1942 | 147 | 1963 | 21 |
| 1943 | 131 | 1964 | 15 |
| 1944 | 120 | 1965 | 7 |
| 1945 | 117 | 1966 | 1 |
| 1946 | 131 | 1967 | 2 |
| 1947 | 153 | 1968 | 0 |
| 1948 | 119 | 1969 | 0 |
| 1949 | 119 | 1970 | 0 |
| 1950 | 82 | | |

[a] Source: U.S. Bureau of Prisons, *National Prisoner Statistics, Executions,* 1930–1968, No. 45, August 1969. Updated by Editor.

lation. The immediate reason for the decline in executions is the increasing unwillingness of juries and courts to impose death sentences. Another reason is the greater readiness of governors to commute death sentences to life imprisonment. Probably behind these factors is the growing public sentiment in the U.S. against the use of the death penalty. Thus juries, judges, and governors are responding to prevailing public opinion.

Because of the long delays involved in the procedures for appeal or consideration for commutation, the prison population includes a steadily growing number of persons who have been sentenced to death. On January 1, 1960, there were 189 such prisoners; on January 1, 1966, there were 351 (see Table 2.8). In the next two years, the figure rose to 434 and then to 479.

From 1930 to 1967 thirty-two women (twenty white and

TABLE 2.8: *Movement of Prisoners Under Sentence of Death: 1961–1970*

| Number of prisoners | 1970 | 1969 | 1968 | 1967 | 1966 | 1965 | 1964 | 1963 | 1962 | 1961 |
|---|---|---|---|---|---|---|---|---|---|---|
| Under sentence of death, Jan. 1 | 524 | 479 | 434 | 415 | 351 | 322 | 298 | 268 | 266 | 219 |
| Received death sentence during year | 116 | 97 | 102 | 85 | 118 | 86 | 106 | 93 | 103 | 140 |
| Other admissions[(a)] | 44 | 33 | 20 | 5 | – | 12 | 3 | 7 | 7 | – |
| Executed during year | – | – | – | 2 | 1 | 7 | 15 | 21 | 47 | 42 |
| Median elapsed time (in months) | – | – | – | – | – | 44.5 | 20.5 | 16.0 | 20.5 | 16.2 |
| Other dispositions | 76 | 85 | 77 | 69 | 53 | 62 | 70 | 49 | 61 | 51 |
| Median elapsed time (in months) | (N.A.) | (N.A.) | 32.6 | 40.8 | 31.7 | 33.3 | 23.5 | 22.4 | 16.6 | 18.7 |
| Commutations | 29 | 20 | 16 | 13 | 17 | 19 | 9 | 16 | 27 | 17 |
| Transfer to mental hospitals | 5 | 1 | 2 | 3 | 3 | 4 | 3 | 1 | 4 | 3 |
| Other[(b)] | 42 | 64 | 59 | 53 | 33 | 39 | 58 | 32 | 30 | 31 |
| Under sentence of death, Dec. 31 | 608 | 524 | 479 | 434 | 415 | 351 | 322 | 298 | 268 | 266 |
| Median elapsed time (in months) | (N.A.) | (N.A.) | 33.2 | 28.9 | 29.5 | 30.8 | 26.8 | 24.0 | 16.7 | 14.4 |

[a] Includes those prisoners previously reported as being "disposed of by other means" as a result of being granted a new trial or being transferred to a mental hospital, who were returned to "death row" during the following or subsequent year.
[b] Includes reversals of judgment, vacated sentences, grants for new trial, suicide, and death from natural causes.
N.A. = not available
Source: U.S. Bureau of Prisons, National Prisoner Statistics, Number 45 (August 1969) and unpublished data provided by the editor.

twelve Negro) were executed.[18] Why so few, in proportion to the number of men? One reason is that women are much less frequently involved in crime. Another is the general attitude toward them which results in their being reported for crimes less frequently than men, arrested less frequently, held for court action less frequently, and found guilty by the courts less frequently. Women are nowhere near as saintly as the thirty-two executions in thirty-eight years seem to suggest: they have men "going for them" in many legitimate and illegitimate ways. It is doubtful that the United States will ever execute another woman.

Of 3,857 persons executed in the United States from 1930 to 1966, inclusive, 1,750 (45.4 per cent) were white; 2,065 (53.5 per cent), Negro; 42 (1.1 per cent), other.[19] The number of Negroes executed was disproportionate to their percentage of the total population of the United States in the thirty-seven years. American criminologists have pointed out the disproportionate involvement of the Negro in most crimes, particularly in crimes against the person. The sociological criminologists see it as a result of a subculture of violence and the stresses and strains imposed on a minority group living in the slums of the large cities. In addition, victims (including Negro victims) are more willing to complain about Negro offenders than about white offenders, police are probably more ready to arrest and hold the Negro offender for court, and the courts tend to sentence Negro defendants more severely than white defendants. To get a commutation or an appeal for a death-sentenced Negro is far more difficult than for a white prisoner.

## No Evidence of Deterrent Effect

### *Homicide Rates in Contiguous States*

Although the proponents of capital punishment assert that it acts as a deterrent to capital crimes (particularly murder), the evidence indicates that it has no discernible effect in the United States, and presumably the same is true in other countries. Sellin

TABLE 2.9: *Rates per 100,000 Population for Murder, Aggravated Assault, and the Major Crimes of Violence, by Contiguous Groupings of the Retention States around the Thirteen Abolition States, 1967*[a]

| *State* | *Murder and Non-negligent Manslaughter* | *Aggravated Assault* | *Violent Crime*[c] |
|---|---|---|---|
| Alaska[b] | 9.6 | 98.2 | 160.7 |
| Hawaii[b] | 2.4 | 52.8 | 80.0 |
| Oregon[b] | 3.1 | 76.1 | 157.4 |
| Washington | 3.1 | 83.7 | 154.0 |
| Idaho | 4.3 | 44.5 | 68.4 |
| California | 5.4 | 172.7 | 352.1 |
| Nevada | 10.8 | 104.7 | 247.7 |
| Minnesota[b] | 1.6 | 54.7 | 132.0 |
| North Dakota[b] | 0.2 | 18.3 | 29.0 |
| South Dakota | 3.7 | 62.0 | 86.9 |
| Iowa[b] | 1.5 | 3.3 | 58.4 |
| Nebraska | 2.7 | 63.6 | 113.2 |
| Missouri | 7.3 | 122.1 | 276.9 |
| Wisconsin[b] | 1.9 | 35.9 | 70.4 |
| Illinois | 7.3 | 168.3 | 394.3 |
| Michigan[b] | 6.2 | 158.5 | 376.8 |
| Indiana | 3.7 | 64.9 | 156.7 |
| Ohio | 5.3 | 74.5 | 185.0 |
| West Virginia[b] | 4.6 | 68.4 | 97.0 |
| Kentucky | 7.2 | 77.2 | 140.6 |
| Virginia | 7.3 | 122.0 | 192.2 |
| Maryland | 8.0 | 261.5 | 474.1 |
| New York[b] | 5.4 | 165.8 | 403.4 |
| Pennsylvania | 3.8 | 63.6 | 138.4 |
| New Jersey | 3.9 | 92.4 | 188.5 |
| Vermont[b] | 3.1 | 11.3 | 20.6 |
| Maine[b] | 0.4 | 43.3 | 59.3 |
| Rhode Island[b] | 2.2 | 90.0 | 128.4 |
| New Hampshire | 2.0 | 20.3 | 31.8 |
| Massachusetts | 2.8 | 65.2 | 127.6 |
| Connecticut | 2.4 | 55.7 | 95.9 |

[a] Source: Federal Bureau of Investigation, U.S. Department of Justice, *Uniform Crime Reports—1967* (Washington, D.C., 1968), pp. 62–79.
[b] An abolition state.
[c] Includes murder, aggravated assault, forcible rape, and robbery.

compared the homicide rates per 100,000 population in abolition states with the rates in contiguous death-penalty states in the period 1920–55 and included in his tabulations the yearly number of executions in each contiguous death-penalty state. He found that homicide rates varied widely among these clusters of states and that within any regional cluster it was "impossible to distinguish the abolition state from the others" since the trends of the homicide rates "of comparable states with or without the death penalty are similar." As he interpreted the evidence, "the inevitable conclusion is that executions have no discernible effect on homicide death rates which, as we have seen, are regarded as adequate indicators of capital murder rates."[20]

Using the data from the 1967 *Uniform Crime Reports,* Table 2.9 groups the thirteen abolition states with contiguous death-penalty states to compare the rates for murder, aggravated assault, and the combined major crimes of violence (including murder, forcible rape, robbery, and aggravated assault). Aggravated assault is listed separately because the main difference between it and murder is that the assault victim does not die: the intent of the assaulter may have been the same as the murderer's. One cannot point to higher sets of rates in the abolition states than in the contiguous retention states. As Sellin pointed out ten years ago, the variation between states in rates of murder and presumably all crimes of violence must be attributed to factors other than the abolition or retention of the death penalty.

However, some interesting comparisons can be singled out of the data in Table 2.9. Selecting nine of the thirteen abolition states (because of readiness of comparability), we can compare each with a contiguous retention state. (See Table 2.10.) For Alaska, since contiguity cannot apply, the comparison is with a geographically large state having a small population.

Perhaps comparisons of this sort are not completely justified, but, even if they are only partly justified, the abolition states have won the argument against deterrence: five to two with two ties, which might be considered a seven-to-two score for abolition. Perhaps the statement should be reversed: retention lost the argument in 1967 in seven out of nine abolition states.

## *Before, During, and After Abolition*

Gathering data from several European countries on homicides in the years before and after abolition of the death penalty or before and after drastic revisions in the law covering capital crimes, Sellin found that there was no clear trend one way or the other —that is, toward increase or decrease after abolition and revision of law.[21]

The impact of abolition in the three earliest abolition states (Michigan, 1846; Rhode Island, 1852; and Wisconsin, 1853), as judged by the number of offenders imprisoned for first-degree murder, was negative. In various combinations of post-abolition years, there was definitely no increase in the yearly averages of convicted first-degree murderers.[22] The data from Maine, which abolished the death penalty in 1876, restored it in 1883, and reabolished it in 1887, indicate no overall increase in murder from one period to another.[23] Ten other states have abolished capital punishment and then have restored it: Arizona, Colorado, Dela-

TABLE 2.10: *Nine Abolition States Compared with Contiguous Death-Penalty States on Rates for Murder, Aggravated Assault, and Combined Major Crimes of Violence*

| *Abolition State* | *Comparison* | *Retention State* |
|---|---|---|
| Alaska | Very close on murder and on aggravated assault | Nevada |
| Oregon | Close on all three rates | Washington |
| Minnesota | Lower on murder and on aggravated assault | South Dakota |
| Iowa | Lower on all three rates | Nebraska |
| Wisconsin | Several times lower on all three rates | Illinois |
| Michigan | Much higher on aggravated assault and major crimes of violence | Ohio |
| Vermont | Higher on murder but lower on the two other rates | New Hampshire |
| New York | Much higher on all three rates | New Jersey |
| West Virginia | Much lower on all three rates | Virginia |

TABLE 2.11: *Murder and Aggravated Assault Rates per 100,000 Population for Selected States, 1962–67*[a]

| | Iowa[b] | | New York[c] | | Oregon[d] | | West Virginia[e] | |
|---|---|---|---|---|---|---|---|---|
| *Year* | *Murder* | *Aggravated Assault* | *Murder* | *Aggravated Assault* | *Murder* | *Aggravated Assault* | *Murder* | *Aggravated Assault* |
| 1962 | 1.1 | 6.7 | 3.6 | 81.3 | 2.9 | 27.8 | 3.7 | 32.9 |
| 1963 | 1.3 | 8.7 | 3.8 | 85.0 | 3.0 | 34.1 | 5.3 | 33.9 |
| 1964 | 1.3 | 19.0 | 4.6 | 104.4 | 1.8 | 56.0 | 3.7 | 50.1 |
| 1965 | 1.3 | 20.1 | 4.6 | 147.8 | 3.4 | 59.3 | 4.0 | 55.4 |
| 1966 | 1.6 | 25.0 | 4.8 | 155.2 | 2.7 | 65.2 | 4.2 | 61.5 |
| 1967 | 1.5 | 30.3 | 5.4 | 165.8 | 3.1 | 76.1 | 4.6 | 68.4 |

[a] Source: *Uniform Crime Reports*, 1962, 1963, 1964, 1965, 1966, 1967.
[b] Abolished the death penalty in 1965.
[c] Abolished the death penalty in 1965.
[d] Abolished the death penalty in 1964.
[e] Abolished the death penalty in 1965.

ware, Iowa (which re-abolished it in 1965), Kansas, Missouri, Oregon (which re-abolished it in 1964), South Dakota, Tennessee, and Washington. Analyzing the statistics for the years before abolition, during abolition, and after restoration of the death penalty, Sellin says: "If any conclusion can be drawn, it is that there is no evidence that abolition of the death penalty generally causes an increase in criminal homicides or that its re-introduction is followed by a decline. The explanation of changes in homicide rates must be sought elsewhere."[24]

Table 2.11 shows the rate of murder and aggravated assault in four states that recently abolished the death penalty, for the two to three years before abolition and the two or three years after abolition. The murder rates show little change, before or after abolition. The trend in the rates of aggravated assault is definitely upward, but this rise seems to be completely unrelated to abolition, as it started in the years before abolition and continued thereafter.

## *Immediately Before and After Execution*

An ingenious test of the impact of executions on the commission of murder was reported by Robert H. Dann, in Philadelphia. Examining all criminal homicide cases in the records of the coroner's office, he selected five (occurring in 1927, 1929, 1930, 1931, and 1932) which had the following characteristic in common: the date of execution for the homicide was preceded by a sixty-day period during which there were no other executions in Philadelphia and was also followed by a sixty-day, no-execution period. "It was found that if the five periods were combined there was a total of 105 days free from homicides during the sixty-day periods before the executions and 74 in the periods after the executions. There was a total of 91 homicides in the 'before execution' periods and 113 in the 'after' periods."[25] (Only nineteen of the 204 homicides resulted in sentences for first-degree murder: nine in the sixty-day periods before and ten in the sixty-day periods after executions.) One could hardly say that executions were having any noticeable deterrent effect.

Several years later, Savitz, conducting a similar study of four murder cases in Philadelphia, examined the eight-week period before and the eight-week period after the day on which the court sentenced the offender to death. In the four eight-week periods preceding pronouncement of the death sentence, there were forty-three so-called "capital" crimes, of which twenty-three were definitely so and twenty were possibly so. In the four eight-week periods after the court imposed the death sentence, there were forty-one "capital" crimes, of which twenty-eight were definitely capital and thirteen possibly so.[26]

Neither study showed any significant increase in murders before or after execution (Dann data) or before and after sentence (Savitz data). One must conclude once again, therefore, that capital punishment has no detectable deterrent effect.

## *Shooting of Police and Killings in Prison*

One of the most persistent claims for capital punishment is that it deters criminals from shooting or killing policemen. Sellin obtained information on 128 killings of municipal police in 264 cities of the United States in the period 1919–54. The cities were located in seventeen states, of which eleven had the death penalty and six did not. The rate of police killings per 100,000 population during the period was 1.3 in the death penalty states and 1.2 in the abolition states. Claims that more police are killed in abolition than in retention states are not supported by the data.[27]

Father Campion, S.J., surveying about half of the state police departments in the United States in 1954, concluded that his data did not support "the claim that the existence of the death penalty in the statutes of a state provides a greater protection to the police than exists in states where the death penalty has been abolished."[28]

Sometimes the claim is made that the death penalty deters prisoners from killing one another in prison and from killing staff members. Sellin requested data from prison administrators in the United States on the number of assaults which took place in their penal institutions in 1965. Of the forty-seven jurisdictions that supplied the required information, ten said no assaults had taken place in their prisons that year. Thirty-seven jurisdictions reported prison assaults having 603 victims, of whom sixty-one—eight officers and fifty-three inmates—died. The sixty-one killings resulted from forty-six incidents (mostly altercations), in which fifty-nine identifiable killers took part.

No fatal assaults occurred in the prisons of six abolition states: Alaska, North Dakota, Oregon, Rhode Island, West Virgina, and Wisconsin. Four other abolition states reported eight fatal assaults (out of the total of sixty-one). Seventeen death-penalty states reported no fatal assaults; nineteen death-penalty states and the federal prison system reported fifty-three prison homicides (out of the total of sixty-one). Certainly Sellin's data do not indicate that abolition of the death penalty encourages prison killings. The explanation of fatal as well as nonfatal assaults in prisons should be sought, according to Sellin, in the hazards of prison life—not in the presence or absence of capital punishment.[29]

Confirmation of Sellin's findings on the relation of prison assaults to the death penalty was made by Akman, using Canadian data for 1964 and 1965. He could find no empirical support for the claim that commutation of death sentences increased the hazards of prison life. "Not only has commutation not led to further violence by those whose sentences have been commuted, but attenuation of the threat of the death penalty resulting from an unprecedented high rate of commutations has not resulted in a general increase of homicidal and assaultive behavior in Canadian prisons."[30]

All these sources—a comparison of homicide rates in abolition states and contiguous retention states, a contrast of murder incidence in states which abolished and later restored capital punishment, the number of homicides just before and just after sentence or execution, the count on killings of policemen in cities of abolition and retention states, and the incidence of fatal assaults in prisons—contain no evidence that the absence or nonuse of the death penalty encourages murder, and no evidence that the presence or liberal use of the death penalty deters capital offenses.

## NOTES

1. Clarence H. Patrick, "The Status of Capital Punishment: A World Perspective," *Journal of Criminal Law, Criminology, and Police Science* (December 1965), pp. 397–411.
2. *Id.*, p. 405.
3. *Id.*, p. 408.
4. *Ibid.*
5. *Id.*, p. 405.
6. *Ibid.*
7. *Id.*, p. 408.
8. *Id.*, pp. 409–410.
9. *Id.*, pp. 410–411.
10. *Id.*, p. 410.
11. James A. McCafferty, *Capital Punishment in the United States: 1930 to 1952,* M.A. thesis, Ohio State University, 1954.
12. *Id.*, pp. 25–28.
13. *Id.*, Table A1, p. 74.
14. U.S. Bureau of Prisons, *National Prisoner Statistics, Executions,* No. 8, April 1953.
15. McCafferty, *op. cit. supra* note 11, pp. 29–36.
16. *Id.*, pp. 36–41.
17. No executions took place in 1968, up to Dec. 1, when this issue went to press.
18. U.S. Bureau of Prisons, *National Prisoner Statistics, Executions,* 1930–1966, No. 41, April 1967, p. 3.
19. *Id.*, p. 9.
20. Thorsten Sellin, *The Death Penalty* (Philadelphia, Pa.: American Law Institute, 1959), p. 34. See also a reprint from this report, bringing the trends in homicide rates for the same group of states up to 1958. See Thorsten Sellin, "Death and Imprisonment as Deterrents to Murder," in Hugo Adam Bedau, *The Death Penalty in America* (Garden City, N.Y.: Anchor-Doubleday, 1964), pp. 274–84.
21. Sellin, *op. cit.* supra note 20, pp. 38–50.
22. *Id.*, pp. 34–35.
23. *Id.*, p. 35.
24. Thorsten Sellin, "Experiments with Abolition," in *Capital Punishment,* Thorsten Sellin, ed. (New York: Harper & Row, 1967), p. 124. The data in this article are taken from Sellin's report, *The Death Penalty, supra* note 20, pp. 34–38.
25. The report by Dann is summarized in Sellin, *supra* note 20, pp. 50–52.

26. Leonard D. Savitz, "A Study in Capital Punishment," *Journal of Criminal Law, Criminology and Police Science,* (November–December 1958) pp. 338–41.
27. Thorsten Sellin, "The Death Penalty and Police Safety," in *Capital Punishment, op. cit. supra* note 24, pp. 146, 154.
28. "Does the Death Penalty Protect State Police?" reprinted in Bedau, *op. cit. supra* note 20, pp. 314–315.
29. Thorsten Sellin, "Prison Homicides," *Capital Punishment, supra* note 24, pp. 154–160.
30. Dogan D. Akman, "Homicides and Assaults in Canadian Prisons," *Capital Punishment, supra* note 24, p. 168.

# II The Issues

In late 1969, William O. Hochkammer, Jr., a student at the Northwestern University School of Law, brought together the pro and con positions on the leading issues of the capital punishment debate. His article places substantial reliance on recent studies and writings by leading writers. Hochkammer discusses five basic issues: (1) deterrence, (2) discrimination, (3) protection of society, (4) role of public opinion, and (5) legal issues.

According to Hochkammer the arguments of the retentionists and the abolitionists regarding the effect of deterrence are mostly inconclusive. Neither argument, when surveys are discounted, has more than its respective opinion to support its position. Hochkammer states that, if discrimination truly exists, the remedy would be to equally apply the punishment and not to reject it. Retentionists declare that only the death penalty can protect society. Abolitionists with considerable documentation maintain that the life sentence is sufficient to safeguard the community.

Though public opinion polls show a diminished support of the death penalty, legislators, who may lag behind the opinion changes of their constituents, have not abolished the death penalty in many jurisdictions. And when the matter of abolition is put to the voters in a referendum the decision can go either way.

In his discussion of legal issues, Hochkammer describes recent efforts to bring the capital punishment controversy into the courts. It has been argued that the Eighth Amendment prohibits punishment that is inherently cruel or cruelly excessive. Until the *Ralph* decision handed down by the Fourth Circuit Court of Appeals, however, this contention was rejected.[1]

To date, courts also have rejected the position that the imposition of the death sentence denies due process. However, though attempts to have capital punishment ruled unconstitutional have failed, several decisions have held some of the procedures used to impose the death sentence to be unconstitutional. Hochkammer describes recent decisions which have restricted the use of the death penalty.

## NOTE

1. Ralph v. Warden Maryland Penitentiary, C.C.A. Fourth Circuit, No. 13, 757, decided December 11, 1970.

# 3

# *The Capital Punishment Controversy*

WILLIAM O. HOCHKAMMER, JR.

The death penalty has been the subject of heated debate in the United States for over 150 years.[1] During this period, both retentionists[2] and abolitionists[3] have developed ritualistic arguments on the key issues of the controversy. Even though most arguments are based on opinion unsupported by facts, both groups have used statistical data and studies to prove the correctness of their respective positions. Confusion has resulted because the line between unsubstantiated opinion and fact has not been clear. This comment will consider some of the major areas of disagreement between retentionists and abolitionists and assess the use of the factual proof presented.

## The Deterrence Issue

A major element of the controversy is whether capital punishment, as claimed by retentionists, is a unique deterrent to crime.[4] Their argument is that most people will not commit a crime if they know they may be executed as a result; this is an outgrowth of man's instinct for self-preservation.[5]

Retentionists attempt to emphasize the logic of this argument by observing that people, when they are absolutely determined to get results frequently resort to the threat of death.[6] Abolitionists note that some people commit crimes for which they may be executed because of a conscious or subconscious desire to commit suicide, a motivation that offsets any deterrent effect the death penalty might have.[7] The retentionists reply that few criminals, especially hardened criminals, want to and expect to be punished for their crimes.[8]

Some abolitionists believe that the death penalty increases the level of serious crime because those who have already committed a capital crime will not hesitate to commit others since they feel they have nothing to lose.[9] Retentionists counter that if a life sentence is substituted for the death penalty, a man who has committed a crime for which he may be sentenced to life imprisonment would be just as likely to commit other serious crimes because he would also know he was already subject to the maximum penalty.[10] Neither position is persuasive.

To the extent it is true that a criminal does not expect to be caught[11] or, if caught, to be convicted or, if convicted, to be the recipient of the maximum sentence, it is also true that the criminal will not be deterred by the most severe sentence the law may impose on him.

The few attempts which have been made to validate these arguments have failed to establish conclusively the existence of a deterrent effect. Consequently abolitionists have concluded either that such an effect does not exist or, if it does, that it is negligible.[12] Retentionists have, however, disputed the validity of these studies[13] by noting that most were conducted by the opponents of capital punishment (apparently making them immediately suspect) and that these studies do not take into account the number of crimes which were actually deterred.[14] The fact that two states, one with capital punishment and the other without, have similar rates of crime does not prove that there is no deterrent effect. It may be that the factors contributing to a high crime rate are so much stronger in the capital punishment state that they are not offset by the death penalty deterrent effect.

Since these studies contain potentially serious defects, they should be accepted only with reservations. They are suspect to the extent they are based on assumptions which, unfortunately, cannot satisfactorily be tested. For example, most studies assume that the rate of capital murder varies proportionally to the fluctuations in the homicide rate. The statistics are based on data for total homicides, rather than for capital murder rates, which are generally unavailable.[15] Thus, when a study indicates that the homicide rate did not increase after the abolition of the death penalty, this does not eliminate the possibility of an increase in the rate of capital murders. An increase in the capital murder rate might simply have been offset by a decrease in the rate of non-negligent homicides.

Recent studies with improved methodology have to some extent quelled this uncertainty. For example, it may now be possible to ascertain more accurately the effect of capital punishment in a comparison of state crime rates. Abolitionists have, in the past, relied on unrefined statistics to show that the homicide rates in states without the death penalty do not differ substantially from rates in death penalty states.[16] Retentionists have countered that factors other than the deterrent effect of the death penalty—race, heredity, regional lines, and standards of housing and education—have an effect on crime rates.[17] Grouping the states according to similarities in the character of the population, urban and industrial development, and geographical proximity, a comparison was made between states in the group which have and those which do not have capital punishment. This study supported the conclusion that those states which fell into each group have similar homicide rates, whether or not they have the death penalty.[18] Nevertheless, this study is inconclusive since it does not consider crimes actually deterred and it assumes there is a relationship between capital murder and homicide rates.

The information presently available does not provide an adequate basis for deciding whether there is a deterrent effect. When the inconclusive surveys are discounted, all that remains are statements of opinion which must be treated with scepticism.

## The Discrimination Issue

Some aspects of the controversy are susceptible to valid statistical analysis. An example is the abolitionist criticism that the death penalty has been discriminatorily applied since it is imposed more frequently on the poor, the ignorant, and minority group members than on other convicted criminals who do not fit into these categories.[19] If capital punishment is not uniformly applied, some say, it should be abolished.

Studies indicate that such discrimination exists. For example, even though women commit about one of every seven murders,[20] of the 3,298 people executed for murder from 1930 through 1962, only 30 were women.[21] There are also clear indications of discrimination on the basis of race. From 1932 through 1957, twice as many Negroes as whites were executed in the South.[22] While crime rates for different races are not equal, the difference in the numbers of executions cannot be explained on this basis.[23] The factor of discrimination becomes especially clear when the numbers of whites and nonwhites who are executed for rape are compared. From 1930 through 1962, 446 people were executed under civil authority in the United States for rape. Of these, 45 were white, 399 Negro, and 2 American Indian. 436 of these executions were in the South—42 white, 392 Negro, and 2 American Indian.[24] This discrimination also appears in a comparison of the success with which Negroes and whites are able to obtain commutations. Between 1914 and 1958 in Pennsylvania, whites received commutations three times as often as Negroes.[25]

Yet, even if the existence of discrimination can satisfactorily be proven, it would be a mistake to argue that capital punishment should be rejected because some discrimination exists. The proper approach is to remedy the defect, not abolish the system. Emphasis should be on insuring uniform application in the future.[26] If there is any justification at all for the death penalty it may well overcome the objection of unequal application which can be remedied by more conscientious administration.

## Protection of Society Issue

Retentionists argue that only the death penalty can adequately protect society; the life sentence alternative does not provide adequate protection because criminals who are given a life sentence are often paroled and thus able to commit other crimes.[27] Abolitionists counter that there is no indication that people who have committed capital crimes are more likely to commit other crimes than those who are guilty of lesser crimes.[28] Furthermore, many who commit repeated capital crimes are adjudged legally insane and are not executed, even in a capital punishment jurisdiction.[29] Besides this, parole boards do not release criminals unless they consider them unlikely to commit additional crimes.[30]

To counter this, the retentionists claim that prison personnel and inmates are put in a position of danger when the life sentence is substituted for capital punishment. Criminals under a life sentence (especially those for whom the possibility of parole is remote) are likely to kill in an attempt to escape since they know their sentences cannot be increased if the attempt fails. Even though this has a surface plausibility, retentionists have been unable to offer proof in support of it. Some people experienced in the handling of prisoners have concluded that murderers, for example, are among the best behaved prisoners.[31] In addition, this argument fails to recognize that nearly all prisoners, including those given a life sentence, will at some time be eligible for parole. It is likely that the loss of the possibility of parole would also be a deterrent against killing to escape from prison.

Statistical information available is limited to that concerning the dangers of paroling life prisoners. Most prisoners sentenced to life imprisonment will at some time be eligible for parole,[32] and statistics show that most such prisoners become successful parolees. Of 36 prisoners under life sentence who were paroled between 1943 and 1958 in New York, only two were returned to prison—one for a technical offense and the other for burglary. Most of these prisoners would have been executed if their sentences had not been commuted.[33] Some retentionists emphasize that a parole board may make a mistake—it may release a person who is in fact very likely to commit other crimes. While this possibility cannot be denied, it does not provide a convincing reason for continued use of the death penalty. One would hardly argue that the right to a jury trial should be suspended in serious cases because the jury might make a mistake and allow a guilty person to go free.

## Other Issues

One of the oldest and most popular arguments for abolition is that innocent people are convicted and may possibly be executed.[34] Retentionists respond that mistakes are unlikely; the presence of the judge at trial and the impartial review upon appeal provide adequate protection.[35] Furthermore, abolitionists have been unable to show many instances in which it has been established that an innocent person actually was executed, although they have pointed to numerous cases in which persons sentenced to prison were later to be found innocent.[36] Perhaps the reason executions of innocent persons seldom come to light is because there is little impetus for a continued investigation once a person has been executed for a crime. Also, where the innocence of an executed person is later established, the police are understandingly hesitant to publicize the fact. But since the death penalty is in fact imposed for only those capital crimes which shock the public and where guilt is clear,[37] and in light of the existing safeguards of appellate review and the possibility of commutation, execution of the innocent is unlikely.

Another argument is that continued use of the death penalty has resulted in the execution of the mentally disturbed.[38] Retentionists agree that the execution of such persons is undesirable, but argue that the mentally disturbed are adequately protected by the existing tests of legal insanity,[39] or alternatively, that if these tests are inadequate, the appropriate solution is to devise better tests, not to abolish the death penalty.

"Pragmatic" arguments also enter the capital punishment controversy. Retentionists claim that it is less expensive to execute a criminal than to confine him for a long period. The abolitionists answer that if there is no possibility of a death sentence, more convictions with fewer delays will result; thus less money and effort will be expended on appeals designed only to delay and hinder.[40] Further, as an incidental effect, fewer guilty people will be freed because juries will no longer have the reluctance to bring in guilty verdicts when there is no possibility of execution. Thus each group claims the least expensive solution, but neither can produce factual support.

These arguments must be carried on at the level of opinion rather than fact, since proof is almost impossible to obtain. The adequacy of existing tests of insanity cannot be proven except by reference to some standard which is in essence nothing more than an opinion which is widely accepted.[41] It might be possible to compare the costs of keeping a criminal in prison with the costs of bringing one to execution, but it would be difficult to test the accuracy of such a comparison. There are difficulties in comparing criminals in different states and in comparing those in the same state at different times. The cost of executing a criminal is increased by delays. The extent of such delays depends upon the skill of attorneys and at times the sympathy of public officials. Because of differences in the importance of these factors in individual cases, cost comparisons are nearly impossible. Such areas of the controversy are likely to remain at the level of conflicting opinions for lack of a factual basis on which they can be resolved.

## Public Opinion

The death penalty has been abolished or severely restricted in only thirteen states.[42] But the abolitionist movement has had an effect in those states which have retained it since, in spite of increases in population and crime rates, the number of annual executions has decreased.[43] From 1930 through 1964 there were 3,848 executions in the United States. A comparison of the average annual executions in selected five year periods shows considerable decrease. There was an average of approximately 110 executions each year during the period. But in the years 1930 through 1934, the average was 155.2; from 1940 through 1944, an average of 129; from 1950 through 1954, an average of 82.6; from 1960 through 1964, an average of 36.2.[44] Since 1964 the level of executions has decreased further.[45]

It is upon state legislatures that primary responsibility for the decision to abolish or retain capital punishment finally rests. When abolition has been considered, the legislatures have generally voted to retain the death penalty. This might be explained either on the basis that legislators lag behind the opinion changes of their constituents, or that the public, as accurately reflected in the legislatures, actually favors the death penalty. In the short run, however, it does not matter which of these reasons is correct; the fact remains that the death penalty has not been abolished in many jurisdictions.

Inconclusive evidence of public opinion is available from those states where a referendum to abolish the death penalty has been taken. A 1958 Oregon referendum was defeated by a close vote, but in 1964 the referendum was carried by a vote of 455,654 to 302,105 and the death penalty was abolished. But in

1966 capital punishment was retained in Colorado by a vote of 389,707 to 193,245.[46]

Most opinion polls are inconclusive, although they do indicate that opposition to capital punishment is increasing. A Gallup Poll conducted in 1953 showed 68% favored the death penalty for persons convicted of murder, 25% opposed it, and 7% were undecided.[47] The same group conducted similar surveys posing the same question in 1960 and 1965. In 1960, 51% favored the death penalty, 36% opposed it, and 13% were undecided.[48] In 1965, 45% were in favor, 43% opposed, and 12% undecided.[49]

These surveys are not as significant as they might appear. Since the question asked only for a reaction to the use of death as a penalty for murder, the results are suspect when used as an indication of support for the use of the penalty for other crimes. More people might have favored it if confronted with a specific gruesome crime. On the other hand, more people might have opposed it if the question used had been framed in terms of an opinion on capital punishment with regard to the broad spectrum of crimes for which this penalty can be imposed. A 1958 Roper Poll bears out this uncertainty. Asked whether the heaviest penalty given people convicted of the "worst" crimes should be death or life imprisonment, 42% favored the death penalty, 50% favored life imprisonment, and 8% were undecided.[50]

It is unlikely that most state legislators would continue to oppose abolition if a substantial majority of people were, in fact, strongly opposed to capital punishment. It is not illogical to conclude, then, that the public has not been convinced by existing studies and the abolitionists' criticism of the deterrence and protection of society arguments. It may be that the public feels a need for retribution which the death penalty satisfies and which serves to justify it in spite of its lack of benefits in other respects.

An important aspect of the capital punishment controversy is centered about the relative importance which should be attributed to the factors of rehabilitation and retribution.[51] If retribution is its primary aim and the public feels that only the death penalty can achieve it, the likelihood that any specific criminal can be rehabilitated is irrelevant. For those who consider rehabilitation the primary aim of punishment and feel it is possible to rehabilitate even those criminals who committed capital crimes, the death penalty must appear harmful. Some criminals can be helped and others cannot. But the mere fact that the only effective way to handle some criminals may be life imprisonment without eligibility for parole does not provide justification for their execution. There is no proof that the level of support for the death penalty in the legislatures is due to an overriding concern for retribution. To the contrary, there is some indication that large segments of the population have repudiated vengeance as a primary aim of punishment. Most religious groups oppose capital punishment and have taken a stand against measures motivated by desire for revenge.[52]

But it is not necessary to conclude that rehabilitation and suitable retribution are mutually exclusive. Confinement alone qualifies as punishment and society's demand that criminals be punished can certainly be met by imposition of prison terms. An argument has been made that society demands the death penalty for certain criminals and that if they are not executed, private action will result. But experience in states which abolished capital punishment has shown no increase in lynchings or similar action has resulted. The South, which has the greatest incidence of private action, is characterized by a high execution level.[53]

## RECENT LEGAL ISSUES

Although the battle over the death penalty has been carried out primarily in the legislatures, the controversy has recently been brought to the courts with greater frequency. The argument that execution is cruel and unusual punishment prohibited by the Eighth Amendment has been unsuccessful.[54] Historically the Eighth Amendment has been used to prohibit punishment which is inherently cruel[55] or cruelly excessive.[56] But punishment by death—at least where it does not add unnecessary pain—has consistently been held outside of the Eighth Amendment prohibition.[57] Courts have also rejected the contention that capital punishment is *per se* a denial of due process. For example, the Washington Supreme Court recently held that:

> . . . The Fifth Amendment refers specifically to "capital cases", and also states . . . that a person may not be deprived of his life without due process. The Fifth Amendment also provides that a person may not be twice put in jeopardy of his life. Implicit in these are their corollaries—that the state may deprive an individual of his life if the proceedings are in accord with the requirements of due process and may place him in jeopardy once for a given offense. Certainly, if the state can call upon the most responsible and law abiding of its young men to sacrifice their lives in battle, it has the power, under the constitution, to execute one who, in a proceeding in which the requirements of due process have been strictly observed, has been found by a jury of his peers to have committed a crime so heinous that, in its opinion, his life should be exacted as a penalty.[58]

While the United States Supreme Court has not recently considered whether capital punishment is *per se* unconstitutional, recent decisions have restricted the use of the death penalty by holding unconstitutional some of the procedures by which its imposition was determined.

In *United States v. Jackson,*[59] a six-Justice majority held the death penalty provision of the Federal Kidnapping Act,[60] which limited the death penalty to cases where the jury recommended it, violated the Fifth and Sixth Amendments. Since the death penalty could be imposed only on defendants who asserted their right to a jury trial, the provision needlessly discouraged defendants from pleading innocent and demanding a jury trial. The majority did not rest its decision upon the assumption that the only *purpose* of this provision was to limit the assertion of basic constitutional rights. The majority was concerned with the effect rather than the purpose of the provision. To them, it was irrelevant whether the chilling effect of these rights was incidental or intentional; the question was whether the chilling effect was unnecessary and thus excessive.[61]

In spite of the fact that some states have provisions similar to the one held unconstitutional in *Jackson,* the effect of this decision has been limited. The highest courts of some states have distinguished *Jackson.* In *State v. Laws*[62] the New Jersey Supreme Court reasoned that the *Jackson* holding was not relevant where the power to reverse and nullify a death sentence is vested in an appellate court. Thus it held that a death sentence resulting from the failure of the jury to recommend mercy in a first degree murder conviction was not unconstitutional since it had the power to reduce such a sentence.[63] In *State v. Peele*[64] the North Carolina Supreme Court held that a provision making the death penalty mandatory upon a rape conviction unless the jury specifically ruled otherwise was constitutional. This court distinguished *Jackson.* The Federal Kidnapping Act allowed an accused kidnapper to escape the possibility of a death sentence either by pleading guilty or by requesting a bench trial. The North Carolina provision allowed the avoidance of a possible death sentence only by a guilty plea; if the plea was accepted by the state with the approval of the court, it had the effect of a guilty verdict with a life recommendation. The court characterized this provision as benefitting the defendant.[65]

In *Witherspoon v. Illinois*[66] the Supreme Court held that putting the power to impose the death penalty in the hands of a jury from which there had been excluded all persons expressing general objections to or religious scruples against capital punishment was violative of the Sixth and Fourteenth Amendments. Unless a venireman states unambiguously that he would vote against the death penalty regardless of what the trial might reveal, he cannot be excluded. If veniremen are excluded on any basis broader than this absolute refusal to impose the death penalty under any circumstances, the imposition of the death penalty is unconstitutional and the sentence cannot be carried out.[67]

If it is true that persons with conscientious or religious scruples against the death penalty will seldom if ever vote to impose it (as Justice Black suggests in his dissent to *Witherspoon*[68]), this decision will undoubtedly decrease the number of such sentences returned. Since the decision is retroactive, it will require resentencing of some defendants now awaiting execution. But Justice White, dissenting in *Witherspoon,*[69] has suggested that the future effect of this decision could easily be avoided by the legislature in any state where the jury now has the power to impose the death penalty by requiring only majority agreement rather than unanimity by the jury on the question of the sentence.

The majority in *Witherspoon* did not go as far as the Fourth Circuit did in *Crawford v. Bounds.*[70] That court held the exclusion of prospective jurors on the basis of their capital punishment views voided both the sentence and the conviction. The majority in *Crawford* was unable to agree on a rationale for this decision. Two judges felt that the systematic exclusion of any identifiable group within the community from which the jury venire is drawn violates the equal protection clause, irrespective of a showing of prejudice.[71] Two other judges felt it was wrong to rely so heavily on the equal protection ground. They reasoned that due process was violated simply because the issue of guilt was submitted to a jury from which every juror with scruples against the death penalty was excluded without inquiring whether these beliefs would preclude a fair consideration of the guilt issue. Three judges apparently based their decision flatly on the essential unfairness of excluding every juror professing an "unexplained scruple" against capital punishment while seating every juror who professed a belief in it.

*Jackson* and *Witherspoon* are significant not only because of their effect on the imposition of the death penalty, but also because they show the United States Supreme Court is now willing to take a constitutional stand in the capital punishment controversy. Perhaps as a result of these decisions, death penalty provisions have since come under increased attack in the state courts; the bases for these attacks have not been limited to the arguments which were successful in *Jackson* and *Witherspoon.* While these attacks have generally not been successful, they may signal a new era: The capital punishment controversy is increasingly being carried on in the courts.

Some state death sentence provisions have recently been attacked as lacking standards for imposition of the death penalty, thus resulting in a denial of due process and equal protection. This contention was raised before and rejected by at least two state supreme courts. The Washington Supreme Court reasoned that it was permissible for a jury to decide whether a particular punishment should be imposed as long as it did not, in so doing, determine the nature of the offense.[72] But a minority of the California Supreme Court argued that statutes without standards for imposition of the death penalty violate due process because, without standards, no meaningful review is possible. It also considered such statutes to be a denial of equal protection since they allow a jury to practice invidious discrimination—persons who commit the same crime and who cannot be classified differently on any reasonable basis can be given fundamentally different sentences.[73]

With these increasing statements by the courts, it is probable that the United States Supreme Court will eventually have to face the question of the *per se* constitutionality of the death penalty. The contention that capital punishment is unconstitutional under the Eighth Amendment is frequently raised.

It has long been recognized that the Eighth Amendment was not designed to eliminate merely physical brutalities.[74] The Supreme Court of the United States has, by reference to "standards of decency more or less universally accepted"[75] and "the evolving standards of decency that mark the process of a maturing society,"[76] recognized that the definition of inherently cruel and cruelly excessive punishment is not static. Since the Court apparently believes that the purview of this Amendment changes with the societal standard for acceptable punishment, the courts may be expected to look to data relevant to that standard.[77] The standard used will probably be based, either directly or tacitly, on public opinion. At least some justices of the Supreme Court have shown an acute awareness of public opinion on the capital punishment issue.[78]

But a court may invalidate a particular punishment only when there is an obvious societal standard which has been violated.[79] Existing public opinion surveys[80] do not provide an adequate indication of a societal standard with regard to use of the death penalty. Thus, unless polls which convincingly show the existence of a societal standard rejecting capital punishment can be offered, such legal attacks must fail and the resolution of the controversy must, by necessity, be left to the legislatures. The legislatures are presumably more responsive to public opinion than the courts. Consequently, if the controversy is to be decided on the basis of what the public thinks is appropriate, the courts should defer to the legislative judgment unless public opinion is obvious.

Some members of the Supreme Court of the United States have indicated a willingness to use, as evidence of a societal standard, the results of polls. In *Rudolph v. Alabama*[81] the Court refused to grant certiorari to consider whether the imposition of the death penalty for rape was prohibited by the Eighth Amendment. Justice Goldberg, joined by Justices Douglas and Brennan, dissented from the refusal. One of the questions the minority would have considered was whether the punishment by death for rape was violative of societal standards, and in doing so, would have considered the results of a survey of sixty-five countries.[82]

At this time, the Goldberg dissent in *Rudolph* has not been used as precedent for a decision on the merits. For example, while the court in *Bell v. Patterson*[83] noted that the scope of the Eighth Amendment was not static, it concluded that it was not broad enough to proscribe the death penalty as cruel and unusual punishment. Interestingly, the basis for this court's holding is somewhat contradictory to the idea that the scope of this amendment changes with societal standards—an idea which this court purports to accept. The court remarked that "[T]he decisions upholding the validity of the death penalty have not been overruled or even determined. Hence the law of the land as of the present moment is that the death penalty does not violate the Constitution of the United States."[84] It would seem that if the scope of the Eighth Amendment is not considered static, earlier decisions on its scope are significant only to the extent that societal standards have not changed.

## CONCLUSION

The 150 year old controversy over the death penalty is in need of settlement. But it is unlikely that such settlement will be reached through another "logical" analysis of the arguments which are as old as the controversy. Nor will settlement be likely to come through the development of new arguments.

Whether the controversy is ultimately settled in the legislatures or in the courts, the resolution will depend upon public opinion. Thus the approach to the controversy of rephrasing the old arguments, changing the emphasis to those currently in vogue, and adding emotional appeals in current fashion must be abandoned, and more emphasis placed on determining what the public actually thinks about capital punishment.

But this does not mean that other issues such as the existence of a deterrent effect, existence of discrimination in application, and the necessity of protecting society can be ignored. Both retentionists and abolitionists can contribute to the resolution of the controversy by presenting empirical evidence to sustain their position on each of these issues. It is by presenting such evidence that public opinion can be changed.

Recent experience may indicate that the death penalty is fast becoming a thing of the past. In spite of the fact that attempts to abolish capital punishment in the legislatures have generally failed, that attempts to have it declared unconstitutional are unsuccessful, and that many death sentences are still being returned, very few criminals have been executed in recent years. But it is unlikely that the controversy over capital punishment will so easily disappear.

### NOTES

1. For a discussion of the historical background of the controversy *see* Bedau, *Death Penalty in America* 7–13 (1st ed. 1964).

2. This term is used to designate those who favor the use of the death penalty.
3. This term is used to designate those opposed to the use of the death penalty. Of course many individuals involved in this controversy do not fit neatly into either the abolitionist or retentionist classification.
4. *See, e.g.,* Sellin, "Capital Punishment," 25 *Fed Prob.* 3 (Sept. 1961).
5. *See* Gerstein, "A Prosecutor Looks at Capital Punishment," 51 *J. Crim. L.C. & P.S.* 252 (1960).
6. *Id.* at 254.
7. *See* Comment, "In Defense of Capital Punishment," 54 *Ky. L.J.* 743 (1966).
8. *See* Schmidelberg, "The Offender's Attitude Toward Punishment," 51 *J. Crim. L.C. & P.S.* 328, 332–33 (1960)
9. *See, e.g.,* Bedau, *supra* note 1, at 273.
10. *See* Comment, "In Defense of Capital Punishment" *supra* note 7, at 744.
11. *See* Schmidelberg, *supra* note 8, at 332–33, and text accompanying note 8.
12. *See* Sellin, *supra* note 4.
13. *See* Reichert, "Capital Punishment Reconsidered," 47 *Ky L.J.* 397 (1958).
14. Gerstein, *supra* note 5 at 252–53. *See also,* Van Den Haag, for comment "On Deterrence and the Death Penalty," 60 *J. Crim. L. C. & P. S.* 141 (1969), a recent article, in which the author argues for the retention of the death penalty. The author notes that the actual number of persons deterred by the penalty is still unknown.
15. Most available statistics on cause of death include the category of homicide, but do not break this into sub-categories. *See* Bedau, *supra* note 1, at 277.
16. *Id.* at 264.
17. *See* Gerstein, *supra* note 5, at 252.
18. Sellin, *supra* note 4, at 6.
19. *See, e.g.,* Comment, "Capital Punishment," 29 *Tenn. L. Rev.* 534, 542–45 (1962).
20. *Id.* at 542.
21. Bedau, *supra* note 1, table 6 at 116–117.
22. Data indicating racial discrimination in the imposition of the death penalty is presented in Comment, *supra* note 19.
23. *See* Bedau, *supra* note 1, at 74–90 for an analysis of criminal homicide by Marvin E. Wolfgang. On the basis of all criminal homicides recorded by the Philadelphia Homicide Squad between January 1, 1948 and December 31, 1952, the rate per 100,000 by race and sex of offenders was: Negro males (41.7), Negro females (9.3), white males (3.4), and white females (.4). Bedau, *supra* note 1, at 78.
24. *Id.* at 116–117.
25. Comment, *supra* note 19, at 543.
26. Some steps which result in greater uniformity of application have already been taken. The indigent are appointed counsel. Gideon v. Wainwright, 372 U.S. 335 (1963). They are also notified of their right of counsel and having this counsel available before trial. Escobedo v. Illinois, 378 U.S. 478 (1964); Miranda v. Arizona, 384 U.S. 436 (1966).

27. *See* Gerstein, *supra* note 5 at 255.
28. *See* Comment, *supra* note 19 at 550.
29. *See* "In Defense of Capital Punishment," *supra* note 7, at 246–47.
30. Whether or not parole boards can make accurate decisions in this regard is open to question.
31. *See* Comment, *supra* note 19, at 548; and Sellin, *supra* note 4 at 6–7.
32. *See* Comment, *supra* note 19 at 549.
33. *Id.* at 550. Paine also reports other examples of success in paroling convicted murderers. For example, in Ohio 94.1% of such paroles were successful as compared with a 74% success level for other paroles in that state. Of the 164 first-degree murderers paroled in Michigan between 1938 and 1961, only four were returned; just one of these four was returned for a new felony. *See also* Sellin, *supra* note 4 at 6–8.
34. *See* "In Defense of Capital Punishment," *supra* note 7 at 745.
35. *Id.*
36. *See* Bedau, *supra* note 1, at 434–52.
37. *See* "In Defense of Capital Punishment," *supra* note 7 at 745.
38. *See, e.g.,* Gaetz, "Should Ohio Abolish Capital Punishment?," *Cleve.-Mar. L. Rev.* 365, 371–72 (1961).
39. Most jurisdictions use either the M'Naughten or Durham rule to determine legal insanity. The M'Naughten rule provides that if the defendant did not know the nature of his act or that it was wrong, he will be declared insane. The Durham rule provides that one accused is not criminally responsible if his unlawful act was the product of a mental disease or defect.
40. *See* McGee, "Capital Punishment as Seen by a Correctional Administrator," 28 *Fed. Prob.* 11, 13 (June 1964). Some writers have suggested that effective use of prison labor power could be made and the cost to the public of imprisonment thus reduced. *See, e.g.,* Sellin, *supra* note 4 at 3.
41. Both the M'Naughten and Durham rules have come under frequent criticism. The objection has often been made that many dangerous offenders are medically insane but do not qualify as legally insane under these tests. For example, in Frigillana v. United States, 307 F. 2d 665, 667 (D.C. Cir. 1962) the court noted: "We submit that under a standard or test based upon the basic concepts of criminal responsibility—that is cognition and volition or capacity to control behavior—there might be some meaningful medical testimony. . . .

    "As we see it the difficulty of the experts in this case arose in large part because they did not understand what 'product' means as stated in our rule, for the term 'product' has no special generally accepted meaning in medicine. And of course it has no special meaning in law."

    For a discussion of the problems these rules present for the psychiatrist "expert witness" called on to testify as to insanity, *see* Halleck, "The Psychiatrist and the Legal Process," *Psychology Today,* Vol. 2, No. 9 at 24 (Feb. 1969).
42. These states are Michigan, Rhode Island (which permits capital punishment only for life term convicts who commit murder), Wisconsin, Maine, Minnesota, North Dakota (which retains the death penalty for murder by a prisoner serving a life term for murder), Alaska, Hawaii, Oregon, Iowa, West Virginia, Vermont, and New York (which retains the death penalty for murder of a police officer

on duty, or of anyone by a prisoner under life sentence). For a discussion of the use of capital punishment in the United States and in foreign countries, *see* Patrick, "The Status of Capital Punishment: A World Perspective," 56 *J. Crim. L.C. & P.S.* 397 (1965).

43. It has not been established whether this decrease is primarily due to the reluctance of juries to bring in a verdict which might result in an execution, the reluctance of judges (where they have discretion) to impose the death penalty, or the fact that more such sentences are reversed on appeal or commuted.
44. Based on figures reported by the U.S. Bureau of Prisons in *National Prisoner Statistics.*
45. For example, there were no executions in 1968, two in 1967, and one in 1966.
46. Bedau, *Death Penalty in America* 233 (rev. ed. 1967).
47. *Id.* at 237. The question asked was: "Are you in favor of the death penalty for persons convicted of murder?"
48. *Id.* at 239.
49. Bedau, *supra* note 46, at 238.
50. Bedau, *supra* note 1, at 234. This poll is of doubtful significance because of the word "worst." The individuals polled may have had widely divergent views on which crimes are worst.
51. Opinion on the issue of whether retribution is a proper aim of punishment splits three ways. One position is that it is never a proper aim and should be avoided in all cases. A second position is that punishment for the sole purpose of vengeance is undesirable, but that this is one of numerous permissible aims of punishment. The third position is that retribution is a proper aim for all punishment and may become the primary concern in appropriate cases, *e.g.,* a person who has committed a crime particularly shocking to the public.
52. *See, e.g.,* Milligan, "A Protestant's View of the Death Penalty," reprinted in Bedau, *supra* note 1, at 175, and Kazis, "Judaism and the Death Penalty," reprinted in Bedau, *supra* note 1, at 171. Whether the official position of such groups is a reflection of its members' opinions or is an attempt to "lead" these opinions is open to question.
53. Comment, *supra* note 19, at 538–39.
54. *See* Bell v. Patterson, 279 F.Supp. 760 (D.Colo. 1968).
55. *See, e.g.,* Rosenberg v. Carral, 99 F.Supp. 630 (S.D.N.Y. 1951) (confinement in death row awaiting execution is not inherently cruel).
56. *See, e.g.,* State v. Evans, 73 Idaho 50, 245 P.2d 788 (1952).
57. *See, e.g.,* In re Storti, 178 Mass. 549 60 N.E. 210 (1901).
58. State v. Smith, 446 P.2d 571, 589 (Wash. 1968).
59. 390 U.S. 570 (1968).
60. 18 U.S.C. §1201 (a).
61. United States v. Jackson, 390 U.S. 570, 581–583 (1968).
62. 51 N.J. 494 242 A.2d 333 (1968).
63. But it does not appear from *Jackson* that the constitutionality of the death penalty provision of the Federal Kidnapping Act would have been saved by the power in an appellate court to reverse or reduce the penalty. In *Jackson,* the Court was concerned with a *needless* chilling effect on the exercise of the right to a jury trial. This objection is not eliminated by such a power in an appellate court. A death penalty is still possible only when the right to a jury

trial has been asserted. Thus the objectionable needless chilling effect is still present.

64. 274 N.C. 106, 161 S.E.2d 568 (1968).
65. Even if the North Carolina court was correct in characterizing this provision as for the benefit of the defendant, it is still objectionable under the *Jackson* reasoning. Since under this provision the possibility of a death sentence could be avoided only by a guilty plea, it has an even stronger chilling effect on basic constitutional rights than the *Jackson* situation. To avoid the possibility of the death penalty, a defendant need not only waive his right to jury trial but must also plead guilty.
66. 391 U.S. 510 (1968).
67. This decision does not prevent the exclusion from the jury of veniremen who make "unmistakably clear . . . that they would *automatically* vote against the imposition of capital punishment without regard to any evidence that might be developed at the trial of the case before them, or . . . that their attitude toward the death penalty would prevent them from making an impartial decision as to the defendant's *guilt*." 391 U.S. at 522–523 n.21. But a high standard for permissible exclusion of veniremen has obviously been set.
68. 391 U.S. at 532.
69. 391 U.S. at 540.
70. 395 F.2d 297 (4th Cir. 1968).
71. Apparently this is also the position taken by Justice Douglas in his separate opinion in *Witherspoon*. 391 U.S. 510, 523 (1968). He would not require a showing of prejudice with respect to guilt since he is willing to assume than in many, if not most, cases of class exclusion some prejudice does result.
72. State v. Smith, 446 P.2d 571 (Wash. 1968).
73. In re Anderson, 73 Cal. Rptr. 21, 447 P.2d 117 (1968). The majority set aside the defendant's death sentence on the basis of *Witherspoon*, but held that the death penalty statutes themselves were not unconstitutional. It felt that absolute discretion as to sentence could be left to the trier of fact and, since the statute did this, the appellate courts could not substitute their judgment on penalty for that of the trier of fact. The majority felt there was adequate protection against arbitrary abuses since the trial judge could review and reduce a sentence on a motion for a new trial and the governor could grant a pardon or commutation.
74. Weems v. United States, 217 U.S. 349 (1910).
75. Louisiana *ex rel* Francis v. Resweber, 329 U.S. 459, 469 (1947).
76. Trop v. Dulles, 356 U.S. 86, 101 (1957).
77. *See* Note, "Constitutional Law—Cruel and Unusual—Capital Punishment," 42 *N.C. L. Rev*. 909 (1964).
78. *See* notes 81–82 *infra* and accompanying text.
79. *See* Note, *supra* note 77.
80. *See* notes 46–50 *supra* and accompanying text.
81. 375 U.S. 889 (1963).
82. The Goldberg dissent in *Rudolph* was critically analyzed in Parker, "Making the Punishment Fit the Crime," 77 *Harv. L. Rev*. 1071 (1964).
83. 279 F.Supp. 760 (D.Colo. 1968).
84. 279 F.Supp. at 765.

# III Proponents of Capital Punishment

This section begins with two articles, "In Favor of Capital Punishment," by Professor Jacques Barzun, of Columbia University, and "On Deterrence and the Death Penalty," by Ernest van den Haag, Adjunct Professor of Philosophy at New York University. The section closes with position papers by Edward J. Allen, Chief of Police at Santa Ana, California, Richard E. Gerstein, State Attorney, Eleventh Judicial Circuit of Florida and James V. Bennett, retired Director of the United States Bureau of Prisons. These latter papers mirror the views of persons responsible for administering criminal justice. Here we have a representative view of a police officer, a state's attorney, and an administrator of one of the largest prison systems in the Western World.

Barzun, a distinguished university educator and author, supports the death penalty on the grounds that it deters crime. Likewise, van den Haag, an educator, psychoanalyst and author, uses deterrence as an uppermost argument. Van den Haag further indicates that murder is not subject to social control, whereas society can provide control over those persons who commit murder by imposing the death sentence. Both authors lend importance to the proponent position because of their noteworthy contributions to the current mainstream philosophy in the United States.

Allen, who presents the view of the police officer, feels that the idea of certain punishment is being repudiated by judges and governors who permit their opinions to delay or stop the imposition of the supreme penalty. In his judgment, "The business of government is justice, not pity—however self-consoling." One of Allen's major issues is the great danger that would befall the law enforcement officer should capital punishment be repealed.

Prosecutor Gerstein identifies heinous crimes that require capital punishment; many of these have overtones of sexual depravation linked to homicide. According to Gerstein, the final argument for the retention of capital punishment is the State's right of self-defense. Society in the name of the State is justified in slaying the evildoer.

The mood of the administrator who must carry out the law when it is his responsibility to execute is described by James V. Bennett. In a conversational exposition of the problem, Bennett portrays some of the most notorious Federal capital punishment cases. These include the case of Arthur Ross Brown, a convicted murderer and rapist who was executed in February 1956 at the Missouri State Prison gas chamber. Obviously Brown had not been deterred by the worldwide publicity given to Carl Austin Hall and Bonnie Brown Heady, who were executed together in the same gas chamber three years earlier.

The near-execution of Charles Bernstein, also discussed by Bennett, illustrates the problem of possible error in the use of the death penalty. A last-minute commutation to life imprisonment spared Bernstein's life. President Franklin D. Roosevelt later gave Bernstein full freedom and he was subsequently pardoned by President Harry S. Truman. Bills to provide compensation to

Bernstein have been introduced in the United States Congress, but to date he has received no award.

The prison administrator's concern with his role in regard to capital punishment is evident as Bennett describes his encounters with Robert Stroud, the "Birdman of Alcatraz," and the Rosenbergs, Julius and Ethel, executed at Sing Sing prison on June 19, 1953 for espionage involving American atomic secrets during World War II.

In the end, the former Director of the Federal prison system sees himself standing on a middle ground in the capital punishment issue.

# 4 *In Favor of Capital Punishment*

## JACQUES BARZUN

A passing remark of mine in the *Mid-Century* magazine has brought me a number of letters and a sheaf of pamphlets against capital punishment. The letters, sad and reproachful, offer me the choice of pleading ignorance or being proved insensitive. I am asked whether I know that there exists a worldwide movement for the abolition of capital punishment which has everywhere enlisted able men of every profession, including the law. I am told that the death penalty is not only inhuman but also unscientific, for rapists and murderers are really sick people who should be cured, not killed. I am invited to use my imagination and acknowledge the unbearable horror of every form of execution.

I am indeed aware that the movement for abolition is widespread and articulate, especially in England. It is headed there by my old friend and publisher, Mr. Victor Gollancz, and it numbers such well-known writers as Arthur Koestler, C. H. Rolph, James Avery Joyce and Sir John Barry. Abroad as at home the profession of psychiatry tends to support the cure principle, and many liberal newspapers, such as the *Observer,* are committed to abolition. In the United States there are at least twenty-five state leagues working to the same end, plus a national league and several church councils, notably the Quaker and the Episcopal.

The assemblage of so much talent and enlightened goodwill behind a single proposal must give pause to anyone who supports the other side, and in the attempt to make clear my views, which are now close to unpopular, I start out by granting that my conclusion is arguable; that is, I am still open to conviction, *provided* some fallacies and frivolities in the abolitionist argument are first disposed of and the difficulties not ignored but overcome. I should be glad to see this happen, not only because there is pleasure in the spectacle of an airtight case, but also because I am not more sanguinary than my neighbor and I should welcome the discovery of safeguards—for society *and* the criminal—other than killing. But I say it again, these safeguards must really meet, not evade or postpone, the difficulties I am about to describe. Let me add before I begin that I shall probably not answer any more letters on this arousing subject. If this printed exposition does not do justice to my cause, it is not likely that I can do better in the hurry of private correspondence.

I readily concede at the outset that present ways of dealing out capital punishment are as revolting as Mr. Koestler says in his harrowing volume, *Hanged by the Neck.* Like many of our prisons, our modes of execution should change. But this objection to barbarity does not mean that capital punishment—or rather, judicial homicide—should not go on. The illicit jump we find here, on the threshold of the inquiry, is characteristic of the abolitionist and must be disallowed at every point. Let us bear in mind the possibility of devising a painless, sudden and dignified death, and see whether its administration is justifiable.

The four main arguments advanced against the death penalty are: *1.* punishment for crime is a primitive idea rooted in revenge; *2.* capital punishment does not deter; *3.* judicial error being possible, taking life is an appalling risk; *4.* a civilized state, to deserve its name, must uphold, not violate, the sanctity of human life.

I entirely agree with the first pair of propositions, which is why, a moment ago, I replaced the term capital punishment with "judicial homicide." The uncontrollable brute whom I want put out of the way is not to be punished for his misdeeds, nor used as an example or a warning; he is to be killed for the protection of others, like the wolf that escaped not long ago in a Connecticut suburb. No anger, vindictiveness or moral conceit need preside over the removal of such dangers. But a man's inability to control his violent impulses or to imagine the fatal consequences of his acts should be a presumptive reason for his elimination from society. This generality covers drunken driving and teen-age racing on public highways, as well as incurable obsessive violence; it might be extended (as I shall suggest later) to other acts that destroy, precisely, the moral basis of civilization.

But why kill? I am ready to believe the statistics tending to show that the prospect of his own death does not stop the murderer. For one thing he is often a blind egotist, who cannot conceive the possibility of his own death. For another, detection would have to be infallible to deter the more imaginative who, although afraid, think they can escape discovery. Lastly, as Shaw long ago pointed out, hanging the wrong man will deter as effectively as hanging the right one. So, once again, why kill? If I agree that moral progress means an increasing respect for human life, how can I oppose abolition?

I do so because on this subject of human life, which is to me the heart of the controversy, I find the abolitionist inconsistent, narrow or blind. The propaganda for abolition speaks in hushed tones of the sanctity of human life, as if the mere statement of it as an absolute should silence all opponents who have any moral sense. But most of the abolitionists belong to nations that spend half their annual income on weapons of war and that honor research to perfect means of killing. These good people vote without a qualm for the political parties that quite sensibly arm their country to the teeth. The West today does not seem to be the time or place to invoke the absolute sanctity of human life. As for the clergymen in the movement, we may be sure from the experience of two previous world wars that they will bless our arms and pray for victory when called upon, the sixth commandment notwithstanding.

"Oh, but we mean the sanctity of life *within* the nation!" Very well: is the movement then campaigning also against the principle of self-defense? Absolute sanctity means letting the cutthroat have his sweet will of you, even if you have a poker handy to bash him with, for you might kill. And again, do we hear any protest against the police firing at criminals on the street—mere bank robbers usually—and doing this, often enough, with an excited marksmanship that misses the artist and hits the bystander? The absolute sanctity of human life is, for the abolitionist, a slogan rather than a considered proposition.

Yet, it deserves examination, for upon our acceptance or rejection of it depend such other highly civilized possibilities as euthanasia and seemly suicide. The inquiring mind also wants to know, why the sanctity of *human* life alone? My tastes do not run to household pets, but I find something less than admirable in the uses to which we put animals—in zoos, laboratories and space machines—without the excuse of the ancient law, "Eat or be eaten."

It should moreover be borne in mind that this argument about sanctity applies—or would apply—to about ten persons a year in Great Britain and to between fifty and seventy-five in the United States. These are the average numbers of those executed in recent years. The count by itself should not, of course, affect our judgment of the principle: one life spared or forfeited is as important, morally, as a hundred thousand. But it should inspire a comparative judgment: there are hundreds and indeed thousands whom, in our concern with the horrors of execution, we forget: on the one hand, the victims of violence; on the other, the prisoners in our jails.

The victims are easy to forget. Social science tends steadily to mark a preference for the troubled, the abnormal, the problem case. Whether it is poverty, mental disorder, delinquency or crime, the "patient material" monopolizes the interest of increasing groups of people among the most generous and learned. Psychiatry and moral liberalism go together; the application of law as we have known it is thus coming to be regarded as an historic prelude to social work, which may replace it entirely. Modern literature makes the most of this same outlook, caring only for the disturbed spirit, scorning as bourgeois those who pay their way and do *not* stab their friends. All the while the determinism of natural science reinforces the assumption that society causes its own evils. A French jurist, for example, says that in order to understand crime we must first brush aside all ideas of Responsibility. He means the criminal's and takes for granted that of society. The murderer kills because reared in a broken home or, conversely, because at an early age he witnessed his parents making love. Out of such cases, which make pathetic reading in the literature of modern criminology, is born the abolitionist's state of mind: we dare not kill those we are beginning to understand so well.

If, moreover, we turn to the accounts of the crimes committed by these unfortunates, who are the victims? Only dull ordinary people going about their business. We are sorry, of course, but they do not interest science on its march. Balancing, for example, the sixty to seventy criminals executed annually in the United States, there were the seventy to eighty housewives whom George Cvek robbed, raped and usually killed during the months of a career devoted to proving his virility. "It is too bad." Cvek alone seems instructive, even though one of the law officers who helped track him down quietly remarks: "As to the extent that his villainies disturbed family relationships, or how many women are still haunted by the specter of an experience they have never disclosed to another living soul, these questions can only lend themselves to sterile conjecture."

The remote results are beyond our ken, but it is not idle to speculate about those whose death by violence fills the daily two inches at the back of respectable newspapers—the old man sunning himself on a park bench and beaten to death by four hoodlums, the small children abused and strangled, the middle-aged ladies on a hike assaulted and killed, the family terrorized by a released or escaped lunatic, the half-dozen working people massacred by the sudden maniac, the boatload of persons dispatched by the skipper, the mindless assaults upon schoolteachers and shopkeepers by the increasing horde of dedicated killers in our great cities. Where does the sanctity of life begin?

It is all very well to say that many of these killers are themselves "children," that is, minors. Doubtless a nine-year-old mind is housed in that 150 pounds of unguided muscle. Grant, for argument's sake, that the misdeed is "the fault of society," trot out the broken home and the slum environment. The question then is, What shall we do, not in the Utopian city of tomorrow, but here and now? The "scientific" means of cure are more than uncertain. The apparatus of detention only increases the killer's antisocial animus. Reformatories and mental hospitals are full and have an understandable bias toward discharging their inmates. Some of these are indeed "cured"—so long as they stay under a rule. The stress of the social free-for-all throws them back on their violent modes of self-expression. At that point I agree that society has failed—twice: it has twice failed the victims, whatever may be its guilt toward the killer.

As in all great questions, the moralist must choose, and choosing has a price. I happen to think that if a person of adult body has not been endowed with adequate controls against irrationally taking the life of another, that person must be judicially, painlessly, regretfully killed before that mindless body's horrible automation repeats.

I say "irrationally" taking life, because it is often possible to feel great sympathy with a murderer. Certain *crimes passionnels* can be forgiven without being condoned. Blackmailers invite direct retribution. Long provocation can be an excuse, as in that engaging case of some years ago, in which a respectable carpenter of seventy found he could no longer stand the incessant nagging of his wife. While she excoriated him from her throne in the kitchen—a daily exercise for fifty years—the husband went to his bench and came back with a hammer in each hand to settle the score. The testimony to his character, coupled with the sincerity implied by the two hammers, was enough to have him sent into quiet and brief seclusion.

But what are we to say of the type of motive disclosed in a journal published by the inmates of one of our Federal penitentiaries? The author is a bank robber who confesses that money is not his object:

> My mania for power, socially, sexually, and otherwise can feel no degree of satisfaction until I feel sure I have struck the ultimate of submission and terror in the minds and bodies of my victims. . . . It's very difficult to explain all the queer fascinating sensations pounding and surging through me while I'm holding a gun on a victim, watching his body tremble and sweat. . . . This is the moment when all the rationalized hypocrisies of civilization are suddenly swept away and two men stand there facing each other morally and ethically naked, and right and wrong are the absolute commands of the man behind the gun.

This confused echo of modern literature and modern science defines the choice before us. Anything deserving the name of cure for such a man presupposes not only a laborious individual psychoanalysis, with the means to conduct and to sustain it, socially and economically, but also a re-education of the mind, so as to throw into correct perspective the garbled ideas of Freud and Nietzsche, Gide and Dostoevski, which this power-seeker and his fellows have derived from the culture and temper of our times. Ideas are tenacious and give continuity to emotion. Failing a second birth of heart and mind, we must ask: How soon will this sufferer sacrifice a bank clerk in the interests of making civilization less hypocritical? And we must certainly question the wisdom of affording him more than one chance. The abolitionists' advocacy of an unconditional "let live" is in truth part of the same cultural tendency that animates the killer. The Western peoples' revulsion from power in domestic and foreign policy has made of the state a sort of counterpart of the bank robber: both having power and neither knowing how to use it. Both waste lives because hyponotized by irrelevant ideas and crippled by contradictory emotions. If psychiatry were sure of its ground in diagnosing the individual case, a philosopher might consider whether such dangerous obsessions should not be guarded against by judicial homicide *before* the shooting starts.

I raise the question not indeed to recommend the prophylactic execution of potential murderers, but to introduce the last two perplexities that the abolitionists dwarf or obscure by their concentration on changing an isolated penalty. One of these is the scale by which to judge the offenses society wants to repress. I can for example imagine a truly democratic state in which it would be deemed a form of treason punishable by death to create a disturbance in any court or deliberative assembly. The aim would be to recognize the sanctity of orderly discourse in arriving at justice, assessing criticism and defining policy. Under such a law, a natural selection would operate to remove permanently from the scene persons who, let us say, neglect argument in favor of banging on the desk with their shoe. Similarly, a bullying minority in a diet, parliament or skupshtina would be prosecuted for treason to the most sacred institutions when fists or flying inkwells replace rhetoric. That the mere suggestion of such a law sounds ludicrous shows how remote we are from civilized institutions, and hence how gradual should be our departure from the severity of judicial homicide.

I say gradual and I do not mean standing still. For there is one form of barbarity in our law that I want to see mitigated before any other. I mean imprisonment. The enemies of capital punishment—and liberals generally—seem to be satisfied with any legal outcome so long as they themselves avoid the vicarious guilt of shedding blood. They speak of the sanctity of life, but have no concern with its quality. They give no impression of ever having read what it is certain they have read, from Wilde's *De Profundis* to the latest account of prison life by a convicted homosexual. Despite the infamy of concentration camps, despite Mr. Charles Burney's remarkable work, *Solitary Confinement,* despite riots in prisons, despite the round of escape, recapture and return in chains, the abolitionists' imagination tells them nothing about the reality of being caged. They read without a qualm, indeed they read with rejoicing, the hideous irony of "Killer Gets Life"; they sigh with relief instead of horror. They do not see and suffer the cell, the drill, the clothes, the stench, the food; they do not feel the sexual racking of young and old bodies, the hateful promiscuity, the insane monotony, the mass degradation, the impotent hatred. They do not remember from Silvio Pellico that only a strong political faith, with a hope of final victory, can steel a man to endure long detention. They forget that Joan of Arc, when offered "life" preferred burning at the stake. Quite of another mind, the abolitionists point with pride to the "model prisoners" that murderers often turn out to be. As if a model prisoner were not, first, a contradiction in terms, and second, an exemplar of what a free society should not want.

I said a moment ago that the happy advocates of the life sentence appear not to have understood what we know they have read. No more do they appear to read what they themselves write. In the preface to his useful volume of cases, *Hanged in Error,* Mr. Leslie Hale, M.P., refers to the tardy recognition of a minor miscarriage of justice—one year in jail: "The prisoner emerged to find that his wife had died and that his children and his aged parents had been removed to the workhouse. By the time a small payment had been assessed as 'compensation' the victim was incurably insane." So far we are as indignant with the law as Mr. Hale. But what comes next? He cites the famous Evans case, in which it is very probable that the wrong man was hanged, and he exclaims: "While such mistakes are possible, should society impose an irrevocable sentence?" Does Mr. Hale really ask us to believe that the sentence passed on the first man, whose wife died and who went insane, was in any sense *revocable?* Would not any man rather be Evans dead than that other wretch "emerging" with his small compensation and his reasons for living gone?"

Nothing is revocable here below, imprisonment least of all. The agony of a trial itself is punishment, and acquittal wipes out nothing. Read the heart-rending diary of William Wallace, accused quite implausibly of having murdered his wife and "saved" by the Court of Criminal Appeals—but saved for what? Brutish ostracism by everyone and a few years of solitary despair. The cases of Adolf Beck, of Oscar Slater, of the unhappy Brooklyn bank teller who vaguely resembled a forger and spent eight years in Sing Sing only to "emerge" a broken, friendless, useless, "compensated" man—all these, if the dignity of the individual has any meaning, had better have been dead before the prison door ever opened for them. This is what counsel always says to the jury in the course of a murder trial and counsel is right: far better hang this man than "give him life." For my part, I would choose death without hesitation. If that option is abolished, a demand will one day be heard to claim it as a privilege in the name of human dignity. I shall believe in the abolitionist's present views only after he has emerged from twelve months in a convict cell.

The detached observer may want to interrupt here and say that the argument has now passed from reasoning to emotional preference. Whereas the objection to capital punishment *feels* that death is the greatest of evils, I *feel* that imprisonment is worse than death. A moment's thought will show that feeling is the appropriate arbiter. All reasoning about what is right, civilized and moral rests upon sentiment, like mathematics. Only, in trying to persuade others, it is important to single out the fundamental feeling, the prime intuition, and from it to reason justly. In my view, to profess respect for human life and be willing to see it spent in a penitentiary is to entertain liberal feelings frivolously. To oppose the death penalty because, unlike a prison term, it is irrevocable is to argue fallaciously.

In the propaganda for abolishing the death sentence the recital of numerous miscarriages of justice commits the same error and implies the same callousness: what is at fault in our present system is not the sentence but the fallible procedure. Capital cases being one in a thousand or more, who can be cheerful at the thought of all the "revocable" errors? What the miscarriages point to is the need for reforming the jury system, the rules of evidence, the customs of prosecution, the machinery of appeal. The failure to see that this is the great task reflects the sentimentality I spoke of earlier, that which responds chiefly to the excitement of the unusual. A writer on Death and the Supreme Court is at pains to point out that when that tribunal reviews a capital case, the judges are particularly anxious and careful. What a left-handed compliment to the highest judicial conscience of the country! Fortunately, some of the champions of the misjudged see the issue more clearly. Many of those who are thought wrongly convicted now languish in jail because the jury was uncertain or because a doubting governor commuted the death sentence. Thus Dr. Samuel H. Sheppard, Jr., convicted of his wife's murder in the second degree, is serving a sentence that is supposed to run for the term of his natural life. The story of his numerous trials, as told by Mr. Paul Holmes, suggests that police incompetence, newspaper demagogy, public envy of affluence and the mischances of legal procedure fashioned the result. But Dr. Sheppard's vindicator is under no illusion as to the conditions that this "lucky" evader of the electric chair will face if he is granted parole after ten years: "It will carry with it no right to resume his life as a physician. His privilege to practice medicine was blotted out with his conviction. He must all his life bear the stigma of a parolee, subject to unceremonious return to confinement for life for the slightest misstep. More than this, he must live out his life as a convicted murderer."[1]

What does the moral conscience of today think it is doing? If such a man is a dangerous repeater of violent acts, what right has the state to let him loose after ten years? What is, in fact, the meaning of a "life sentence" that peters out long before life? Paroling looks suspiciously like an expression of social remorse of the pain of incarceration, coupled with a wish to avoid "unfavorable publicity" by freeing a suspect. The man is let out when the fuss has died down; which would mean that he was not under lock and key for our protection at all. He *was* being punished, just a little—for so prison seems in the abolitionist's distorted view, and in the jury's and the prosecutor's, whose "second-degree" murder suggests killing someone "just a little."[2]

If, on the other hand, execution and life imprisonment are judged too severe and the accused is expected to be harmless hereafter—punishment being ruled out as illiberal—what has society gained by wrecking his life and damaging that of his family?

What we accept, and what the abolitionist will clamp upon us all the more firmly if he succeeds, is an incoherence which is not remedied by the belief that second-degree murder merits a kind of second-degree death; that a doubt as to the identity of a killer is resolved by commuting real death into intolerable life; and that our ignorance whether a maniac will strike again can be hedged against by measuring "good behavior" within the gates and then releasing the subject upon the public in the true spirit of experimentation.

These are some of the thoughts I find I cannot escape when I read and reflect upon this grave subject. If, as I think, they are relevant to any discussion of change and reform, resting as they do on the direct and concrete perception of what happens, then the simple meliorists who expect to breathe a purer air by abolishing the death penalty are deceiving themselves and us. The issue is for the public to judge; but I for one shall not sleep easier for knowing that in England and America and the West generally a hundred more human beings are kept alive in degrading conditions to face a hopeless future; while others—possibly less conscious, certainly less controlled—benefit from a premature freedom dangerous alike to themselves and society. In short, I derive no comfort from the illusion that in giving up one manifest protection of the law-abiding, we who might well be in any of these three roles—victim, prisoner, licensed killer—have struck a blow for the sanctity of human life.

## NOTES

1. Editor's note: See Sheppard v. Maxwell, 346 F.2d 707 which reversed defendant Sheppard's conviction. Released from prison, Dr. Sheppard later succumbed following a brief illness.
2. The British Homicide Act of 1957, Section 2, implies the same reasoning in its definition of "diminished responsibility" for certain forms of mental abnormality. The whole question of irrationality and crime is in utter confusion, on both sides of the Atlantic.

# 5

# *On Deterrence and the Death Penalty*

ERNEST VAN DEN HAAG

## I

If rehabilitation and the protection of society from unrehabilitated offenders were the only purposes of legal punishment the death penalty could be abolished: it cannot attain the first end, and is not needed for the second. No case for the death penalty can be made unless "doing justice," or "deterring others," are among our penal aims.[1] Each of these purposes can justify capital punishment by itself; opponents, therefore, must show that neither actually does, while proponents can rest their case on either.

Although the argument from justice is intellectually more in-

Reprinted by Special Permission of the *Journal of Criminal Law, Criminology and Police Science* (Northwestern University School of Law), Copyright © 1969, Vol. 60, No. 2.

teresting, and, in my view, decisive enough, utilitarian arguments have more appeal: the claim that capital punishment is useless because it does not deter others, is most persuasive. I shall, therefore, focus on this claim. Lest the argument be thought to be unduly narrow, I shall show, nonetheless, that some claims of injustice rest on premises which the claimants reject when arguments for capital punishment are derived therefrom; while other claims of injustice have no independent standing: their weight depends on the weight given to deterrence.

## II

Capital punishment is regarded as unjust because it may lead to the execution of innocents, or because the guilty poor (or disadvantaged) are more likely to be executed than the guilty rich.

Regardless of merit, these claims are relevant only if "doing justice" is one purpose of punishment. Unless one regards it as good, or, at least, better, that the guilty be punished rather than the innocent, and that the equally guilty be punished equally,[2] unless, that is, one wants penalties to be just, one cannot object to them because they are not. However, if one does include justice among the purposes of punishment, it becomes possible to justify any one punishment—even death—on grounds of justice. Yet, those who object to the death penalty because of its alleged injustice, usually deny not only the merits, or the sufficiency, of specific arguments based on justice, but the propriety of justice as an argument: they exclude "doing justice" as a purpose of legal punishment. If justice is not a purpose of penalties, injustice cannot be an objection to the death penalty, or to any other; if it is, justice cannot be ruled out as an argument for any penalty.

Consider the claim of injustice on its merits now. A convicted man may be found to have been innocent; if he was executed, the penalty cannot be reversed. Except for fines, penalties never can be reversed. Time spent in prison cannot be returned. However a prison sentence may be remitted once the prisoner serving it is found innocent; and he can be compensated for the time served (although compensation ordinarily cannot repair the harm). Thus, though (nearly) all penalties are irreversible, the death penalty, unlike others, is irrevocable as well.

Despite all precautions, errors will occur in judicial proceedings: the innocent may be found guilty,[3] or the guilty rich may more easily escape conviction, or receive lesser penalties than the guilty poor. However, these injustices do not reside in the penalties inflicted but in their maldistribution. It is not the penalty—whether death or prison—which is unjust when inflicted on the innocent, but its imposition on the innocent. Inequity between poor and rich also involves distribution, not the penalty distributed.[4] Thus injustice is not an objection to the death penalty but to the distributive process—the trial. Trials are more likely to be fair when life is at stake—the death penalty is probably less often unjustly inflicted than others. It requires special consideration not because it is more, or more often, unjust than other penalties, but because it is always irrevocable.

Can any amount of deterrence justify the possibility of irrevocable injustice? Surely injustice is unjustifiable in each actual individual case; it must be objected to whenever it occurs. But we are concerned here with the process that may produce injustice, and with the penalty that would make it irrevocable—not with the actual individual cases produced, but with the general rules which may produce them. To consider objections to a general rule (the provision of any penalties by law) we must compare the likely net result of alternative rules and select the rule (or penalty) likely to produce the least injustice. For however one defines justice, to support it cannot mean less than to favor the least injustice. If the death of innocents because of judicial error is unjust, so is the death of innocents by murder. If some murders could be avoided by a penalty conceivably more deterrent than others—such as the death penalty—then the question becomes: which penalty will minimize the number of innocents killed (by crime and by punishment)? It follows that the irrevocable injustice, sometimes inflicted by the death penalty would not significantly militate against it, if capital punishment deters enough murders to reduce the total number of innocents killed so that fewer are lost than would be lost without it.

In general, the possibility of injustice argues against penalization of any kind only if the expected usefulness of penalization is less important than the probable harm (particularly to innocents) and the probable inequities. The possibility of injustice argues against the death penalty only inasmuch as the added usefulness (deterrence) expected from irrevocability is thought less important than the added harm. (Were my argument specifically concerned with justice, I could compare the injustice inflicted by the courts with the injustice—outside the courts—avoided by the judicial process. *I.e.*, "important" here may be used to include everything to which importance is attached.)

We must briefly examine now the general use and effectiveness of deterrence to decide whether the death penalty could add enough deterrence to be warranted.

## III

Does any punishment "deter others" at all? Doubts have been thrown on this effect because it is thought to depend on the incorrect rationalistic psychology of some of its 18th and 19th century proponents. Actually deterrence does not depend on rational calculation, on rationality or even on capacity for it; nor do arguments for it depend on rationalistic psychology. Deterrence depends on the likelihood and on the regularity—not on the rationality—of human responses to danger; and further on the possibility of reinforcing internal controls by vicarious external experiences.

Responsiveness to danger is generally found in human behavor; the danger can, but need not, come from the law or from society; nor need it be explicitly verbalized. Unless intent on suicide, people do not jump from high mountain cliffs, however tempted to fly through the air; and they take precautions against falling. The mere risk of injury often restrains us from doing what is otherwise attractive; we refrain even when we have no direct experience, and usually without explicit computation of probabilities, let alone conscious weighing of expected pleasure against possible pain. One abstains from dangerous acts because of vague, inchoate, habitual and, above all, preconscious fears. Risks and rewards are more often felt than calculated; one abstains without accounting to oneself, because "it isn't done," or because one literally does not conceive of the action one refrains from. Animals as well refrain from painful or injurious experiences presumably without calculation; and the threat of punishment can be used to regulate their conduct.

Unlike natural dangers, legal threats are constructed deliberately by legislators to restrain actions which may impair the social order. Thus legislation transforms social into individual dangers. Most people further transform external into internal danger: they acquire a sense of moral obligation, a conscience, which threatens them, should they do what is wrong. Arising originally from the external authority of rulers and rules, conscience is internalized and becomes independent of external forces. However, conscience is constantly reinforced in those whom it controls by the coercive imposition of external authority on recalcitrants and on those who have not acquired it. Most people refrain from offenses because they feel an obligation to behave lawfully. But this obligation would scarcely be felt if those who do not feel or follow it were not to suffer punishment.

Although the legislators may calculate their threats and the responses to be produced, the effectiveness of the threats neither requires nor depends on calculations by those responding. The predictor (or producer) of effects must calculate; those whose responses are predicted (or produced) need not. Hence, although legislation (and legislators) should be rational, subjects, to be deterred as intended, need not be: they need only be responsive.

Punishments deter those who have not violated the law for the same reasons—and in the same degrees (apart from internalization: moral obligation) as do natural dangers. Often natural dangers—all dangers not deliberately created by legislation (*e.g.*, injury of the criminal inflicted by the crime victim) are insufficient. Thus, the fear of injury (natural danger) does not suffice to control city traffic; it must be reinforced by the legal punishment meted out to those who violate the rules. These punishments keep most people observing the regulations. However, where (in the absence of natural danger) the threatened punishment is so light that the advantage of violating rules tends to exceed the disadvantage of being punished (divided by the risk), the rule is violated (*i.e.,* parking fines are too light). In this case the feeling of obligation tends to vanish as well. Elsewhere punishment deters.

To be sure, not everybody responds to threatened punishment. Non-responsive persons may be a) self-destructive or b) incapable of responding to threats, or even of grasping them. Increases in the size, or certainty, of penalties would not affect these two groups. A third group c) might respond to more certain or more severe penalties.[5] If the punishment threatened for burglary, robbery, or rape were a $5 fine in North Carolina, and 5 years in prison in South Carolina, I have no doubt that the North Carolina treasury would become quite opulent until vigilante justice would provide the deterrence not provided by law. Whether to increase penalties (or improve enforcement) depends on the importance of the rule to society, the size and likely reaction of the group that did not respond before, and the acceptance of the added punishment and enforcement required to deter it. Observation would have to locate the points—likely to differ in different times and places—at which diminishing, zero, and negative returns set in. There is no reason to believe that all present and future offenders belong to the *a priori* non-responsive groups, or that all penalties have reached the point of diminishing, let alone zero returns.

## IV

Even though its effectiveness seems obvious, punishment as a deterrent has fallen into disrepute. Some ideas which help explain this progressive heedlessness were uttered by Lester Pearson, then Prime Minister of Canada, when, in opposing the death penalty, he proposed that instead "the state seek to eradicate the causes of crime—slums, ghettos and personality disorders."[6]

"Slums, ghettos and personality disorders" have not been shown, singly or collectively, to be "the causes" of crime.

(1) The crime rate in the slums is indeed higher than elsewhere; but so is the death rate in hospitals. Slums are no more "causes" of crime, than hospitals are of death; they are locations of crime, as hospitals are of death. Slums and hospitals attract people selectively; neither is the "cause" of the condition (disease in hospitals, poverty in slums) that leads to the selective attraction.

As for poverty which draws people into slums, and, sometimes, into crime, any relative disadvantage may lead to ambition, frustration, resentment and, if insufficiently restrained, to crime. Not all relative disadvantages can be eliminated; indeed very few can be, and their elimination increases the resentment generated by the remaining ones; not even relative poverty can be removed altogether. (Absolute poverty—whatever that may be—hardly affects crime.) However, though contributory, relative disadvantages are not a necessary or sufficient cause of crime: most poor people do not commit crimes, and some rich people do. Hence, "eradication of poverty" would, at most, remove one (doubtful) cause of crime.

In the United States, the decline of poverty has not been associated with a reduction of crime. Poverty measured in dollars of constant purchasing power, according to present government standards and statistics, was the condition of ½ of all our families in 1920; of ⅕ in 1962; and of less than ⅙ in 1966. In 1967, 5.3 million families out of 49.8 million were poor—1/9 of all families in the United States. If crime has been reduced in a similar manner, it is a well kept secret.

Those who regard poverty as a cause of crime often draw a wrong inference from a true proposition: the rich will not commit certain crimes—Rockefeller never riots; nor does he steal.

(He mugs, but only on T.V.) Yet while wealth may be the cause of not committing (certain) crimes, it does not follow that poverty (absence of wealth) is the cause of committing them. Water extinguishes or prevents fire; but its absence is not the cause of fire. Thus, if poverty could be abolished, if everybody had all "necessities" (I don't pretend to know what this would mean), crime would remain, for, in the words of Aristotle, "the greatest crimes are committed not for the sake of basic necessities but for the sake of superfluities." Superfluities cannot be provided by the government; they would be what the government does not provide.

(2) Negro ghettos have a high, Chinese ghettos have a low crime rate. Ethnic separation, voluntary or forced, obviously has little to do with crime; I can think of no reason why it should.[7]

(3) I cannot see how the state could "eradicate" personality disorders even if all causes and cures were known and available. (They are not.) Further, the known incidence of personality disorders within the prison population does not exceed the known incidence outside—though our knowledge of both is tenuous. Nor are personality disorders necessary, or sufficient causes for criminal offenses, unless these be identified by means of (moral, not clinical) definition with personality disorders. In this case, Mr. Pearson would have proposed to "eradicate" crime by eradicating crime—certainly a sound, but not a helpful idea.

Mr. Pearson's views are part as well of the mental furniture of the former U.S. Attorney General, Ramsey Clark, who told a congressional committee that " . . . only the elimination of the causes of crime can make a significant and lasting difference in the incidence of crime." Uncharitably interpreted, Mr. Clark revealed that only the elimination of causes eliminates effects—a sleazy cliche and wrong to boot. Given the benefit of the doubt, Mr. Clark probably meant that the causes of crime are social; and that therefore crime can be reduced "only" by non-penal (social) measures.

This view suggests a fireman who declines fire-fighting apparatus by pointing out that "in the long run only the elimination of the causes" of fire "can make a significant and lasting difference in the incidence" of fire, and that fire-fighting equipment does not eliminate "the causes"—except that such a fireman would probably not rise to fire chief. Actually, whether fires are checked, depends on equipment and on the efforts of the firemen using it no less than on the presence of "the causes": inflammable materials. So with crimes. Laws, courts and police actions are no less important in restraining them than "the causes" are in impelling them. If firemen (or attorneys general) pass the buck and refuse to use the means available, we may all be burned while waiting for "the long run" and "the elimination of the causes."

Whether any activity—be it lawful or unlawful—takes place depends on whether the desire for it, or for whatever is to be secured by it, is stronger than the desire to avoid the costs involved. Accordingly people work, attend college, commit crimes, go to the movies—or refrain from any of these activities. Attendance at a theatre may be high because the show is entertaining and because the price of admission is low. Obviously the attendance depends on both—on the combination of expected gratification and cost. The wish, motive or impulse for doing anything —the experienced, or expected, gratification—is the cause of doing it; the wish to avoid the cost is the cause of not doing it. One is no more and no less "cause" than the other. (Common speech supports this use of "cause" no less than logic: "Why did you go to Jamaica?" "*Because* it is such a beautiful place." "Why didn't you go to Jamacia?" "*Because* it is too expensive." —"Why do you buy this?" "*Because* it is so cheap." "Why don't you buy that?" "*Because* it is too expensive.") Penalties (costs) are causes of lawfulness, or (if too low or uncertain) of unlawfulness, of crime. People do commit crimes because, given their conditions, the desire for the satisfaction sought prevails. They refrain if the desire to avoid the cost prevails. Given the desire, low cost (penalty) causes the action, and high cost restraint. Given the cost, desire becomes the causal variable. Neither is intrinsically more causal than the other. The crime rate increases if the cost is reduced or the desire raised. It can be decreased by raising the cost or by reducing the desire.

The cost of crime is more easily and swiftly changed than the conditions producing the inclination to it. Further, the costs are very largely within the power of the government to change, whereas the conditions producing propensity to crime are often only indirectly affected by government action, and some are altogether beyond the control of the government. Our unilateral emphasis on these conditions and our undue neglect of costs may contribute to an unnecessarily high crime rate.

## V

The foregoing suggests the question posed by the death penalty: is the deterrence added (return) sufficiently above zero to warrant irrevocability (or other, less clear, disadvantages)? The question is not only whether the penalty deters, but whether it deters more than alternatives and whether the difference exceeds the cost of irrevocability. (I shall assume that the alternative is actual life imprisonment so as to exclude the complication produced by the release of the unrehabilitated.)

In some fairly infrequent but important circumstances the death penalty is the only possible deterrent. Thus, in case of acute *coups d' état,* or of acute substantial attempts to overthrow the government, prospective rebels would altogether discount the threat of any prison sentence. They would not be deterred because they believe the swift victory of the revolution will invalidate a prison sentence and turn it into an advantage. Execution would be the only deterrent because, unlike prison sentences, it cannot be revoked by victorious rebels. The same reasoning applies to deterring spies or traitors in wartime. Finally, men who, by virtue of past acts, are already serving, or are threatened, by a life sentence, could be deterred from further offenses only by the threat of the death penalty.[8]

What about criminals who do not fall into any of these (often ignored) classes? Prof. Thorsten Sellin has made a careful study of the available statistics: he concluded that they do not yield evidence for the deterring effect of the death penalty.[9] Somewhat surprisingly, Prof. Sellin seems to think that this lack of evidence for deterrence is evidence for the lack of deterrence. It is not. It means that deterrence has not been demonstrated statistically—not that non-deterrence has been.

It is entirely possible, indeed likely (as Prof. Sellin appears willing to concede), that the statistics used, though the best available, are nonetheless too slender a reed to rest conclusions on. They indicate that the homicide rate does not vary greatly between similar areas with or without the death penalty, and in the same area before and after abolition. However, the similar areas are not similar enough; the periods are not long enough; many social differences and changes, other than the abolition of the death penalty, may account for the variation (or lack of) in homicide rates with and without, before and after abolition; some of these social differences and changes are likely to have affected homicide rates. I am unaware of any statistical analysis which adjusts for such changes and differences. And logically, it is quite consistent with the postulated deterrent effect of capital punishment that there be less homicide after abolition: with retention there might have been still less.

Homicide rates do not depend exclusively on penalties any more than do other crime rates. A number of conditions which influence the propensity to crime, demographic, economic or generally social changes or differences—even such matters as changes of the divorce laws or of the cotton price—may influence the homicide rate. Therefore variation or constancy cannot be attributed to variations or constancy of the penalties, unless we know that no other factor influencing the homicide rate has changed. Usually we don't. To believe the death penalty deterrent does not require one to believe that the death penalty, or any other, is the only, or the decisive causal variable; this would be as absurd as the converse mistake that "social causes" are the only, or always the decisive factor. To favor capital punishment, the efficacy of neither variable need be denied. It is enough to affirm that the severity of the penalty may influence some potential criminals, and that the added severity of the death penalty adds to deterrence, or may do so. It is quite possible that such a deterrent effect may be offset (or intensified) by non-penal factors which affect propensity; its presence or absence therefore may be hard, and perhaps impossible to demonstrate.

Contrary to what Prof. Sellin *et al.* seem to presume, I doubt that offenders are aware of the absence or presence of the death penalty state by state or period by period. Such unawareness argues against the assumption of a calculating murderer. However, unawareness does not argue against the death penalty if by deterrence we mean a preconscious, general response to a severe, but not necessarily specifically and explicitly apprehended, or calculated threat. A constant homicide rate, despite abolition, may occur because of unawareness and not because of lack of deterrence: people remain deterred for a lengthy interval by the severity of the penalty in the past, or by the severity of penalties used in similar circumstances nearby.

I do not argue for a version of deterrence which would require me to believe that an individual shuns murder while in North Dakota, because of the death penalty, and merrily goes to it in South Dakota since it has been abolished there; or that he will start the murderous career from which he had hitherto refrained, after abolition. I hold that the generalized threat of the death penalty may be a deterrent, and the more so, the more generally applied. Deterrence will not cease in the particular areas of abolition or at the particular times of abolition. Rather, general deterrence will be somewhat weakened, through local (partial) abolition. Even such weakening will be hard to detect owing to changes in many offsetting, or reinforcing, factors.

For all of these reasons, I doubt that the presence or absence of a deterrent effect of the death penalty is likely to be demonstrable by statistical means. The statistics presented by Prof. Sellin *et al.* show only that there is no statistical proof for the deterrent effect of the death penalty. But they do not show that there is no deterrent effect. Not to demonstrate presence of the effect is not the same as to demonstrate its absence; certainly not when there are plausible explanations for the non-demonstrability of the effect.

It is on our uncertainty that the case for deterrence must rest.[10]

## VI

If we do not know whether the death penalty will deter others, we are confronted with two uncertainties. If we impose the death penalty, and achieve no deterrent effect thereby, the life of a convicted murderer has been expended in vain (from a deterrent viewpoint). There is a net loss. If we impose the death sentence and thereby deter some future murderers, we spared the lives of some future victims (the prospective murderers gain too; they are spared punishment because they were deterred). In this case, the death penalty has led to a net gain, unless the life of a convicted murderer is valued more highly than that of the unknown victim, or victims (and the non-imprisonment of the deterred non-murderer).

The calculation can be turned around, of course. The absence of the death penalty may harm no one and therefore produce a gain—the life of the convicted murderer. Or it may kill future victims of murderers who could have been deterred, and thus produce a loss—their life.

To be sure, we must risk something certain—the death (or life) of the convicted man, for something uncertain—the death (or life) of the victims of murderers who may be deterred. This is in the nature of uncertainty—when we invest, or gamble, we risk the money we have for an uncertain gain. Many human actions, most commitments—including marriage and crime—share this characteristic with the deterrent purpose of any penalization, and with its rehabilitative purpose (and even with the protective).

More proof is demanded for the deterrent effect of the death penalty than is demanded for the deterrent effect of other penalties. This is not justified by the absence of other utilitarian purposes such as protection and rehabilitation; they involve no less uncertainty than deterrence.[11]

Irrevocability may support a demand for some reason to expect more deterrence than revocable penalties might produce, but not a demand for more proof of deterrence, as has been pointed out above. The reason for expecting more deterrence lies in the greater severity, the terrifying effect inherent in finality. Since it seems more important to spare victims than to spare murderers, the burden of proving that the greater severity inherent in irrevocability adds nothing to deterrence lies on those who oppose capital punishment. Proponents of the death penalty need show only that there is no more uncertainty about it than about greater severity in general.

The demand that the death penalty be proved more deterrent than alternatives can not be satisfied any more than the demand that six years in prison be proved to be more deterrent than three. But the uncertainty which confronts us favors the death penalty as long as by imposing it we might save future victims of murder. This effect is as plausible as the general idea that penalties have deterrent effects which increase with their severity. Though we have no proof of the positive deterrence of the penalty, we also have no proof of zero, or negative effectiveness. I believe we have no right to risk additional future victims of murder for the sake of sparing convicted murderers; on the contrary, our moral obligation is to risk the possible ineffectiveness of executions. However rationalized, the opposite view appears to be motivated by the simple fact that executions are more subjected to social control than murder. However, this applies to all penalties and does not argue for the abolition of any.

## NOTES

1. Social solidarity of "community feeling" (here to be ignored) might be dealt with as a form of deterrence.
2. Certainly a major meaning of *suum cuique tribue.*
3. I am not concerned here with the converse injustice, *which I regard as no less grave.*
4. Such inequity, though likely, has not been demonstrated. Note that, since there are more poor than rich, there are likely to be more guilty poor; and, if poverty contributes to crime, the proportion

of the poor who are criminals also should be higher than that of the rich.

5. I neglect those motivated by civil disobedence or, generally, moral or political passion. Deterring them depends less on penalties than on the moral support they receive, though penalties play a role. I also neglect those who may belong to all three groups listed, some successively, some even simultaneously, such as drug addicts. Finally, I must altogether omit the far from negligible role problems of apprehension and conviction play in deterrence—beyond saying that by reducing the government's ability to apprehend and convict, courts are able to reduce the risks of offenders.
6. *N.Y. Times,* Nov. 24, 1967, at 22. The actual psychological and other factors which bear on the disrepute—as distinguished from the rationalizations—cannot be examined here.
7. Mixed areas, incidentally, have higher crime rates than segregated ones. *See, e.g.,* Ross & van den Haag, *The Fabric of Society,* 102–4 (1957). Because slums are bad (morally) and crime is, many people seem to reason that "slums spawn crime"—which confuses some sort of moral with a casual relation.
8. Cautious revolutionaries, uncertain of final victory, might be impressed by prison sentences—but not in the acute stage, when faith in victory is high. And one can increase even the severity of a life sentence in prison. Finally, harsh punishment of rebels can intensify rebellious impulses. These points, though they qualify it, hardly impair the force of the argument.
9. Prof. Sellin considered mainly homicide statistics. His work may be found in his *Capital Punishment* (1967), or, most conveniently, in Bedau, *The Death Penalty in America* (1964), which also offers other material, mainly against the death penalty.
10. In view of the strong emotions aroused (itself an indication of effectiveness to me: might murderers not be as upset over the death penalty as those who wish to spare them?) and because I believe penalties must reflect community feeling to be effective, I oppose mandatory death sentences and favor optional recommendations by juries after their finding of guilt. The opposite course risks the non-conviction of guilty defendents by juries who do not want to see them executed.
11. Rehabilitation or protection are of minor importance in our actual penal system (though not in our theory). We confine many people who do not need rehabilitation and against whom we do not need protection (*e.g.,* the exasperated husband who killed his wife); we release many unrehabilitated offenders against whom protection is needed. Certainly rehabilitation and protection are not, and deterrence is, the main actual function of legal punishment, if we disregard non-utilitarian purposes.

# 6 Capital Punishment: Your Protection and Mine

EDWARD J. ALLEN

In the previous discussion on capital punishment (*The Police Chief,* March 1960), it was pointed out that the wisdom of the ages, as revealed in Holy Scripture and spoken through the saints and sages, approved and advocated the death penalty for certain heinous crimes.

In our own times the people of California have repeatedly (16 times from 1933 to 1960) turned back the constantly recurring repeal attempts of a militant minority and their malinformed minions. Yet, the present governor, with a seeming fixation, has vowed that he will foist the matter upon the California Legislature at succeeding sessions . . . and the same old tired arguments will be trotted out again:

1. Capital punishment does not deter crime.

From *The Police Chief,* June 1960, International Association of Chiefs of Police, Inc., Publisher.

2. It "brutalizes" human nature.
3. The rich and powerful often escape the death penalty.
4. Swift and certain punishment is more effective.
5. Society is to blame for the criminal's way of life, so we ought to be more considerate of him.

Let us, then, apart from the demands of pure justice, which should be the only determining factor, examine the above claims for validity and provability.

## Capital Punishment Does Not Deter Crime?

If this be true, then why do criminals, even the braggadocian Chessman type, fear it most? Why does every criminal sentenced to death seek commutation to life imprisonment? Common sense alone, without the benefit of knowledge, wisdom, and experience, convinces that we are influenced to the greatest degree by that which we love, respect or fear to the greatest degree—and that we cling most tenaciously to our most valued possessions. Life is indisputably our greatest possession. Additionally, there is no definitive proof anywhere that the death penalty is not a deterrent. There are merely the gratuitous statements of wishful thinkers, some of whom, because of the responsible duties of their positions, ought not be making unprovable or misleading statements.

Parole and probation people, an occasional governor, prison wardens (some prefer to be called penologists), criminal defense attorneys, and oftentime prison chaplains advance this "no deterrent" point of view. None doubts their sincerity, but they are hardly qualified to speak on the matter authoritatively or with pure objectivity. How can they *possibly* know how many people are NOT on death row because of the deterrent effect of the death penalty? Neither do they see the vicious, often sadistic despoiler or the cold-blooded professional killer plying their murderous trades. They encounter these predatory creatures after their fangs have been pulled; after they have been rendered harmless, deprived of the weapons and the opportunities to commit additional crimes. Naturally, in their cages they behave more like sheep than ravenous wolves.

Prison wardens are housekeepers, custodians of criminals after they have been convicted under our system of justice; hence, they see them when they are docile by compulsion but certainly cunning enough to know that to "spring" themselves they must "make friends and influence people" of power and authority *inside* the prison walls, since their own criminal lives on the outside have deservedly brought upon them the judgment of society. It is neither the duty nor the prerogative of wardens or chaplains to decide matters of criminal justice. This has already been accomplished by the people, and their jobs, respectively, are to keep the gate locked, to feed, to clothe, and to guard—and to counsel, console, and convert. True, it is altogether human to develop sympathy for even a depraved and chronic criminal. I suppose a zoo keeper develops a fondness for the wild animals which the taxpayers pay him to feed and guard. Yet, what kind of a zoo keeper would he be if he opened the cage doors and released the voracious beasts to prey upon the public? This very act would throw a community into terror and alarm. Even so, if a wild beast attacked a human being, there would be less guilt attached, since such an animal acts from instinct and not malice aforethought. Not so, a rational human being who deliberately murders or defiles his fellowman. It might serve a good purpose if these "bleeding hearts" could accompany those whose duty it is to examine first-hand, at the scenes of their crimes, the gruesome handiwork of those for whom they intercede. This might give them pause to properly weigh the public interest in their private scales of justice.

It is also put forth by those who would weaken our laws and, perforce, our ability to protect the innocent, that many murderers on death row claim they did not think of the death penalty when they committed their crimes. This is undoubtedly true. That is precisely the point. If they had thought of it, they would not have committed their crimes. Here we have the spectacle of a minute minority of convicted murderers convincing intelligent people that capital punishment is wrong because of their own failure to realize the consequences of their murderous conduct. Are we then to base our laws on this reasoning? What of the countless others who *were* deterred from murder through fear of the penalty? The implication is clear: even those murderers who didn't think of the death penalty would have been deterred had they given it consideration. Our laws are made for reasonable creatures, not to satisfy an abnormal handful. It is hardly the part of wisdom to be guided by the counsel and advice of an infinitesimally small band of bestial criminals. Further, the cunning individual and conspiratorial group who plot murder always imagine themselves too clever to get caught, or if caught, convicted.

## It Brutalizes Human Nature?

But the opposite is true. Wanton *murder* brutalizes human nature and cheapens human life, not the penalty for its perpetration. Capital punishment is the guarantee against murder and the brutalization of human nature. It places an inestimable value on human life—the forfeiture of the life of the despoiler. To allow heinous criminals to commit their crimes without the commensurate reparation of the death penalty would surely brutalize and degrade human nature and reduce society to a state of barbarism. True Christian charity is based upon justice, the proper concern for the weak and innocent, not upon a soft-headed regard for despicable and conspiratorial killers. Let us resort to right reason and view retribution and reparation in proper perspective.

## The Rich and Powerful Generally Escape?

There is truth in this statement and it is equally applicable to other penalties, not the death penalty alone. No one decries this discrimination more than law enforcement. The deals which allow criminals to escape justice are consummated by courts and attorneys. Attorneys present evidence to the courts and judges hand down sentences. Responsibility also devolves upon citizen jurors to return proper verdicts. If some citizens, courts, and lawyers fail in their duty, is the law itself to blame? Rather it is their administration of it. Surely, bribery, social position, or political pull ought not to influence the administration of justice, but admittedly they often do. Since this is so, it would be as logical to advocate the repeal of the entire criminal code. If one person escapes justice, is it unjust that another does not? Since justice does not *always* prevail, ought we abandon our striving for its attainment? Who would advocate the abolition of the Ten Commandments because they are honored more in their breach than in their observance? Justice is still justice if no man is just! The defect, in this instance, lies in men, not in the law! Law enforcement firmly believes that all men should be treated equally at the bar of justice. There are attorneys, judges, governors, parole boards and that peculiar phenomena called "Adult and Juvenile Authorities" who decree otherwise.

## Jurors and Governors and Judges

Let us take the matter of justice, including capital punishment, a step further. In selecting a murder jury each prospective juror is asked if he has a conscientious objection to returning a death penalty verdict. If so, such a person is summarily excused as unqualified. No injustice obtains from this practice, since a private citizen has a right to his own opinion.

*But* this does not apply to judges and governors who have the duty of sentencing and the right of commutation, since their consciences must be guided by the law which they have sworn to uphold. Therefore, if a judge or state governor has such a conscientious objection to the death penalty that he "creeps through the serpentine windings of utilitarianism to discover some advantage that may discharge him from the justice of punishment or even from the due measure of it," then such a judge or governor has disqualified himself, and ought, in all justice to the commonwealth he serves, to vacate his lofty position and return it to the people to whom it belongs. Then, as a private citizen, he can campaign to his heart's content for the abolition of whatever law he doesn't happen to like. In the meantime, however, he ought not attempt to substitute the minority decisions of our Supreme Courts for majority decisions or be persuaded by the opinions of condemned criminals on murderer's row. Further, to incessantly inveigh from high office against the law of the land, particularly a law ingrained in the tradition of our Judeo-Christian culture, smacks of arbitrary dictation. The business of government is justice, not pity—however self-consoling.

## Life Imprisonment

In most of our states life imprisonment simply does not exist. In truth and justice the term ought to be discarded since it does not mean what it says. In the State of California, for example, the State Constitution provides that the governor, under his commutation powers, may set aside the words "without parole" with respect to life imprisonment. It would take a constitutional amendment to abolish that power. In other states life imprisonment means merely a varying number of years.

## Death Penalty Seldom Used

The argument that the death penalty is seldom used argues for its retention, not its abolition. It proves that juries and courts are exercising extreme leniency, even with vicious murderers. Yet, there are certain heinous crimes regarding which the very stones would cry out for the death penalty were it abolished. Therefore, it should be retained as just punishment and reparation for these and as a deterrent for other malignant criminals. It would be a better argument for the abolitionists if they could say that the death penalty was capriciously or routinely being returned for every homicide.

## Specious Arguments

Two of the reasons advanced for the abolition of the death penalty have no validity whatsoever. One is an attempt to equate human slavery with capital punishment. The argument is this: Slavery was once rampant, but now an enlightened society favors its abolition; therefore, we ought to do away with capital punishment, since we "moderns" are more "enlightened" than our forebears.

Firstly, slavery never was, or never will be, morally right or justifiable or just. The death penalty *is* morally right and justifiable and just. So these sophists are merely advancing a completely false and odious comparison. Here is another "beaut" from a university psychiatrist: The death penalty could be society's way of "projecting its own crime into the criminal." Now, I submit that the longer we permit this type of nonsense to be spread abroad, the more ridiculous our nation is going to appear in the eyes of the world. I understand that there is a growing resentment among those in the medical profession against this type of gobble-de-gook, and about time.

It is obvious to anyone who believes in the moral and natural law (as clearly stated in the law of the land) that first-degree murder requires personal premeditation and the full consent of the will, hence, its punishment should be meted out to the criminal or criminals personally responsible. To argue otherwise is to argue the unnatural, but admittedly, this is the day of the unnatural logician.

We argue that the unnatural in sex is natural and point to fables for proof. Thus, we have the Oedipus and Electra complexes, situations culled from Greek drama and foisted upon us as Freudian truisms. No use talking about free will, we just can't help ourselves. So today there is no crime, really, and no criminals —just "complexes." And these "complexes" are so "complex" we must all eventually succumb to their "complexity"—and employ a psychoanalyst. (Physician, heal thyself!) Truly, it is possible for people, even with exceptionally high IQ's, to be nuttier than fruitcakes, or vice versa, as the case may be. We had better be careful in these "modern" times (which condone the criminal immorality of ancient Greece and Rome) or we, too, will abandon our reason altogether. Mainly because of their sexual excesses, aberrations and perversions, St. Paul told the Romans (1st Epistle to the Romans) that they had gone blind and no longer knew the difference between right and wrong. Neither does this generation in many respects, and we will degenerate further if we continue to give ear to certain types of psychoanalytical professors and their automorphic automatons who impute to all of us (including themselves?) the guilt for the personal crimes of individual criminals.

## Swift and Certain Punishment

Swift and certain punishment is assuredly a crime deterrent, but only when coupled with commensurate severity, otherwise the statement is an absurdity. Suppose a bank robber was very swiftly and very surely sentenced to five days in the county jail; or a rapist swiftly and certainly given a $25 fine. Would such punishment(?) be a deterrent to either the bank robber or the rapist? Surely, the deterrent value is in the severity as well as the swiftness and the certainty. However, if one had to choose but one of the three, then the severity of the punishment must needs be selected.

Once again, we must reiterate that some lawyers and courts and the criminals themselves have caused the "swiftness and certainty" of justice to have almost vanished from the American scene. The same sources would now abolish the severity. Yet, those lawyers who, through capricious, dilatory tactics continually postpone justice are the very ones who prattle about swiftness and certainty as a substitute for severity. The Chessman case is a prize example of how lawyers, judges and a governor can foul up "swift and certain" punishment. The irony of it is that Chessman and his attorneys and the present governor, who were responsible for the seemingly interminable postponements, now cry to the high heavens that such postponements are "cruel and unusual punishment." No wonder Hamlet cited the "law's delay" as one of the problems that was driving him nuts. Chessman himself became so disgusted with the publicity-seeking antics of one lawyer who injected himself into the case that he fired him, publicly. However, this did not delay the redoubtable attorney, and he is still trying to make a career of the case. Wonder what further "deterrent" he needs?

## Individual States and Capital Punishment

A study of the statistics on murder in the 48 states in 1958 produced some interesting results with respect to the capital crime. The proponents for abolition make much of the fact that there were seven states in 1958 (nine since the admission of Alaska and Hawaii) which have abolished capital punishment. These proponents make no mention of the fact that eight other states in the Union once abolished capital punishment and have returned to it.

The states which abolished capital punishment and after an unhappy experience restored it are: Kansas, Iowa, Colorado, Washington, Oregon, Arizona, Missouri, and Tennessee. It is noted that three of these states border on California: Arizona, continguous to the southeast; Oregon, contiguous to the north on the coast; and Washington, further north and also on the west coast. Since these comprise the area surrounding and abutting California, it is the most revealing and significantly important statistic for California residents. Of the states which have abolished capital punishment, two are now in New England: Maine and Rhode Island. Maine had one of the highest murder rates in New England in 1958, with an average of 2.5 per 100,000 population (all averages are quoted using this population figure). The six New England states have an average of 1.6, the lowest murder rate of any section of the country, yet only two of the six states have abolished the death penalty, and one of them has a rate half again as high as the average. New Hampshire, which has the death penalty, compares with the lowest, 0.7.

Seven midwestern states: Iowa, Kansas, Minnesota, Nebraska, North Dakota, South Dakota and Missouri, have an average of 2.2 murders for 1958. It is noted that three of these states returned to capital punishment after having abolished it, and two of the seven still have no capital punishment.

In the 11 far western states, the average percentage in 1958 was 3.7, oddly enough the exact percentage for the State of California. Four of these states returned to the death penalty. The other seven states have always had capital punishment.

Eleven northeastern states had an average of 3.1 murders in 1958.

The highest murder rate of the geographical groups of states was the southern group of 13 states. They had the exceptionally high rate of 9.0. Admittedly, the South has a problem, but the removal of the death penalty would only aggravate it. Of these states only Tennessee ever tried to get along without capital punishment and has since returned to it.

It would appear that the permeance of racial, ethnic and religio-political cultures influence crime rates, including murder, in the various geographical sections of our country. Common sense dictates that more severe punitive sanctions are necessary in those states or sections where serious crime is more prevalent. Conversely, where the crime is minimal because of the law-abiding nature of the people, murder is less frequent. Thus it is that the New England States have a low murder rate while the South has an unusually high rate. It would be the height of folly therefore to advocate the removal of the death penalty throughout the Southern States where the crime of murder is a serious threat.

Where crime and murder are at a low level and where community life is governed by respect and reverence for law, rather than by its enforcement, then severe punitive measures may be relaxed, but not abolished. (Such a state presages the millennium.) On the other hand, where crime and murder are a serious problem, then the removal of stringent punitive measures further aggravates it. The eight states which re-enacted the death penalty after a trial period without it, discovered this to their own dismay.

The seven states within the corporate United States which do not have the death penalty are among the smallest, in territory and/or population: Delaware, Maine, Michigan, Minnesota, North Dakota, Rhode Island, and Wisconsin. There is among them only one really large state, Michigan, whose 1958 population of 7,865,547 exceeds by more than a half-million the combined total of the six other states. Michigan's 1958 murder rate per 100,000 population was 3.1, not only the highest of these seven states, but higher than both Pennsylvania and New York, two of the three most populous states in the Union—with over eleven to sixteen million respectively. California, in the top three, has approximately twice the population of Michigan. New York has a 2.8 rate and Pennsylvania 2.5. The experience has been that the larger states with crime problems have found it necessary to return to the death penalty. And to re-emphasize, three of these states either border on California, or are on the west coast, or both.

## California Officers Murdered on Duty

I do not have the figures for the other states, but in California a review of the number of police officers killed in line of duty during the past ten years is of significance. From 1950 through 1959 there have been 35 law enforcement officers shot and killed while performing law enforcement duties, i.e., protecting the lives and property of California citizens. Even more alarming is the fact that of the 35, approximately twice as many were murdered during the latter half of the decade than were killed during the first half. Twelve were killed from 1950 through 1954 and 23 from 1955 through 1959. In the last three years 17 of these 23 were murdered while on duty.

At a time in our national and state history when crime is increasing alarmingly and when the murder of police officers in the State of California is reaching new heights, we have powerful figures and groups advocating the abolition of capital punishment

—almost an invitation for murderous thugs to kill more police officers whose duty it is to protect (even at the expense of their own lives) the very citizens who advocate leniency for their murderers. Where is the reciprocal regard for the life of a police officer in the minds and hearts of these paragons of Christian charity, in or out of the governor's office, in or out of our courtrooms, on or off our judicial benches, or in or out of the Humpty-Dumpty (egghead) claque in politics, entertainment, television, journalism, and education? (By "eggheads" I do not mean authentic intellectuals, but the poseurs.)

Perhaps we are arriving at a governmental philosophy which considers the lives of police officers expendable, but not so the lives of the vicious criminals who murder them. Rather, we must protect the latter, since to punish them too severely would be "projecting society's crime into the criminal." Would it not be more sensible and accurate to state that "society" is to blame for the murder of its police officers unless it insists upon the retention of the death penalty as a protection for its own protectors, ergo, society itself? Unmistakably, without militant police protection the whole of society would overnight become a criminal jungle.

## Conclusion

Of course, the overwhelming statistic (for those who wish to decide on statistics alone) is that 41 of the 50 states and the majority of the nations in the world have the death penalty.

However, even though statistics, per se, unquestionably favor the retention of the death penalty, mere numbers, pro and con, ought not be the deciding factor. The deciding factor should be the consideration of justice—the primary, if not the sole business of government. All of the erudition, wisdom, experience, and knowledge of history reveals that the death penalty is morally and legally just. For the just man or nation this should be sufficient. Even so, justice is still justice, if no man is just—were it not so, God would have told us.

# 7

# *A Prosecutor Looks at Capital Punishment*

RICHARD E. GERSTEIN

At the outset I would like to make my personal position clear. As a Prosecuting Attorney in this state in which the law provides for capital punishment I have always believed that I could best objectively do my job if I did not become known as an avid advocate of capital punishment. Conversely, I could not fulfill my duty under the law if I was opposed to capital punishment. Therefore, I have refrained from taking any personal position on this question. During the course of this presentation I will endeavor to convey a composite of the arguments in favor of the retention of capital punishment, since almost without exception, prosecutors, both in the State of Florida and throughout the Nation, with whom I have discussed this issue, have been strongly in favor of the retention of capital punishment.

Reprinted by Special Permission of the *Journal of Criminal Law, Criminology and Police Science* (Northwestern University School of law), Copyright © 1960, Vol. 51, No. 2.

The most convincing and most widely used argument in favor of capital punishment is that it acts as a deterrent. Deterrence is usually defined as the preventive effect which actual or threatened punishment of offenders has upon potential offenders. This principle has influenced our penal codes since ancient times when torturous deaths and mutilations were exacted with the thought of making an example of the malefactor. The deterrence concept governed the Romans in their use of crucifixion as a means of execution, and it led the English to employ the ingenious device of drawing and quartering to warn the potential criminal of the consequences of his proposed action. In Colonial America the use of the pillory and stocks served to remind those with criminal ideas that the course of lawlessness had its disadvantages. In short, it may be said that the deterrence concept has been evident through the ages in Western thought concerning crime and punishment.

As do many members of our profession, I take the position that deterrence is necessary for the maintenance of the legal system and the preservation of society. As clearly stated by Sir John Salmond:

> Punishment is before all things deterrent, and the chief end of the law of crime is to make the evil doer an example and a warning to all who are like-minded with him.[1]

There can be no argument with the fact that capital punishment is totally effective as a deterrent in so far as convicted criminals are concerned. The murderer who has been permanently deterred by execution no longer poses a threat to society.

Therefore, the basic question to be resolved is whether or not the death penalty acts as a deterrent upon potential offenders. It is the contention of virtually all prosecutors that the death penalty does have this desired effect, although it must be admitted at the outset that most of the statistical evidence available does not support this position, for, according to statistics, in jurisdictions where the penalty has been abolished the number of murders has not increased and may even have decreased. For example, Maine, which abolished capital punishment in 1870, has the lowest murder rate of any State in the Union, and Wisconsin and Minnesota, which abandoned the death penalty in 1854 and 1911, respectively, have far lower homicide rates than most of the other states.[2] However, it should be emphasized that criminologists and sociologists agree that statistics are an unsatisfactory indication of the deterrent effect of the death penalty because murder is a complex sociological problem, as well as a crime, and contributing factors, such as race, heredity, regional lines, standards of housing and education, are intangibles, the value of which is difficult to assess. Furthermore, it is obvious that statistics cannot tell us how many potential criminals have refrained from taking another's life through fear of the death penalty. As Judge Hyman Barshay of New York stated:

> The death penalty is a warning, just like a lighthouse throwing its beams out to sea. We hear about shipwrecks, but we do not hear about the ships the lighthouse guides safely on their way. We do not have proof of the number of ships its saves, but we do not tear the lighthouse down.[3]

The contention that statistics are not necessarily the controlling factor in resolving the issue at hand was apparently shared by the Royal Commission on Capital Punishment which was set up on May 4, 1949. Under the chairmanship of Sir Ernest Gowers, their terms of reference were to consider and report, among other things, on "whether liability under the criminal law in Great Britain to suffer capital punishment for murder should be limited or modified." This inquiry extended over a long period and a most comprehensive report was submitted, with which I cannot deal in detail but which I commend to your perusal. Their terms of reference precluded the committee from considering whether the abolition of capital punishment would be desirable, but they did consider its deterrent effect, as the Report stated in part as follows:

> We recognize that it is impossible to arrive confidently at firm conclusions about the deterrent effect of the death penalty, or

> indeed of any form of punishment. The general conclusion which we reach, after careful review of all the evidence we have been able to obtain as to the deterrent effect of capital punishment may be stated as follows: Prima facie the penalty of death is likely to have a stronger effect as a deterrent to normal human beings than other forms of punishment, and there is some evidence (though no convincing statistical evidence) that this is in fact so.[4]

The evidence to which the Royal Commission refers is the testimony of law enforcement officials concerning their experiences in the apprehension and prosecution of criminals. This evidence clearly illustrates the inadequacy of the claim that capital punishment is not a deterrent, as is seen by the following:

(1) Criminals who have committed an offense punishable by life imprisonment, when faced with capture, refrained from killing their captor though by killing, escape seemed probable. When asked why they refrained from the homicide, quick responses indicated a willingness to serve a life sentence, but not risk the death penalty.

(2) Criminals about to commit certain offenses refrained from carrying deadly weapons. Upon apprehension, answers to questions concerning absence of such weapons indicated a desire to avoid more serious punishment by carrying a deadly weapon, and also to avoid use of the weapon which could result in imposition of the death penalty.

(3) Victims have been removed from a capital punishment State to a non-capital punishment State to allow the murderer opportunity for homicide without threat to his own life. This in itself demonstrates that the death penalty is considered by some would-be killers. Statistics cannot tell us how many lives have thus been saved.

Frank S. Hogan, District Attorney for the County of New York, wrote to me recently and with the letter he enclosed a memorandum representing the thinking of eight of ten of his associates, all of whom have had considerable experience in the prosecution of murder cases. Their collective opinion as to the deterrent value of capital punishment is clearly set forth in the following excerpt from that memorandum:

We are satisfied from our experience that the deterrent effect is both real and substantial . . . for example, from time to time accomplices in felony murders state with apparent truthfulness that in the planning of the felony they strongly urged the killer not to resort to violence. From the context of these utterances, it is apparent that they were led to these warnings to the killer by fear of the death penalty which they realized might follow the taking of life. Moreover, victims of hold-ups have occasionally reported that one of the robbers expressed a desire to kill them and was dissuaded from so doing by a confederate. Once again, we think it not unreasonable to suggest that fear of the death penalty played a role in some of these intercessions.

"On a number of occasions, defendants being questioned in connection with homicide, have shown a striking terror of the death penalty. While these persons have in fact perpetrated homicides, we think that their terror of the death penalty must be symptomatic of the attitude of many others of their type, as a result of which many lives have been spared.

In further support of this argument, it is interesting to note that eight States which previously abolished the death penalty have found it necessary to re-adopt it for its deterrent value. In Washington, for example, the death penalty was repealed in 1913 and re-enacted in 1919. According to John R. Cranson, warden of the Washington State Penitentiary, "Records available . . . indicate that there was an increase in the number of capital crimes . . . during that period".[3] This increase, plus a scandalous trial in 1917, convinced Washingtonians that abolition of the death penalty was a mistake. The trial involved a man accused of a brutal murder. He boasted throughout his trial that the State could do nothing to him but board him up for the rest of his life.

For what purpose was capital punishment restored in these states, who urged it and why, if not to serve notice on people who might be tempted to murder that on conviction their lives would be forfeited?

It is argued that the professional criminal does not take the death penalty seriously due to the lack of consistency with which it is applied. For example, out of an estimated 23, 370 cases of murder, non-negligent manslaughter, and rape in the year 1949, there were only 119 executions carried out in the entire United States. In 1953 there were sixty-two persons executed in this country. In that same year there were over 7,000 cases of murder and non-negligent manslaughter. At that rate the criminal's chances of escaping execution are better than 100 to 1.[5]

While this factor must of necessity affect the deterrent value of capital punishment, it is the contention of prosecutors that the potential killer will refrain from taking a life if there is the slightest possibility that the death penalty may be invoked against him.

It is clear that for normal human beings no other punishment deters so effectively from committing murder as the punishment of death. The threat of death is the one to which resort has always been made, when there is an absolute determination to produce some result.

The Commissioner of Police of London, England, in his evidence before the Royal Commission on Capital Punishment, told of a gang of armed robbers who continued operations after one of their members was sentenced to death and his sentence commuted to penal servitude for life, but the same gang disbanded and disappeared when, on a later occasion, two others were convicted of murder and hanged.[4]

Surely it is a common sense argument, based on what is known of human nature, that the death penalty has a deterrent effect particularly for certain kinds of murderers. Furthermore, as the Royal Commission opined the death penalty helps to educate the conscience of the whole community, and it arouses among many people a quasi-religious sense of awe. In the mind of the public there remains a strong association between murder and the penalty of death. Certainly one of the factors which restrains some people from murder is fear of punishment and surely, since people fear death more than anything else, the death penalty is the most effective deterrent.

Another factor in support of the retention of capital punishment is that the public is in favor of it. A poll on this issue by the American Institute of Public Opinion in 1955 showed these results: In favor of the death penalty, 68 per cent; opposed, 25 per cent; no opinion, 7 per cent.[3] The reason for this may be seen in the following excerpts from the report of the Royal Commission on Capital Punishment:

> Moreover, we think it must be recognized that there is a strong and widespread demand for retribution in the sense of reprobation—not always unmixed in the proper mind with that of atonement and expiation. As Lord Justice Denning put it: "The punishment inflicted for grave crimes should adequately reflect the revulsion felt by the great majority of citizens for them. It is a mistake to consider the object of punishment as being deterrent or reformative or preventive and nothing else. . . . The ultimate justification of any punishment is not that it is a deterrent but that it is the emphatic denunciation by the community of a crime; and from this point of view there are some murders which, in the present state of public opinion, demand the most emphatic denunciation of all, namely the death penalty.[4]

That this opinion is shared by those of us who are called upon to prosecute for heinous crimes may be seen in the experience of J. Frank Adams, State Attorney for the Fourteenth Judicial Circuit of Florida. In his recent letter to me, he described the following three cases which he prosecuted:

> 1. The defendant had raped and murdered his victim and afterwards attempted to have intercourse with her body;
> 2. The defendant unnaturally assaulted two young boys and then abandoned them in St. Andrews Bay;
> 3. The defendant raped the mother, killed her husband and one small child and left two other children for dead. In each of these cases, the defendant received the death penalty, and in speaking in justification of these sentences, State Attorney Adams said: "I feel that in all three of these cases imprisonment would not have been much punishment to these defendants nor would it have satisfied the public." In concluding his letter, he made the following statement in support of capital punishment:
> In my career as a prosecuting attorney, I have had occasions to talk to many defendants, some of them hardened criminals, and they all fear the chair and to many of them being in the penitentiary merely furnished security. Therefore, I believe it would be a terrible mistake to abolish capital punishment or to weaken it in any way in the State of Florida.

Much of the opposition to the retention of capital punishment is based on the ideas of the fallibility of a single jury in a murder trial, of the possibly inflamed atmosphere in which a trial might take place, and of the personal disposition of a single Judge in directing the jury in such a trial. However, under appeals acts, a person convicted of murder may appeal his conviction, and in the serene and impartial atmosphere surrounding an appellate court he may have the conviction set aside and a judgment and verdict of acquittal entered, or may be granted a new trial; or he may have the capital charge reduced to a lesser crime, if the jury, on the evidence, could have found him guilty of such an offense. We must not forget the importance of the American citizen and the role he plays as a jurist. It's not a duty he takes lightly, nor do the attorneys and judges. No man on trial for murder is given a superficial trial. I therefore feel that there is little chance for an innocent man to be sentenced to death.

The prosecutors' final argument for the retention of capital punishment is the State's right of self-defense. Just as the individual has the right to defend his life against the attacks of an unjust aggressor, so the State has the right to defend itself against external enemies (by waging war) and internal enemies (by capital punishment), who by their crimes undermine the very foundations of the social order. "The slaying of an evildoer is lawful," says St. Thomas Aquinas, "inasmuch as it is directed to the welfare of the whole community."

A man who has committed murder deliberately has proved himself unfit for society, and regardless of all the duties which belong to it. The safety of society is most effectually guarded by cutting him off from the power of doing further mischief. If his life be not taken away, the only other means left are confinement for life or exile for life. Neither of these is a perfect security against the commission of other crimes. It is true that the latter punishments leave open the chance of reform to the offender, but we must not forget that reformation is an enjoyable by-product, not the sole goal of punishment. Suppose a criminal has proved unable to be reformed in spite of many honest attempts. Logic demands refraining from further punishment, as its alleged end cannot be attained. But the law demands his punishment and an especially severe one, life imprisonment, and this fact proves that not reformation but protection is the desired aim of punishment.[6]

Society must also consider what effect the abolition of capital punishment could have upon the philosophy of the youth of our country. Many of them might very well look upon the criminal code, including that part of it forbidding murder, as a mere convention of society which advanced thinking and progressive social theories permit them to set aside as a matter of no consequence. This theory leads to the belief that each is a law unto himself; that each may choose the laws which he will obey, and that he may violate the rest. This type of thinking would eventually lead us into virtual anarchy.

The moralist argues that the State has no right to take away a human life, for in doing so, the State is "playing God." This argument was eloquently answered by Richard H. Rovere in his review of Arthur Koestler's book *Reflections on Hanging,* as he wrote:

> Man must play God, for he has acquired certain Godlike powers, among them a considerable degree of mastery over life and death, and he cannot avoid their exercise. Science has put into our hands—and politics has required us to grasp firmly—instruments that force a human judgment on whether or not the entire race is to be executed; even in benign employment, these instruments can affect the very image of man many millenia hence, and for that matter, the duration of all life. In a less awesome—but an awesome enough—way, modern medicine has been usurping prerogatives once held to be God's alone. It has learned to cheat death not merely by the prolongation of life but by calling men back to life after several hours on the other shore. The judge who orders an execution is no more guilty of playing God than the doctor who, having decided that a human being has been summoned to eternity too soon, restores him to the world of time and suffering and sin.[7]

## Conclusion

Any case for the retention of the death penalty does not rest upon sentiment or hysteria. It is based quite simply on the fact that, human nature being what it is, potential criminals are most effectively deterred from crime by what they fear most. The penalty of death is obviously the most dreaded punishment; obviously it is more dreaded than life imprisonment, else why does every murderer sentenced to death thankfully accept a life sentence if and when he is reprieved? And even the strongest opponents of capital punishment admit that it is necessary to provide the death penalty for murders committed by men under life sentences. This in itself is a complete admission that life imprisonment does not produce sufficient horror in the mind of the killer to deter him.

There is no question that there are some murders committed upon sudden passion, so strong that the existence of no penalty would be sufficient to stay the hand of the murderer. But this is not an argument against capital punishment, as the abolitionists would have us believe. Indeed, it may be that men so dangerous that they kill when they lose their tempers should be executed for the safety of other people. Moreover, we must remember that all murders are not committed under sudden impulse; and, because of those cases in which men do turn over in their minds the dreadful throught of murder, it is necessary that the most powerful and effective deterrent should be retained. As Daniel Webster said:

> . . . When the guilty, therefore, are not punished, the law has so far failed of its purpose; the safety of the innocent is so far endangered.[8]

## NOTES

1. *Journal of Criminal Law, Criminology and Police Science,* 46:347, "The Deterrence Concept in Criminology and Law," John C. Ball.
2. *Kentucky Law Journal,* 47:397, "Capital Punishment Reconsidered," W.O. Reichert.
3. *Senior Scholastic,* 71:6 "Capital Punishment: Pro and Con."
4. Great Britain, *Royal Commission on Capital Punishment. Report.* London: H.M. Stationary Office, 1953.

5. *Journal of Criminal Law, Criminology and Police Science,* 44:695, "Capital Punishment Reconsidered," Evelle J. Younger.
6. *Chitty's Law Journal,* 8:146, "Capital Punishment," Kurt Soelling.
7. *New Yorker,* September 14, 1957, Review of *Reflections on Hanging,* Richard H. Rovere.
8. *The Congressional Digest,* August–September 1927.

# 8 *The Death Penalty*

JAMES V. BENNETT

*The mood and the temper of the people with regard to the treatment of crime and criminals is one of the unfailing tests of the civilization of any country.*

Sir Winston Churchill

The grisly nature of the death penalty first became evident to me early in my career while I was leafing through a pile of papers on my desk in the Justice Department. Amid the house-keeping documents, I found a bill for five dollars, for the acid and cyanide used in the execution of a man named Arthur Ross Brown. How pointless it seemed. Brown was a kidnapper, rapist, and murderer. He had been put on trial on a Monday morning and on Wednesday the jury found him guilty, adding a recommendation that the death penalty be imposed. One month and a day later, we carried out the sentence in the gas chamber. Not even Brown's mother, loyal and loving to the last, would tease out a series of appeals she knew would be useless.

The whole sad business was handled quietly and expeditiously. Only one man protested, not against the execution, but against my decision not to allow him to photograph the proceedings in the gas chamber. The following morning, only a few paragraphs in the newspapers reported the event. If the point of the death penalty was to deter, I asked myself, who did the execution of Brown deter? Who even knew about it, and who cared?

Another morning I was visiting with Director Bates when his secretary slipped into the room and handed him an imposing looking document. "Mr. Bates," she said, "It's from the President and he's . . ." She stopped speaking and appeared almost to be holding her breath. Bates perused the paper swiftly. "Jim," he said, "the President has commuted Bernstein's sentence to life imprisonment." There was a silence. Charles Bernstein was due to be executed that day, in fact, in fifteen minutes' time.

Sanford Bates picked up the telephone and asked to be put through to the District of Columbia jail where the sentence was to be carried out. He hung over the phone, poised to speak the moment the call went through. "But, operator," he said suddenly, "you'll have to cut in." His face turned white and his fingers drummed on the desktop. The lines to the jail were all busy.

My mind ran over the complex details of the case. Bernstein was a young burglar and pickpocket who had served nine years in a state prison for allegedly stealing some bonds from a bank robber. The governor had pardoned him and set him free on grounds of innocence. Several years later Bernstein was "identified" as a man who had been seen committing a murder in Washington, according to the police. Whether or not he had actually been seen was a highly disputed point, but in any case he was a convenient fall guy with a prison record. He was arrested, convicted, and sentenced to death. Humanitarian agencies and government officials challenged the identification. The weather bureau clinched the issue when it said the foliage at that time of year was dense, and that Bernstein could not possibly have been seen through some trees as the alleged witness had claimed. President Roosevelt apparently had not seen the case until the very day of the execution although it had been under investigation and study for three years. At almost the last moment he had commuted the sentence to life imprisonment.

Bates cut into my thoughts. "The operator says she's sorry," he said, shoving the phone to me. "Jim, maybe you can get through. I'm going to tell Bill Hammack and we'll each grab a cab and run down to the jail. We don't have much time." I now had the responsibility for trying to save the life of a man at the other end of a telephone line that was busy.

I made a fresh phone call and told the operator to hurry. It was now ten to twelve, the appointed hour of the execution. "The line is still busy," she said. I told her: "Cut in now. A man's life is involved." Her voice came back as mechanically as only a telephone operator's can: "What is the nature of the emergency?"

I swore and told her: "This is the Department of Justice and in ten minutes a man is going to be executed. The President has just commuted his sentence. We've got to get through and stop the execution." She told me to hang on and she would do her best.

The operator cleared the lines and as soon as I heard a voice, I shouted, "Call off the execution. The President has commuted the sentence." The voice asked who was speaking. "Bennett-- Department of Justice." The man said: "I'm just the officer on the desk. I'll connect you with the superintendent." There was more delay. Then: "I'm sorry, sir, but the superintendent seems to be tied up somewhere in the prison. I'll get one of the sergeants."

One, two, three, four, five more minutes ticked by. My hand was tight on the receiver and the sweat ran down my wrist. The phone went dead. Surely we had not been cut off. Then another voice, a man identifying himself as a sergeant, asked what he could do for me. I shouted again, "Call off the execution," and identified myself. Another minute passed before the sergeant said genially, "We'll take care of it, sir. You can rest easy." Neither Bates's nor Hammack's cabs reached the jail before twelve. I had saved Bernstein's life.

Not long afterward, we were told through the underworld

grapevine that Bernstein was a fall guy and that the murder had been committed by a small-time thug for pay. Roosevelt then commuted Bernstein's sentence to time served and set him free. President Truman subsequently pardoned him unconditionally. Bernstein went to work in a government job and dropped by to see me once in a while, though he had little to say.

How would we have felt if this man had been executed? How many others have died in similar miscarriages of justice we will never know. But we do know that Queen Elizabeth granted a pardon to Timothy Evans on the grounds of innocence fifteen years after he was executed. And dozens of pardons have been granted to condemned men on the ground their confessions were coerced or their conviction based on perjured testimony or mistaken identification.

Then there was the revolting execution of Anthony Chebatoris in the federal institution at Milan, Michigan. Chebatoris had been convicted of murder in a federal court after an attempted bank robbery in Michigan. The death penalty had been long outlawed in that state, but it was Chebatoris's luck that the circumstances of the robbery brought it under federal jurisdiction. Throughout his lengthy trial, he insisted he had not shot and killed a bystander, as charged, but that a police officer must have fired a stray round. Chebatoris was found guilty and condemned to be hanged.

Warden John Ryan of the Milan institution was given the job of carrying out the sentence. Reluctantly, he erected a gallows in the interior of the prison and surrounded it with a canvas screen. Then he located a man said to be an expert hangman. At two A.M. on the day of the execution, Ryan called me at home. "Is it all over?" I asked. Ryan replied, "I wish to God it was. The hangman arrived about an hour ago. He's gloriously drunk and he's got three friends with him, just as potted. We've given him enough coffee to sober him up a bit, but he says he isn't going to do the job unless we let his friends watch. He wants them to see what a 'pro' he is."

I reminded Ryan that nobody was permitted to attend the execution except official witnesses, but Ryan said, "I've been talking to him and he keeps threatening to pack up his stuff and get out if we don't let his friends in. They're all drunk. They can hardly walk." When I told Ryan he would have to carry out the execution himself in accordance with regulations if a hangman could not be found, he blew up at me: "No, sir, I'm against the whole business anyway. We haven't had a hanging here in the state in a hundred years and the whole institution's on edge. You and the attorney general can have this job right now."

We talked on some more, and eventually Ryan said he would go back to try to talk the hangman into executing Chebatoris. Somehow he realized that the hangman was too drunk to see whether his friends were in the darkened execution chamber or not. Ryan then told the hangman he would let the friends watch from the back of the room, whereupon the man agreed to execute Chebatoris. Afterward, another uproar began when the hangman asked his friends what they thought of the job, and they complained that the warden had kept them outside. The hangman promptly accused Ryan of trickery and deception, adding that he was not fit to run a federal institution. At this, Ryan's patience finally broke, and he threw the drunks out of the prison gate.

For obvious reasons, we decided to keep this episode a secret, announcing only that the execution had been carried out. There was something inherently disgusting about the death penalty that led to these excesses, I thought. Small wonder that prison wardens, not only John Ryan, but Lewis Lawes of Sing Sing, James Johnston of Alcatraz, and Clinton Duffy of San Quentin, were in the forefront of those who wanted to abolish capital punishment.

In 1935, while I was serving as an assistant director of the Bureau of Prisons, I decided to make up a list of the 184 executions that had taken place in the federal and state jurisdictions during the year. I noted that executions were being carried out at a rate of eighteen for every thousand homicides.

In 1964, the year in which I retired, I compiled a similar list. There were twenty-one executions, at a rate of three per thousand homicides.

Since then, the actual use of the death penalty has declined further. In 1965, sixty-seven men were condemned to death by the courts and sixty-two were reprieved. In 1966, only one man was executed in the whole country, and in 1967, there were two. In 1968, for the first year on record, there were no executions in the United States. Today more than four hundred condemned men wait in their death cells while their attorneys maneuver through the appellate processes. It is safe to say that most of them will be reprieved or their convictions set aside because they were denied a fair trial.

Despite this historical trend, however, the debate about the death penalty rages on. Of our fifty states, only thirteen have clearly repealed capital punishment. Delaware abolished the death penalty in 1958 but reinstated it in 1961. Colorado voted in a statewide referendum in 1966 to retain the death penalty. President Johnson's Commission on Law Enforcement reported: "Some members favor the abolition of capital punishment while others favor its retention." In this case, as in other sections of its report, the commission sidestepped the issue by declaring that capital punishment was a matter of policy for each state to decide for itself.

Overseas, there is almost as much contention. Great Britain suspended capital punishment in 1965, but only for a five-year trial. Most of the other countries of western Europe, and Japan, have abolished the death penalty unequivocally, while many of the underdeveloped countries maintain it. Canada held a parliamentary debate on the subject in 1965 and decided to retain capital punishment as a deterrent to murder.

Over the years, I found myself increasingly appalled by the nature of the penalty I was often responsible for carrying out. There was little question in my mind, as my experience increased, that the death penalty was revolting, susceptible to miscarriage of justice, and ineffective in the sense that it was not a deterrent to murder. I was affronted by the macabre methodology of capital punishment. I was shocked by the fact that men sentenced to death were generally penniless, friendless, and, disproportionately, Negroes. The death penalty also lent itself to erratic procedures in the courts. As Attorney General Robert H.

Jackson put it: "When the penalty is death, appellate judges are tempted to strain the evidence and, in close cases, the law, in order to give doubtfully condemned men another chance."

On the other hand, I remain a convinced member of the majority of the public that wonders what other punishment may reasonably be imposed for such atrocious crimes as mass murder, the bombing of churches, schools, and aircraft in flight, and the assassination of the President. During my term in office, all of these occurred.

The heart of the argument in favor of the death penalty, of course, lies within Old Testament tradition. How can reverence for human life be protected if those who willfully take it are not themselves condemned? The death penalty is the cornerstone of ancient and medieval justice and, even as recently as the reigns of Henry VIII of England (seventy-two thousand executions) and Queen Elizabeth I (nineteen thousand executions), death was enacted in public spectacles intended to deter witnesses from breaking the law. One such episode, depicted by Lytton Strachey, was the execution of three men, in 1594, for high treason against Good Queen Bess.

> The three culprits, bound to hurdles, were dragged up Holborn, past one of the men's homes, to Tyburn Tree. There, before a crowd in festive spirits, one of the condemned attempted to make a last oration from the scaffold, but was shouted down. The mob howled with laughter when he asserted he loved his mistress more than Jesus Christ, and nothing more was heard until he was hurried to the gallows. There he was hanged and cut down while still living. He was thereupon castrated, disembowelled and quartered. The death sentence was carried out on the second man in like fashion.
>
> But the third man, Tinoco, had seen what was to be his fate, twice repeated. His ears were filled with the shrieks and moans of his companions and his eyes with every detail of the contortions and the blood. Hanged, but cut down too soon, he recovered his feet. He was lusty and desperate and fell upon his executioners. The crowd was wild with excitement and cheered him on, breaking through the soldiers and forming a ring to watch the fight. But before long, the instincts of law and order reasserted them-

selves. Two stalwart men rushed forward to help the executioners. Tinoco was felled with a blow on the head and held down firmly. Then he too was castrated, disembowelled and quartered.

One hundred years afterward, the Earl of Ferrers was executed at Tyburn for the murder of his steward. This was the day, perhaps, in which capital punishment was in its blackest flower.

Dressed in the dove-colored embroidered coat and breeches that he had worn on his wedding day, the Earl rode to Tyburn in his own luxurious tandem, drawn by six gaily bedecked horses. Behind him in procession rode the sheriffs and other officials who had been designated to carry out the sentence. Next followed a coach bearing one or two high-ranking mourners and, at the end, a hearse drawn by six horses draped in the nobleman's black funeral regalia. At the gallows, the hangman and his assistant came forward and begged the Earl's forgiveness for what was about to be done. The Earl forgave them and, in an added gesture of generosity, drew five guineas from his pocket with apparent intent to reward the hangman.

But the Earl gave the five guineas to the hangman's assistant instead. The hangman promptly dropped him through the trap without any more ceremony and began to argue with the assistant about the five guineas. The assistant would not give up the money and, according to one observer, "An unseemly dispute arose between these unthinking wretches which the sheriff quickly silenced."

The modern United States was not incapable of putting on a capital punishment show, such as the shocking execution of Bonnie Brown Heady and Carl Austin Hall for the kidnapping and murder of young Bobby Greenlease. They were allowed to die together in the gas chamber, side by side, and they prepared for the execution as their last date. Bonnie Heady plucked her eyebrows, marcelled her hair and chose her shade of lipstick carefully. Meanwhile the question arose as to what she should be permitted to wear. Because a surfeit of clothing retains poison gas, it was first decided to let her wear only a bra and shorts and a pair of prison slippers, while Hall would wear shorts and slippers. Information obtained from the state of California indicated that gassed people could wear more, provided that the bodies were properly decontaminated. So Bonnie Heady was given a light green prison dress to wear over her underclothes, and Hall a gray prison suit. In the final hours, she wrote an endearing letter to Hall about the honeymoon they would enjoy in the hereafter, which Hall read impassively, and did not answer. When they entered the gas chamber together, he was stony-faced and indifferent, and she was as radiant as a middle-aged bride.

Although the execution was hideous, the cold-blooded murder of ten-year-old Bobby Greenlease while his father was gathering the ransom was one of the atrocious crimes for which the death penalty might be retained. How else to punish the Greenlease kidnappers, or the men who blow up airliners, or Lee Harvey Oswald? How else to punish killers such as Carl Panzran, who boasted he had killed twenty-two people and vowed he would murder a prison guard to make it twenty-three. In Leavenworth, he accomplished his threat, and was executed.

Peering through the bars of a cell opposite Panzran's at Leavenworth was another murderer, Robert Stroud, the so-called Birdman of Alcatraz. He committed his first murder in Juneau, Alaska, at the age of nineteen, when he killed a man in an argument about how much money should be paid to a prostitute for whom he was working as a pimp. Sentenced to twelve years' imprisonment in the federal penitentiary at McNeil Island, he attacked and wounded another prisoner with a knive. He was given another six months and was transferred to Leavenworth. There Stroud attacked a prison officer in the presence of twelve hundred men in a dining hall at the Sunday midday meal. He pulled a double-edged dagger from inside his jacket and plunged it into the guard's heart because, he said later, the man had reported him for violating prison regulations. Stroud was tried and convicted three times of murder in the first degree, but the prosecution made so many errors in the presentation of the case that the first two trials were set aside by the court of appeals. Finally, Stroud was sentenced to death, but President Woodrow Wilson, in 1920, commuted the sentence to life imprisonment. Wilson's attorney general ordered that Stroud should be kept in solitary confinement so he would not be able to kill again.

One of the less formal aspects of imprisonment in those days was that men were sometimes allowed to keep pets in their cells. Stroud became interested in raising canaries and he was permitted to increase his flock. The Leavenworth officials even let him have a second cell in which he could set up a laboratory. He repaid them for these privileges by smuggling out letters, defying the rules, and one day slugging the doctor who was treating him. Then they searched the cell thoroughly and found a lethal knife dug into the edge of his table in such a way that it could be quickly unsheathed and used on anyone who came near him. When Stroud's behavior continued to be recalcitrant he was transferred to Alcatraz, where he extended his studies and won his famous nickname, "Birdman of Alcatraz."

Under my administration, Stroud's case was repeatedly reviewed by attorneys general and parole boards, by members of the judiciary, and by our own classification committees, but none of us believed he was anything but a psychopathic killer. Attorney General Biddle wrote: "Stroud loves birds and hates men." Shortly before his death in our federal mental health institution at Springfield, Missouri, Stroud penned his own epitaph in the form of a dedication of one of his books on bird disease:

> "To my friends and enemies, whose mean, little or thriving souls, actuated by spite, bigotry, jealousy, sadism, vindictiveness or ignorance, by their very opposition, have stimulated me to greater effort and accomplishment than would otherwise have been possible for me."

During the 1950's, I wrote a series of articles for legal and criminological journals in which I attempted to draw upon my experience to clarify my position on capital punishment. Now, as then, I hold to what might be termed the middle ground of the argument.

I am convinced that capital punishment is no deterrent to rape, kidnapping, armed robbery, or most homicides, and the five states with the lowest murder rates (Wisconsin, Minnesota, Iowa, North Dakota, Vermont) have in fact abolished the death penalty.

Another time-honored argument used by my colleague, J. Edgar Hoover, is the one quoted by Sir Robert Grimstone in opposing the abandonment of the death penalty in England. He said: "No one can ever know how many people have refrained from murder because of the fear of being hanged." This sounds logical, but it does not hold when examined closely. All studies of the murder rate since 1920 have shown that the states which abolished the death penalty experienced no increase in willful killings; furthermore, their homicide rates are almost identical to those of contiguous states retaining capital punishment. A public policy of inducing fear of execution as a way to reduce the murder rate is a snare and a delusion.

Another tenuous argument is that to abolish the death penalty would indicate a softening approach to the control of crime and violence. Yet it has been made clear time and again by riots, police brutality, and unrestrained gunfire that violence begets violence. When a state is guilty of violence—as it is when it legalizes murder—it encourages the individual to be guilty of a violent act. That violence inevitably follows a war, or an execution, has been shown to be the case.

The courts are moving into the controversy. They have at last agreed that a person cannot be excluded from a jury because he is opposed to the death penalty. There are to be no more juries like the one described in Truman Capote's *In Cold Blood,* which was confronted with the question of the mental condition of one or both of the defendants. Soon I predict that our Supreme Court will decide whether the death penalty is "cruel and unusual punishment" of the kind forbidden by our Constitution. Surely, it is unusual, and it may be that in the light of present-day attitudes, morals, and value concepts surrounding the administration of justice, it is also cruel.

The least we can and should do is reduce the number of categories of crime for which the death penalty may be imposed, specifically ruling out the death penalty for most types of murder, armed robbery, and rape. As a concession, we may perhaps retain the death penalty for high treason, mass murder or multiple murders, the assassination of the President, murder for hire, the kidnapping and/or rape of children under fourteen years of age, and the murder of law enforcement officers engaged in the performance of their duties.

It would, I realize, be no easy job to draft a statute that would meet constitutional requirements of definiteness. What is mass murder, for instance, or how can you decide what is multiple murder? Is it killing two people, or must there be three or more as in the Speck case, in which a man killed six nurses? What standards should we apply to determining whether a kidnapping was actually the seizure of a person for ransom? In any event we must provide that before the death penalty can be imposed the jury must have full information about the convicted murderer or rapist included a psychiatric examination. They must also be permitted to hear the defendant at a separate trial devoted exclusively to hearing witnesses and the defendant as to the reasons for the crime, its motivation, and any and all mitigating information.

Even with this compromise, we should rewrite the death penalty statutes to provide that capital punishment may never be imposed by a single judge, acting alone, and that three-man panels of judges must be convened to pass on capital cases when the jury so recommends. It goes without saying that in capital cases the federal and state laws ought to be brought into harmony.

During my days of soul-searching on this issue, I was suddenly plunged into the most controversial double execution of the century. This was the electrocution of Julius and Ethel Rosenberg on charges of atomic espionage against the United States during World War II. I was responsible for carrying out the sentence of the courts and for months I tried to stave off the black day. Assuming, as I did, that the Rosenbergs were enemy agents who had transferred atomic secrets to the Soviet Union, I nonetheless doubted that the imposition of the death penalty was justified. I did not believe the country should be asked to pay the price of emotional confusion and division. I thought the Rosenbergs ought not be placed on the national conscience or given the martyrdom they unswervingly sought.

Early in May 1953, I gave Attorney General Brownell a letter I had received from a woman. A passage in the letter read: "Americans are disposed to be just and merciful. I believe there must be many who may now have some qualms about the justice of destroying these two particular young people—among so many known agents, saboteurs and subversives—and surely some legal authority must know whether, in protesting their perfect innocence, they have lied or not. If they have not been reasonable in their answers to questions of known fact, they should be helped to release themselves from the bondage of a mistaken loyalty to a false cause. I believe that the American people would be greatly relieved in conscience if a true statement could be obtained from the Rosenbergs which would warrant their reprieve." Brownell was impressed and he authorized me to proceed on my own to see if I could persuade them to be more cooperative.

The strategy I determined upon, and discussed with Brownell, was to open a channel to the Rosenbergs that would enable them to speak directly with Brownell and through him to President Eisenhower. This channel would bypass the FBI, the U.S. attorney and the other agencies that the Rosenbergs had said they felt to be responsible for their arrest and "false" conviction, and might make it simpler for them to "release themselves from the bondage of a mistaken loyalty."

There was also a possibility that the case had become frozen. The Rosenbergs, arrested in the summer of 1950, had been sentenced to death by Federal Judge Irving Kaufman in May 1951, and their case had been before the Supreme Court seven times. If the Rosenbergs were indeed looking for a way out of their allegiance, I might be able to provide it. Brownell authorized me to interview Julius and Ethel Rosenberg in Sing Sing prison at once.

Three days later I reported on the interviews in this memorandum to Brownell:

> On Tuesday, June 2, I interviewed Julius and Ethel Rosenberg in the death house at Sing Sing. I talked first with Julius Rosen-

berg in an interview room which was made available to me by the Warden. Following a short preliminary conversation about his health and the status of his case, I told Rosenberg that it was part of my official duty to arrange for any visits he might care to request with government officials familiar with the details of his case. I told him that there seemed to be a feeling on the part of some government agencies that he was in possession of information which would be helpful in solving some as yet unanswered questions. I stressed the importance of early disclosure of any such information he might have and giving government agents an opportunity to check on whatever statement he might make in view of the fact that the execution date was only two weeks away.

I had scarcely made known the purpose of my meeting when Rosenberg launched in a quite emotionally charged tirade to the effect that he and his wife were victims not only of a gross miscarriage of justice but a "deal" by the government on the one hand and his brother and sister-in-law, David and Ruth Greenglass, on the other. He asserted that Attorney General McGrath was the architect of the plot and had somehow influenced the selection of Judge Kaufman as the trial judge and was generally responsible for the outcome. He was very bitter also toward his sister-in-law, Ruth Greenglass, and laid great stress on the fact that she got off scot-free while his wife Ethel received the death sentence.

I questioned some of his statements and repeatedly told him that he ought somehow to be able to disabuse those familiar with the case of the feelings he had failed to make a full disclosure and had not been cooperative. Each time he protested his innocence. He also claimed that he was convicted on the basis of perjured testimony and trickery on the part of the prosecutor. He laid considerable stress on the fact that David Greenglass was supposed to have made the drawings involved from memory. He said it was impossible for a person of as little education and experience and knowledge of engineering as his brother-in-law David to do this. He said this in the course of his request that he and his wife be given another opportunity to appear in court so that all of the facts could be brought out. He somehow apparently believed that if he could have had another opportunity for public trial he could have vindicated himself.

This third part of his conversation consisted of a denunciation of Judge Kaufman and the sentence he gave. How, he asked, could it have been possible under any circumstances that a death sentence be meted out to him and his wife in the face of the sentence of thirty years given to Harry Gold and fifteen years to David Greenglass, who were admittedly arch-conspirators in an espionage plot. He contended that he was in no sense guilty of espionage and that the sentence was savage in the extreme.

Rosenberg lacked the detached calmness and self-assurance that characterized my former conversation with him. He no longer seemed to have the attitude of the martyr, which I felt marked his conversation the previous time I saw him. (This was a routine interview when the Rosenbergs were brought into federal custody; though held in a New York State penitentiary, the Rosenbergs were federal prisoners.)

Notwithstanding the fact that he told me several times that he understood I was not there to make any deal with him or put him on the rack, as he phrased it, he nevertheless was quite belligerent, excitable and made some statements that on questioning he was willing to modify. He talked much of Fascist tactics used in his case and inferred the sentence was not what one could expect of a great democracy, that he and his wife were of such small importance peoples abroad would never be able to understand our action in condemning them to death.

I next went to the women's cellblock where I saw Mrs. Rosenberg. I followed about the same approach in telling her that the purpose of my visit was to see how she was getting along and also to ascertain whether she wanted me to put her in touch with the proper government agents so that she could have an opportunity to make any statement or give any information about her case that would be helpful to the government in solving some unanswered questions relating to the whole matter. Evidently she and Julius had anticipated some such inquiry, because her attitude and her statements were substantially the same as those of her husband, although she wasn't quite as verbose or excited as he was. She said that obviously the government could not prove whatever suspicions they had about certain aspects of the case or we would not be turning to her for cooperation, and that she had no intention of putting her finger on somebody else or giving false or misleading information even though it might have the effect of staying her own execution. She said that if the government wanted her testimony on any matter she would have to be brought into open court.

Realizing that I wasn't getting anywhere, I asked the Warden to bring in Julius and to be present while I again repeated the purpose of my presence in the institution and told him that I would appreciate it if he would transmit promptly any message that either Julius or Ethel wished to have brought to the attention of the Department. Both Rosenbergs again protested that they would have no messages and no information and that the only thing I could do for them would be to present to the Attorney General a recommendation that their sentence be commuted. My final word to Julius was that I would be around the institution for an hour or so and that if he wished to see me again before I left to notify the guard. He said that he only wished to see me in the event I had some good news for him.

In the course of the interview Rosenberg asked me if I had consulted his attorney or advised him of my visit. When I told him I had not he requested me to do so, which I did later. I informed Mr. Bloch by telephone as soon as he could be reached, which was about 6 P.M., June 2, of my visit and my offer to expedite any request the Rosenbergs had bearing on a further explanation of the facts involved in their activities. Mr. Bloch expressed surprise that he had not been informed of the visit and invited to be present. I told him I was merely acting as intermediary and in my official capacity as the one to whom responsibility for their safe-keeping had been delegated. He made no further protest and merely said something to the effect that he would see the Rosenbergs the next day about some legal moves he had in mind.

After I had transmitted my memorandum to Brownell, I felt I had done all I could. He evidently deemed he had also done everything possible and I received no further instructions on the matter.

The evening of the execution, I joined the death watch in FBI Director Hoover's office. From the windows we watched the sad and bedraggled pickets parading up Pennsylvania Avenue to the White House. Some denounced President Eisenhower as a murderer. Others jeered the Rosenberg pickets as Communists and supporters of traitors who would soon burn. The police kept order while we waited beside an open phone line from Sing Sing, hoping to the end that the Rosenbergs would talk.

None of us said much, and I found myself mulling over the day's frantic efforts to locate the official executioner. In one of the customary, obscene snafus associated with capital punishment, the executioner had taken the day off and disappeared into the Catskill Mountains, telling nobody where he was going. There had been another last-minute delay in the Supreme Court and the man did not expect to have to work that evening. Only by the purest chance did we find him in one of his favorite haunts in the Catskills and we brought him back by helicopter to Sing Sing. He arrived just in time to perform his task before the Jewish Sabbath began at sundown.

For two hours we waited in Hoover's office for word on the open line. The Rosenbergs had been told for the last time that, if they spoke out, they might get a stay. One of my assistants was on duty in the warden's office at Sing Sing to relay any breaks to Hoover and me. In the White House, President Eisenhower was on hand waiting to the end for any word from us. At 7:55 P.M., Daylight Saving Time, my assistant at Sing Sing informed me there would be no change, and the final seconds ticked away.

At 8:20 P.M., we were told it was all over, and we dispersed. Not until the following morning did I learn that the execution had been a rough one and that electrical currents had been passed through Mrs. Rosenberg for seven minutes until she was dead. Witnesses said a spiral of smoke went up from her head.

Into my office in the Bureau of Prisons a few days later two documents were brought special delivery. The first was the official record, signed by the U.S. marshal of the Southern District of New York, that the execution had been carried out. The second was a bill from Sing Sing:

| | |
|---|---|
| Board, cell and special female guards<br>for Ethel Rosenberg,<br>801 days at $38.60 per day | $30,918.60 |
| Board and cell<br>for Julius Rosenberg,<br>736 days at $4.43 per day<br>and 31 days at $38.60 per day | $3,399.98 |
| Two executions at $150 each | $300.00 |

# IV Opponents of Capital Punishment

Somewhat back to back with Director Bennett's statement is one by Richard A. McGee who for many years held increasingly responsible positions in the California State Corrections System. While serving as the Administrator for the California Youth and Adult Corrections Agency, McGee wrote a strong article opposing the death sentence. This article is reprinted in Chapter 9.

McGee believes that the "issues involved in the death penalty are fundamental to our whole present system of criminal law." His arguments about the inability of capital punishment to deter could be used as a response to those views put forward by Chief of Police Allen and State's Attorney Gerstein. McGee also believes that the death penalty is not necessary for the protection of prison personnel; he further argues that having prisoners confined for long periods awaiting the death sentence may provide a greater danger to prison personnel than if the inmates were serving life sentences. One study has shown that among those prisoners committing prison homicides only half had a sentence of 10 years or less and only one prisoner had a life sentence.

McGee's arguments go to the heart of the concept of rehabilitation. He opposes punishment because the better response is prevention. Should this fail, McGee states, society could utilize imprisonment. He believes that capital punishment is both unnecessary and irrational since it undermines the larger goal of rehabilitation.

Perhaps the most forthright statement ever made by a high public official in opposition to the death sentence was made by Attorney General Ramsey Clark, who in July 1968 testified in support of a bill which would have abolished capital punishment in Federal jurisdictions. Calling upon the resource literature on capital punishment and the government's statistical series on executions, the Attorney General stated that, when the State uses capital punishment, "thou shalt not kill loses the force of the absolute."

The recommendation of the President's Commission on Law Enforcement and Administration of Justice in 1967 (Chapter 11) leaves the matter of capital punishment to be determined by the individual states. Abandonment of capital punishment is suggested when the death penalty, though imposed by juries, is never carried into effect. Many felt that the Commission could have made a stronger recommendation for abolition. It has been said, however, that the Commission decided to avoid stirring up controversy on the capital punishment issue because so many strong feelings surround the subject. Under such conditions, public attention might have focused only on the death penalty issue and tended to overlook the many less sensational, but highly important matters with which the Commission had concerned itself.

In January 1971, after winding up a 3½-year study, the National Commission on Reform of the Federal Criminal Laws called for life imprisonment as the maximum criminal penalty.[1] The recommendation presented here would set aside the death penalty as a Federally imposed sentence for murder, rape, bank robbery where injury results, kidnaping, treason, assassination of the President or Vice President, selling heroin to a juvenile, causing death by transporting explosives for criminal purposes, espionage, and aircraft hijacking causing death.

An editorial that appeared in the January 1969 issue of *Judicature,* the Journal of the American Judicature Society, is reprinted in Chapter 12. This statement is an outright call for removal of the death sentence as a means of punishment in the United States.

Of the many articles that capture the spirit of the struggle over capital punishment, "For Whom the Chair Waits" by Mrs. Sara R. Ehrmann, former Executive Director for the American League to Abolish Capital Punishment, is perhaps the best. Mrs. Ehrmann, wife of the Assistant Defense Counsel for Sacco and Vanzetti, has for more than 40 years beseeched and cajoled legislators, business men, community leaders, and the press to heed her arguments opposing the death sentence. It is said that Sara Ehrmann has been instrumental in preventing execution in the Commonwealth of Massachusetts since 1943.

Mrs. Ehrmann is one of only a handful of women who have examined the capital punishment issue. She strikes out at capital punishment on the ground that it has been used to execute the mentally ill, the friendless and the poor and youthful offenders. She is also firmly convinced that there is the "ever present danger of executing the innocent."

Victor Evjen, former editor of *Federal Probation,* strongly condemns capital punishment as part of a primitive blood vengeance which has no place in today's administration of justice. In a style reminiscent of testimony presented before state legislative committees, Evjen gives short and direct responses to the eight questions constantly asked about the penalty of death.

## NOTE

1. National Commission on Reform of Federal Criminal Laws, *Final Report to the President and Congress,* Washington, D.C.: U.S. Government Printing Office, 1971.

# 9 Capital Punishment as Seen by a Correctional Administrator

RICHARD A. McGEE

The continuing debate over capital punishment has obscured that which it should have illuminated—that we need to re-examine the whole philosophic base of our criminal law.

Capital punishment, itself, obscures more significant issues involved in the administration of criminal justice by furthering the notion that punishment is the simple, easy solution to the complex problem of crime.

That notion is the root attitude that brings forth the branches: Probation is just a slap on the wrist; filthy jails are what criminals deserve; a prison with a rehabilitation program is a country

The author wishes to express his appreciation to Walter L. Barkdull, executive officer of the California Board of Corrections, for assistance in the development of this article.

From *Federal Probation Quarterly*, June 1964, Administrative Office of the United States Courts, pp. 11–16.

club; and, the real answer is to get tough. But the broad view is screened from sight by the narrow focus of the debate on a minute number of offenders, a tiny segment of offenses, and an experience that touches few persons directly.

Even in corrections, few persons are directly involved. Of the more than 9,000 employees of the California Youth and Adult Corrections Agency, less than 70 have duties that bring them into contact with the condemned or require their participation in an execution. Another small number may have known the victim of a murderer or have viewed a murder scene.

As a consequence, opinion surveys of Department of Corrections employees indicate their attitudes toward the death penalty are pretty much the product of their upbringing, education, and associations rather than their correctional experience or study of the issues involved.

On the other hand, personal experience seems more likely to elicit an emotional response than the desire for detached study.

This is unfortunate because the issues involved in the death penalty are fundamental to our whole present system of criminal law. The arguments *for* the death penalty, in particular, throw a harsh light on the concepts of the criminal codes and the relative emphasis of each. The emphasis revealed in this supposedly enlightened day should cause us some concern. Certainly from a purely practical standpoint it is one of the major stumbling blocks in improving the correctional apparatus—probation, jails, prisons, and parole.

The basic arguments advanced for the death penalty are retribution, deterrence, and rehabilitation, with the latter stated negatively—that efforts at rehabilitation are largely fruitless. The same three concepts are the pillars upon which rests, however unevenly, the basic criminal law of the Western civilization. Therefore, if the arguments are unsound favoring the death penalty, perhaps, the whole proposition needs rethinking.

California's Legislature has considered the death penalty in 7 of the past 10 years and the legislative hearings have become just as ritualistic as the execution of the death penalty, itself.

Retribution is not considered a very nice word at such hearings. A witness seldom advocates the death penalty on grounds of retribution and when he does, he is quickly disowned by the other proponents.

## Fails as a Deterrent

It is the unique deterrent value capital punishment is presumed to possess that provides the mainstay of the arguments for retention of the death penalty. That this is true has been refuted year after year before the Legislature by a variety of witnesses—statistical experts, police officials from abolition states, psychiatrists, and criminologists among others.

I need not review for this readership the studies of Dr. Thorsten Sellin and others in comparing homicide rates between jurisdictions with and without capital punishment. A review of these studies must inevitably bring any person who is more influenced by facts than by emotion to the conclusion that the argument for the death penalty as a deterrent is without merit. Indeed, there is evidence that the death penalty encourages homicide in the disordered minds of some. One must conclude that there are many factors other than the presence or absence of the death penalty which result in a higher or lower incidence of murder.

Then the argument turns slightly. The public must be protected from known killers. This is the concept of rehabilitation expressed in the negative. The killer must be exterminated because otherwise he will be released to kill again. Even life without possibility of parole is not certain, the argument runs.

A damaging side effect has been, in the words of the California Supreme Court, that "the jury sometimes lamentably has 'tried' the Adult Authority"[1] because zealous prosecutors have heavily stressed the possibilities of parole. While, of course, there have been instances when a paroled murderer killed again, study after study has shown that the rate of parole violation for the homicide group is the lowest of any offense category.

The fact that there are first degree murderers to be paroled exposes the biggest flaw in the extermination-type argument: the random invocation of the penalty. That, in turn, strikes another blow at the deterrent theory.

California annually has some 600 homicides. There are about 100 convictions for first degree murder for which the defendant (none of whom was deterred) could be sentenced to death. Approximately one-fifth are sentenced to death and, perhaps, a tenth are ultimately executed. There are counties that never pronounced the death sentence. Minority race members are over-represented among those executed. The wealthy never reach Death Row.

This is more like Russian Roulette than the even hand of justice.

## Not Necessary to Protect Prison Personnel

A corollary set of arguments proclaims that the death penalty is necessary for the protection of prison personnel. All of them conveniently ignore the experience of states and countries without capital punishment.

One version is that the life-term prisoner can be controlled only by the ultimate threat of death. This argument displays a pitiful ignorance of both prisons and prisoners. There are innumerable sanctions and measures short of death that will provide just as effective control.

The argument also must assume that although the threat of death is not an effective deterrent in the outside community, it somehow is in the prison community. Any logical analysis must show the opposite to be true in view of the kinds of persons collected in prison: none of them has been deterred by the law.

Experience shows that it is not the life-term prisoner who kills prison officers or inmates, anyway. In California one officer has been killed in the past 10 years. He was killed by two Youth Authority wards who technically were not even serving sentences and who would normally have been released in a year. Incidentally, they were found guilty of second degree murder which does not carry a death sentence. The term is 5 years to life with parole eligibility in 20 months.

A review of all California prison homicides during the past 2 years shows that of the known killers, 50 percent had a maximum term of 10 years or less. Only one had a definite life sentence.

Another version of the argument is that those persons sentenced to death are so dangerous they could not be kept in prison without great risk. The fact is that many of the persons condemned would not pose the least problem as ordinary prisoners. There are, indeed, some very dangerous persons sentenced to death. But for every one of these there are at least a half-dozen equally dangerous persons sent to prison with sentences of less than death.

Perhaps the most dangerous person held in a California prison in modern times—a man who was known to have killed four persons and anxious to add to his score—was not sentenced to prison at all, but was being held for the Department of Mental Hygiene.

But perhaps the biggest fallacy of the argument that the death penalty protects prison officers is the implicit assumption that either those to be executed do not come to prison or that they are executed immediately upon arrival. Nothing could be further from the truth. As a consequence, the death penalty, itself, creates a very dangerous prison situation.

If there were any merit to the argument that persons sentenced to life terms would feel free to act as they please because nothing further could be done to them, then certainly this would apply with even greater force to those actually sentenced to death.

California had 45 persons in prison under sentence of death December 31, 1963. Not only that, two of them had been on condemned row for more than 6 years, another almost 5 years, and three more had been under sentence of death for more than 3 years. This is not unusual. One man spent more than 11 years on condemned row and no one has been executed in less than 8 months after arrival in the past dozen years. The median is 15 months for those executed.

These long periods of confinement under sentence of death not only endanger officers and create a whole series of management problems, but also certainly reduce any possible deterrent effect of the death penalty.

As the ritual of the legislative hearing proceeds, proponents of capital punishment present two side approaches: capital punishment would be effective if we but used it more, and, what they call the "common sense" approach.

The first conveniently ignores thousands of years of bloody history and the second is actually nonsense.

## Death Penalty Once Widely Used

Society *has* used the death penalty extensively. Only 150 years ago when the population of England and Wales totaled half that of California's population today there were more than 100 public executions a year in the London and Middlesex district alone. It has been stated that during the reign of Henry VIII (1509–47) some 72,000 were executed in England. Whether this is an accurate figure or not, it does indicate the extreme use of the penalty.

It cannot be said that the penalty has been insufficiently employed. Furthermore, the death penalty was carried out in a variety of hideous ways well into the 19th century—gibbeting, drawing and quartering, removal of the bowel and heart while the condemned was yet alive, and castration followed by hanging were some of the methods.

But as Beccaria noted in 1764, the human mind adjusts "like fluids to the objects around them" making the protection of society by terror impossible.

Capital punishment tried in enormous volume, in the most terrifying ways and as publicly as possible, failed.

## COMMON SENSE OR NONSENSE

The "common sense" argument for capital punishment is epitomized in the following quotation from a transcript of a hearing before a committee of the California Legislature:

"I don't claim to be a statistician, and I hope I won't be cross-examined on statistics, because, frankly, I don't know anything about them and I don't care to, and I don't think anybody else can draw any valid conclusions from statistics," said this District Attorney of long experience.

"What evidence do we have that the death penalty is a deterrent?" he asked. Then, answering his own question: "First of all, common sense and logic. . . . the universal experience of mankind is that death is the most fearsome thing a human being can face and it, therefore, theoretically, logically, historically and, as a matter of common sense, is the greatest deterrent." (If this were remotely true, no Californian would ever get in his auto in a state where more than 4,000 persons a year are killed on the highways.)

Characteristic of his inverted logic was his further statement that "the fact that men are hung for murder is one great reason why murder is considered so dreadful a crime."

Yes, it is "common sense" to ignore history while citing it, to conclude that because one does not understand statistics himself they prove nothing, to display total lack of man's knowledge of human behavior and to dismiss experience.

One of the problems, parenthetically, is that great weight is given as to the opinion of judges and lawyers who, because of the rigorous demands of their own specialty, have had little, if any, opportunity to study human behavior formally. Few have studied criminology and many have made little study even of criminal law.

One of California's most respected schools of law, for example, requires no study of any of the behavioral sciences for admission or graduation; but it does require completion of a course in accounting. For graduation, only three units out of a minimum of 81 are required in criminal law and procedure.

## Imprisonment is Not Cheaper

There is also the argument of cost. Why support some murderer for the rest of his life when we could execute him and save all that money, the argument goes.

Like so many arguments favoring the death penalty, this does not hold up under factual analysis. The actual costs of execution, the cost of operating the super-maximum security condemned unit, the years spent by some inmates in condemned status, and a pro-rata share of top level prison official's time spent in administering the unit add up to a cost substantially greater than the cost to retain them in prison the rest of their lives.

Furthermore, perhaps half of those condemned could make highly useful prisoners. It is a common experience that many long-term prisoners settle down to responsible jobs in the prison community which could conservatively be valued at a minimum of half the salary of an employee in industrial, maintenance, clerical and other roles. This would more than pay for both their own keep and that of the other half.

Thus, our studies indicate that just on the basis of prison costs alone, it would actually be cheaper to do away with the death penalty. When the other costs of death penalty cases are added —the longer trials, the sanity proceedings, the automatic and other appeals, the time of the Governor and his staff—then there seems no question but that economy is on the side of abolition.

## The Ugly Possibility

Those favoring abolition also have their subsidiary arguments.

One is the ugly possibility of executing an innocent man. I do not know that this has ever happened in California. We had one homicide case in 1959 where the convicted man, John Fry, was later found unquestionably to be innocent. He had not been sentenced to death, but it illustrates the possibility. Furthermore, death sentences have not infrequently been reduced to life by the courts on appeal. In at least two cases in the past 10 years acquittals resulted from appeals.

It is also true that in a number of cases stays of execution have come too late—the execution was underway. I do not contend these persons were innocent, but theoretically, at least, further proceedings might have resulted in a lesser sentence or even freedom.

These last-second stays are one of the harrowing aspects of administering the death penalty for both staff and condemned. It has become, unfortunately, almost a standard operating procedure for attorneys to rush into court, any court, 5 or 10 minutes before the scheduled execution, with a writ or an appeal, many of them without merit, with the hope the court will see no alternative but to stay the execution. Sometimes this results in months of delay. Other times it produces an off-again, on-again situation that inflicts a frightful emotional strain on the prisoner.

## Why the Death Penalty is Not Abolished

To summarize a moment: Capital punishment does not deter and may incite homicide, it is not necessary for the protection of the public or of prison officers, it is randomly invoked and tends to fall most heavily on minorities and those without wealth, there are inordinate delays in its execution, it costs more than other alternatives, it poses the frightening possibility of inflicting an irreversible penalty on an innocent person, and centuries of experience show it does not work.

Why then, if these arguments are so persuasive has the California Legislature repeatedly refused to abolish capital punishment?

First, it should be realized that the Legislature has not unanimously rejected the arguments. There have been close votes. I think there have been a number of reasons for the "no" votes: Frequently some sensational individual case has beclouded the broader issue; complex testimony concerning human motivation has been difficult to understand; the solid stand of peace officers and district attorneys *is* impressive; the press and bar largely favor retention; and many of the Legislators are accurately reflecting the attitude of their districts.

Unfortunately, the public view reflects far more of the cave man than the space man.

And, inevitably, as the witnesses defending capital punishment at the hearings proceed, they fall back on the argument of retribution although they deny this.

But these excerpts are fair samples of their testimony:

> . . . the murderer who has deliberately, wantonly, killed another man, woman or child, brutally, sadistically, in cold blood, with malice aforethought, with premeditation . . . men who have seen the victims and their battered, mutilated bodies . . . men who have talked . . . to the loved ones left behind to grieve.

or

> Having seen so much human blood out on pavements, watched policemen lying there dead, knowing they had wives and children—I don't think there's anything funny about capital punishment.

or

> If you had seen the manner in which Stephan Nash disemboweled an innocent 10-year-old boy and stabbed him repeatedly for his own sexual gratification, I'm sure you—and perhaps some of the abolitionists—would have agreed that the verdict (death) of that jury was proper . . . they want the penalty to fit the crime and the individual.

And that is the most appealing argument for the retention of the death penalty: simple, elemental retribution.

Some crimes are so horrifying, so shocking to the human conscience that there seems to be no answer short of the death penalty. Indeed, some feel that even death as it is administered is too slight a penalty. It would be easy to pursue the argument of retribution and revenge to the point of imposing the ultimate penalty by a process of torture.

I have not been a stranger to violence or violent men. I have walked through the cooling blood of murdered men on more than one occasion. These experiences arouse in me, and I believe, in most normal men, a sense of outrage and an elemental desire to take retributive action.

I've been physically assaulted in the course of my work and I know how it feels to want to return violence with violence. But, I knew, too, that as a warden, my example might have profound effects on several hundred subordinates. It would be easy to turn loose a veritable storm of violence and brutality.

If my personal example might do this, of how much greater influence is the law itself? Unless the penal law itself provides restraint and high example, how can we be sure that the very measures we adopt to prevent violent crime may not, in fact, be contributing to it?

I believe that capital punishment is brutalizing and meets needs in the minds of people which are among their basest instincts—instincts we have brought to modern life from the caves and jungles of antiquity.

## PUNISHMENT

But then, if capital punishment is brutalizing and ineffective, what about the whole concept of punishment?

We tend to be quite irrational about punishment. When punishment does not work, we cry for harsher punishment. This generally is even less effective and so the wheel turns and has turned throughout history.

Take the following statement:

> It is probable that in early times the penalties for the greatest offenses were less severe, and that, as these were disregarded,

> the penalty of death has been by degrees in most cases arrived at, which is itself disregarded in like manner. Either then some means of terror more terrible than this must be discovered, or it must be owned that this restraint is useless; and that as long as poverty gives men the courage of necessity, or plenty fills them with the ambition which belongs to insolence and pride, and the other conditions of life remain each under the thralldom of some fatal and master passion, so long will the impulse never be wanting to drive men into danger. Hope also and cupidity, the one leading and the other following, the one conceiving the attempt, the other suggesting the facility of succeeding, cause the wildest ruin and, although invisible agents, are far stronger than the dangers that are seen. Fortune, too, powerfully helps the delusion, and by the unexpected aid she sometimes lends, tempts men to venture with inferior means. . . . In fine, it is impossible to prevent, and only great simplicity can hope to prevent, human nature doing what it has once set its mind upon, by force of law or by any other deterrent force whatsoever.

Some modern day "egghead" speaking? No, that was Diodotus arguing against massacring the Mitylenians as punishment for revolt at an assembly of the citizens of Athens in 427 B.C. some 2,390 years ago. Incidentally, he won the day by a narrow vote.

I do not know that I would go quite as far as Diodotus. Punishment has some value, but its use must be kept in perspective. The law of diminishing returns sets in early with punishment. Punishment has differing effects on different persons. It works best on the persons who need it least and frequently, not at all on the disordered personalities to whom it is most often directed.

The witness who talked of Nash described him as "an odd individual and abnormal." As a matter of fact, Nash was an excellent example of the type of person who would be undeterred by the death penalty and probably stimulated by it.

## Purpose of the Criminal Law

From the very first it has been realized that the concepts behind the criminal law were imperfect, but instead of seeking new approaches, we have fallen into the trap of taking extremes of a false premise. We must ask ourselves what is the purpose of the criminal law?

A society's prime concern is its own protection. It develops a variety of institutions to achieve this end. Some inspire actions considered beneficial to society, some repress actions believed inimical to society, and some do both.

The criminal law is, of course, one of those institutions designed to inhibit conduct detrimental to society's best interests. The basic method chosen in punishment—punishment as our revenge on the offender, punishment in the hope it will frighten others from committing the offense, and punishment in the hope it will reform the offender.

But the moment punishment was chosen as the basis for the criminal law, it was recognized there were segments of the population for which it would be ineffective and to which it should not apply.

The difficulty of defining who should be *punished* and who not has increased with the growth of our knowledge of human behavior with the result that many of our leading legal scholars and medical experts believe the legal definitions are badly out-of-date. However, proposals for change evoke great controversy.

I believe the basic problem is that having accepted punishment as the basic tool of the criminal law, the exceptions from punishment must be few. In efforts to define who these minor exceptions should be and to make sure the exceptions do in fact remain in the minority, the lawmakers become enmeshed in the concept of criminal responsibility. Basic to that is the complex philosophic, theological, and moral argument over free will.

The debate over free will versus determinism not only poses an insoluable problem, but may also be a problem we do not need to solve if only we will take the undue emphasis off punishment. Punishment will be had in any event. The arrest, the trial, the notoriety, loss of reputation, the costs in money are all punishment. Certainly any loss of liberty, the enforced separation from family and friends through institutionalization, is a high penalty no matter how therapeutic the program. The practical question is, perhaps, how much more punishment do we need and what price we should pay for it.

The price we are paying for placing such faith in excessive punishment is a continuing high rate of crime and a continuing high rate of failure by our correctional apparatus. The price we pay is excessive caseloads for probation officers, dilapidated jails, a lack of diagnostic facilities in the community, lack of treatment resources, inadequate personnel, prison idleness, and overcrowding. I'll not endeavor to explore the submerged needs excessive punishment satisfies in the society that administers it, but I will say that its ineffectiveness and its cost make dependence on it a luxury we can no longer afford.

In selecting punishment as the basis for our criminal law, we not only yielded to a dark, atavistic emotion but, more significantly, we picked an indirect method of accomplishing our objective instead of taking the direct.

What we really want to do is control human behavior. If we can do this through prevention, excellent. If we can do it through reforming the offender, fine. If we cannot reform him, we can at least manage him. Manage him either in an institution or out. Manage him by substituting external controls for the ones he lacks. Manage him by manipulating his environment.

California's civil narcotics addict commitment program provides a good example. This is a nonpunitive program. Persons are committed to the program as addicts, not as criminals, although for most of them the proceedings started with conviction of a crime. A mandatory minimum of 6 months residential treatment is required and a total period of control up to 10 years is provided except as the addict may demonstrate this is unnecessary. He can win his release from control by abstaining from the use of narcotics for a period of 3 consecutive years in the community.

Institutional and outpatient treatment is intensive by the usual correctional standards. A trained counselor—with a master's degree in sociology, psychology, or social work—is assigned to each 60 residents. These are backed up by supervising counselors and by the medical and psychiatric staff.

The patient's status, whether in residence, out-patient or discharged, is determined, with staff advice, by a board consisting of a former law-enforcement official, a sociologist, and a psychiatrist with extensive experience in the treatment of addiction.

The outpatient caseworkers have caseloads of 30. Home environment is checked and families counseled. Halfway houses similar to one already in operation by the Department of Corrections are being readied to control the initial environment in some cases. Frequent nalline testing provides an external control to the former addict as well as a means of detecting any relapse. Relapse means removal from the community. It is not my intent to describe the program in detail here, only to illustrate some of the rehabilitation and control methods employed.

The program has not been in effect long enough to demonstrate whether it is effective in rehabilitating addicts, but I think there is no question that it affords a far more effective social control of the addict than a merry-go-round of punitive jail sentences.

## SUMMARY

I believe that punishment for punishment's sake is and should be repugnant to modern civilized man. Punishment, whether it be the ultimate or the most minor penalty, should be a byproduct of society's systems of control and not its central purpose. In this context capital punishment is both unnecessary and irrational.

### NOTE

1. The California parole board for adult males.

# 10 *To Abolish the Death Penalty*

## RAMSEY CLARK

We live in days of turbulence. Violence is commonplace: murder an hourly occurrence.

In the midst of anxiety and fear, complexity and doubt, perhaps our greatest need is reverence for life—mere life: our lives, the lives of others, all life. Life is an end in itself. A humane and generous concern for every individual, for his safety, his health and his fulfillment, will do more to soothe the savage heart than the fear of state-inflicted death which chiefly serves to remind us how close we remain to the jungle.

"Murder and capital punishment are not opposites that cancel one another, but similars that breed their kind," Shaw advises.

Statement by Attorney General Ramsey Clark before the Subcommittee on Criminal Laws and Procedures of the Senate Judiciary Committee on S. 1760. To abolish the Death Penalty. July 2, 1968.

When the state itself kills, the mandate "thou shalt not kill" loses the force of the absolute.

Surely the abolition of the death penalty is a major milestone in the long road up from barbarism. There was a time when self preservation necessitated its imposition. Later inordinate sacrifices by the innocent would have been required to isolate dangerous persons from the public. Our civilization has no such excuse.

Today more than seventy nations and thirteen of our states have generally abolished the death penalty. While most states and the federal system reserve the ultimate sanction, it has been rarely used in recent years. There were 199 executions in the United States in 1935. There was only one in 1966; two in 1967. Only one person has been executed under any of the 29 federal statutes authorizing death in the past decade. He can be the last.

Our history shows the death penalty has been unjustly imposed, innocents have been killed by the state, effective rehabilitation has been impaired, judicial administration has suffered, crime has not been deterred. Society pays a heavy price for the penalty of death it imposes.

Our emotions may cry vengeance in the wake of a horrible crime. But reason and experience tell us that killing the criminal will not undo the crime, prevent other crimes, or bring justice to the victim, the criminal, or society. Executions cheapen life. We must cherish life.

Extensive studies show that the death penalty does not deter crime. A comprehensive study by Professor Thorsten Sellin concludes, "it has failed as a deterrent." A United Nations report finds from all available information that abolition of the death penalty has no effect on murder rates. With, or without, they are much the same. Why should we expect a deterrent value? Most capital crimes are committed on impulse in a moment of passion without thought of gain or loss. No punishment deters unpremeditated crime. Premeditated crime is committed by people who believe they will not be caught no matter what the penalty. The best deterrent is swift apprehension, prosecution and conviction. The need is to build better law enforcement—to professionalize police, to bring science and technology to criminal justice. The death penalty is considered by some to be incentive for mentally unstable persons to commit capital crimes.

The death penalty's impact on the administration of justice has been malign. Mr. Justice Frankfurter strongly opposed it for this reason. "When life is at hazard in a trial," he said, "it sensationalizes the whole thing almost unwittingly." He regarded as "very bad" the effect on juries, the bar, the public and the judiciary. President Johnson's Crime Commission found that the sensationalism "destroys the fact finding process." In a capital case, realization of the consequences of error permeates the entire proceedings. A jury might acquit because of its fear of the death penalty rather than the weight of evidence. Mr. Justice Jackson observed that appellate courts in capital cases "are tempted to strain the evidence and even, in close cases, the law in order to give a doubtfully condemned man another chance."

Fear of mistake produces excruciating delays in executions. Of the 435 men now on death row, who range in age from 16 to 68, half have been waiting death more than 29 months since being sentenced. Such delays add immeasurably to the inhumanity of capital punishment. Combined with the infrequency of actual imposition, delay eliminates a deterrent effect the penalty might otherwise be thought to have. Moreover, as the American Bar Foundation found in a 1961 study, it weakens public confidence in the law. The President's Crime Commission noted: "The spectacle of men living on death row for years while their lawyers pursue appellate and collateral remedies tarnishes our image of humane and expeditious justice."

The death penalty is irrevocable. For this reason, Lafayette vowed to oppose capital punishment until "the infallibility of human judgment" was demonstrated to him. Innocent persons have been executed. Mental defectives and incompetents have been executed. A judicial determination that a person is legally responsible for his act is not yet precise.

A small and capricious selection of offenders have been put to death. Most persons convicted of the same crimes have been imprisoned. Experienced wardens know many prisoners serving life or less whose crimes were equally, or more atrocious, than those of men on death row.

Death has been visited in a discriminatory fashion. Clarence Darrow observed that, "from the beginning, a procession of the poor, the weak, the unfit, have gone through our jails and prisons to their deaths. They have been the victims." It is the poor, the weak, the ignorant, the hated who are executed. Racial discrimination occurs in the administration of capital punishment. Since we began keeping records in 1930, there have been 2,066 Negroes and 1,751 white persons put to death, although Negroes made up only one-eighth of our population. Of the 455 men executed for rape, 405 were Negroes.

As a people, we are committed to the rule of law. We obey the law, not because we are forced to or fear not to, but because we want to. The law therefore must be just. It must offer hope to all our people. When it suggests vengeance or inhumanity, it loses the respect that is necessary if a free people are to fix it in their hearts.

Modern penology offers effective methods of protecting society. We are at last beginning to realize what can be accomplished through rehabilitation, achieved in confinement and in limited custody or supervision in open society. Community treatment centers, halfway houses and work release programs are evidence of the thrust toward community programs. Their potential is great. They are the future of corrections. It is a sad commentary on how much we care that this wealthy nation spent 95% of all funds for corrections on custody, the remaining 5% on education, therapy and other rehabilitation techniques—while still killing those who offend us the most.

If an offender cannot adapt to community programs, he need not be a burden to society. Through employment in industries within the prison he can be productive. If he is unable or unwilling to work, he can be treated humanely, allowed to live, and society can be fully protected. We do not need to kill from fear.

Murderers, the most likely candidates for execution, generally make well behaved prisoners. There is nothing to indicate that the death penalty is needed to protect prison personnel from murderous assaults by life-termers. One study covered 121 assaults with intent to kill in the prisons of 27 states during the 1940's. Only 10 were committed by prisoners serving life for murder.

The death penalty is inconsistent with the purposes of modern penology. It is a costly substitute for the effort and money needed to develop correctional knowledge and skills.

Our difficult days call for rare courage: the willingness to disenthral ourselves, to think anew and act anew. There is no justification for the death penalty. It cheapens life. Its injustices and inhumanity raise basic questions about our institutions and purpose as a people. Why must we kill? What do we fear? What do we accomplish besides our own embitterment? Why cannot we revere life and in so doing create in the hearts of our people a love for mankind that will finally still violence?

The death penalty should be abolished.

# 11 *Capital Punishment: The Challenge of Crime in a Free Society*

## PRESIDENT'S COMMISSION ON LAW ENFORCEMENT AND ADMINISTRATION OF JUSTICE

As the abolition or the retention of the death penalty is being widely debated in the States, it is appropriate to point out several aspects of its administration that bear on the issue.

The most salient characteristic of capital punishment is that it is infrequently applied. During 1966 only 1 person was executed in the United States; the trend over the last 36 years shows a continual decline in the number of executions, from a high of 200 in 1935 to last year's low of one. Furthermore, all available data indicate that judges, juries, and governors are becoming increasingly reluctant to impose, or authorize the carrying out of a death sentence. Only 67 persons were sentenced to death by the

From *The Challenge of Crime in A Free Society,* A Report by the President's Commission on Law Enforcement and Administration of Justice, United States Government Printing Office, Washington, D.C. February 1967, p. 143.

courts in 1965, a decline of 31 from the previous year, and 62 prisoners were reprieved from their death sentences. In a few States in which the penalty exists on the statute books, there has not been an execution in decades.

The decline in the application of the death penalty parallels a substantial decline in public support for capital punishment. The most recent Gallup Poll, conducted in 1966, revealed that less than half of those interviewed favored retaining the death penalty. In the last 3 years, 5 States either totally abolished capital punishment or severely limited its use, thus bringing to 13 the number of States which have effectively repealed capital punishment. Great Britain experimentally suspended the death penalty for 5 years in 1965. The trend toward abolition has not been uniform, however. Capital punishment was abolished in Delaware in 1958 but restored in 1961. And in 1966 a constitutional amendment abolishing capital punishment was rejected by the voters in Colorado. In 1965 the Canadian Parliament rejected a move to abolish the death sentence.

It is impossible to say with certainty whether capital punishment significantly reduces the incidence of heinous crimes. The most complete study on the subject, based on a comparison of homicide rates in capital and noncapital jurisdictions, concluded that there is no discernible correlation between the availability of the death penalty and the homicide rate. This study also revealed that there was no significant difference between the two kinds of States in the safety of policemen. Another study of 27 States indicated that the availability of the death sentence had no effect on the rate of assaults and murders of prison guards.

Whatever views one may have on the efficacy of the death penalty as a deterrent, it clearly has an undesirable impact on the administration of criminal justice. Capital cases take longer to litigate at the trial level; the selection of a jury often requires several days, and each objection or point of law requires inordinate deliberation because of the irreversible consequences of error. In addition, the inherent sensationalism of a trial for life distorts the factfinding process and increases the danger that public sentiment will be aroused for the defendant, regardless of his guilt of the crime charged. This distortion is not restricted to the trial level. As Mr. Justice Jackson noted: "When the penalty is death . . . [appellate] judges are tempted to strain the evidence and even in close cases, the law, in order to give a doubtfully condemned man another chance."

Furthermore, the imposition of a death sentence is but the first stage of a protracted process of appeals, collateral attacks, and petitions for executive clemency. At the end of 1965 there were 331 prisoners awaiting execution in the United States, and since then this number undoubtedly has increased. These prisoners then were under sentence for an average of 30.8 months, and the average time between imposition and execution was almost 4 years. The spectacle of men living on death row for years while their lawyers pursue appellate and collateral remedies tarnishes our image of humane and expeditious justice. But no one seriously proposes to limit the right of a condemned man to have errors at his trial corrected or to obtain the mercy of the executive.

Finally there is evidence that the imposition of the death sentence and the exercise of dispensing power by the courts and the executive follow discriminatory patterns. The death sentence is disproportionately imposed and carried out on the poor, the Negro, and the members of unpopular groups.

Some members of the Commission favor the abolition of capital punishment, while other members favor its retention. Some would support its abolition if more adequate safeguards against the release of dangerous offenders were devised. All members of the Commission agree that the present situation in the administration of the death penalty in many States is intolerable for the reasons stated above.

## The Commission Recommends:

The question whether capital punishment is an appropriate sanction is a policy decision to be made by each State. Where it is retained, the types of offenses for which it is available should be strictly limited, and the law should be enforced in an evenhanded and nondiscriminatory manner, with procedures for review of death sentences that are fair and expeditious. When a State finds that it cannot administer the penalty in such a manner, or that the death penalty is being imposed but not carried into effect, the penalty should be abandoned.

# 12 *Thou Shalt Not Kill*

## JUDICATURE

Capital punishment is one of a number of controversial issues on which the Supreme Court of the United States may hand down a ruling during its present term. The time has come for this relic of barbarism to be banished from the United States courts.

Nobody should take seriously the contention that the death penalty is necessary for the sake of its deterrent effect on other persons who may be tempted to commit crime. Centuries of history leave any deterrence at all a matter of doubt, and psychology confirms that persons contemplating commission of crime are either not thinking of punishment or are confident that it will not happen to them.

From *Judicature,* The Journal of the American Judicature Society, January 1969, p. 227.

A murderer who is hanged is not going to commit any more murders, true enough, but there are better ways of obtaining that assurance than by committing another homicide.

No alleged justification of capital punishment can excuse or disguise the inconsistency and the horror of the state declaring an act a crime and then making it a part of the state's policy to commit the same act itself. Those who think it does should be willing to concede the right of a prosecuting attorney to use fraudulent evidence in court although the defense may not do so, or the right of Internal Revenue to cheat to increase a taxpayer's tax while forbidding him to cheat to reduce it. If there is to be any difference between moral standards for the individual and for the state, then the state, representing organized society, should apply a higher standard to itself, not a lower one.

Old Testament scripture is cited in defense of capital punishment. The same authority may be used to support bigamy and genocide. We need not condemn Solomon for his thousand wives, or Samuel for utterly destroying the Amalekites and hewing Agag to pieces, but neither do we have to emulate them. Every time human life is intentionally destroyed by fellow man, whether in anger, in war, or in execution of a sentence of a court of justice, mankind is degraded and admits kinship with the beasts.

Any homicide, however committed or under whatever auspices, is an act of violence. There is abundant evidence, psychological and sociological, that violence begets violence. At a time in our national history when crimes of violence have increased to the point of becoming a national emergency, let us tell the world, but mostly let us tell ourselves, that we are too civilized to tolerate the death penalty in our courts any longer.

# 13 *For Whom the Chair Waits*

SARA R. EHRMANN

The recent articles in *Federal Probation* by Professor Thorsten Sellin and James A. McCafferty give excellent statements of the general sociological data which show that capital punishment is much overrated as a deterrent to murder[1] and that the prevailing trend in the United States today is toward gradual abolition.[2] Mr. Ralph G. Murdy deals realistically with some of the practical problems involved in passing legislation.[3] But the "human" side of capital punishment has hardly been discussed at all.

In this article, I shall attempt to give some of this much

The author wishes to express her appreciation to Dr. Hugo A. Bedau, Harvard Law School, for his kind help in revising this article for publication.

From *Federal Probation Quarterly,* March 1962, Administrative Office of the United States Courts, pp. 14–25.

needed information concerning the nature of the offenders who are convicted of capital crimes. Most of the data to be reported are drawn from the files kept by the Massachusetts Council for the Abolition of the Death Penalty and the American League to Abolish Capital Punishment, both active in this field since 1927. Since most of my life has been spent in Massachusetts, I am naturally more familiar with cases there. Yet the facts about capital offenders and the difficulties which face the administration of justice in capital cases seem to be little different there than in the other states which retain the death penalty. So my frequent choice of examples from Massachusetts will not be misleading as to the national picture.

## The Need for Information

The kinds of difficulties one runs into can be illustrated in this way. In 1958, for instance, 48 prisoners were legally executed in the United States, the lowest recorded number of executions. Since I have been engaged for over 30 years in attempting to collect facts about capital punishment, I tried to obtain information concerning these 48 persons who suffered the extreme penalty —who they were and something of their personal histories. The only reliable information available about them was reported in the "Executions" Bulletin prepared by the Federal Bureau of Prisons.[4] The Bulletin showed that the executions had taken place in 15 states, as follows: 6 each in California, Georgia, Ohio, Texas; 4 in New York; 3 each in Florida, Mississippi, Virginia; 2 each in Arizona, Louisiana, North Carolina, West Virginia; 1 each in Alabama, Illinois, Utah. There were no executions in the other 33 states (including the 6 which had abolished capital punishment). The Bulletin also showed that of the 48, none was a woman, 19 were Negroes, 1 was a Filipino. We knew that their ages ran from 20 years to 54. Seventeen were between 20 and 24 when they were executed. Forty were executed for murder, 7 for rape (all Negroes), and 1 prisoner was executed in Texas for robbery with a firearm. Elapsed time between sentence to death and execution ranged from 3 months and under (6 prisoners) to 49 months and over (6 prisoners).

Beyond these data nothing further could be learned. So we are left with no knowledge of the personal histories of these 48 persons who were executed, the events which led to their crimes, or their mental state or social or economic status. Yet such information is vital to the public assessment of capital punishment as it actually exists in our society today. This situation illustrates one of the difficulties confronting those who wish to bring the facts about capital punishment to the American public. There is no central bureau of information to collect or to publish these and other important facts. The result is that the public gets its impressions on the value of the death penalty from the utterances of public officials as quoted in the press, and from news reports on crimes of violence and on prison disturbances.

These opinions are often erroneous. For instance, advocates of capital punishment frequently brand prisoners who are condemned to die as "ruthless killers," "wild beasts," "mad dogs," and the like, as if they were not individual human beings at all but belonged to a special class of dangerous criminals engaged in the practice of murder. Many newspapers constantly encourage this opinion in their reports of sensational crimes.

Actually, among those who incur death sentences, very few could be so-called "professional killers." Such men are either not caught, or, if apprehended and convicted, frequently manage to get lesser sentences through astute criminal representation. As for the wild beasts, they are usually adjudged insane and are committed. Some are executed. The careful study by Professor Reinhardt of Charles Starkweather,[5] the Nebraska slayer of 11 men, women, and children, should provide greater understanding of this "ruthless" killer because it tells the full story that never got into the newspapers.

The need for this usually unavailable information can be seen from the importance that is attached to it in debates over whether to retain or to abolish capital punishment. For instance, a recent article by James V. Bennett, director of the Federal Bureau of Prisons,[6] quotes at length from Herbert Cobin of the Delaware Bar, who in 1958 prepared a concise statement for the Delaware legislature of the main reasons why the death penalty ought to be abolished:

> 1. The evidence clearly shows that execution does not act as a deterrent to capital crimes.
> 2. The serious offenses are committed, except in rare instances, by those suffering from mental disturbances; are impulsive in nature; and are not acts of the "criminal" class. Of those executed in Delaware, 50 percent had had no previous conviction.
> 3. When the death sentence is removed as a possible punishment, more convictions are possible with fewer delays.
> 4. Unequal application of the law takes place because those executed are the poor, the ignorant and the unfortunate without resources.
> 5. Convictions of the innocent do occur and death makes a miscarriage of justice irrevocable. Human judgment cannot be infallible.
> 6. The state sets a bad example when it takes a life. Imitative crimes and murder are stimulated by executions.
> 7. Legally taking a life is useless and demoralizing to the general public. It is also demoralizing to the public officials, who, dedicated to rehabilitating individuals, must callously put a man to death. The effect upon fellow prisoners can be imagined.
> 8. A trial where a life may be at stake is highly sensationalized, adversely affects the administration of justice, and is bad for the community.
> 9. Society is amply protected by a sentence of life imprisonment.

Of these nine arguments, half at least refer implicitly to the "human" facts which are so rarely available about the capital offenders themselves. In the rest of this article I shall illustrate some of these facts, particularly those bearing on the conduct of life-term prisoners, on the opinions of those most closely acquainted with abolition of the death penalty, and on the sentencing and execution of innocent and mentally ill persons.

## CONDUCT OF LIFE-TERM PRISONERS

"They all get out and commit more murders" is far from true. Twenty-five years ago Warden Lewis E. Lawes found that the chief objection to abolishing capital punishment was the fear that the condemned prisoners would be released if they were not executed, but he found no validity in these fears. He said, "As a matter of fact, pardons for 'natural lifers' are very rare. In the 7 years I have been warden of Sing Sing only one commutation has been granted to a lifer, and this man had been in prison over 19 years."[7] More recently, Warden Lawes had this to say about the general problem of incarceration and subsequent release of life-term prisoners:

> Lifers, contrary to popular belief, are model prisoners. I have been in contact with hundreds of them during my years in penal work. They are industrious, as a rule, and give a warden the least trouble. Many of them are first offenders. Some committed murder during a moment of blind fury and have never ceased repenting their misdeeds. I have found, too, that lifers seldom, if ever, violate their parole. Granted freedom, they have become hard-working normal citizens. . . . There is need for remedial legislation concerning lifers.[8]

These views of the late Warden Lawes are definitely supported by the facts.

In order to illustrate the general situation involving the post-conviction conduct of life-term prisoners, it is useful to look at the data available from Massachusetts. Before the Massachusetts Legislature's hearing in 1961, an inquiry was made concerning the conduct of prisoners at Walpole Correctional Institution whose death sentences have been commuted to life. The following reply was received from the office of the superintendent: "None of these men whose death sentences were commuted to life imprisonment have been any greater disciplinary problem than any of the other inmate population."

Professor Zechariah Chafee, Jr., of the Harvard Law School, wrote:

> It is not the occasional pardon to a murderer that endangers society but rather the fact that indictments of first degree so often lead to acquittal. Undoubtedly ten murderers are free on our streets due to lack of apprehension and conviction to every one who is pardoned after careful consideration.[9]

In January 1936, at a parole hearing, Warden Lanagan (of the Charlestown Prison) complained, "They moved the best prisoners, the lifers, to Norfolk. This is one cause of unrest at Charlestown." Five years earlier, Charlestown Prison Warden Hoggsett had said to me, "The life prisoners at Charlestown Prison are the best prisoners, as a class. They are the most trustworthy. Very few of them were ever arrested before for any offense. . . ."

An unpublished study in my files of paroled lifers is especially revealing.[10] Between 1911 and 1940, 75 (out of a total of approximately 242) Massachusetts prisoners serving life sentences were released on parole. All (except 1—convicted as "habitual criminal" in 1933) were serving convictions for murder, and 4 had been commuted from a death sentence. The reasons cited for granting the paroles by the governors and executive councillors were as follows: 13 committed murder under great provocation (including sex), 12 were intoxicated at the time of the crime and under great provocation (2 of these attempted suicide), 11 were either acting in self-defense or were possibly erroneously convicted, 11 pleaded to murder where the indictment should have been for manslaughter, 2 were accessories, 12 were being deported to their native land, 7 were quite old and had records of excellent conduct, 6 were insane, and 1 was released at the request of the sentencing judge. These reasons show that in many cases a serious miscarriage of justice was rectified only many years after conviction. This would have been impossible if these prisoners had been executed.

Governor Joseph B. Ely, who was responsible for most of these releases, stoutly defended his exercise of executive clemency for prisoners serving life sentences and for shorter sentences. Upon assuming office in 1931, Governor Ely found many cases of men who had been in jail 25, 30, and 35 years. In a statement published in the *Boston Herald,* October 26, 1932, Governor Ely said that, "In practically every instance the prisoner had but one bad day in his whole life. . . . His previous record was in almost every case without blemish. . . ." Governor Ely said that in the 65 cases of clemency granted during his first two years in office, "not one has broken the terms and the conditions upon which release was given—not a single solitary instance. . . . I shall exercise the pardon power in order that justice may be finally tempered with mercy."

More recent studies[11] support the same conclusion that Governor Ely reached 30 years ago. Between January 1, 1900 and December 31, 1958 there have been 101 convictions for murder in the first degree in Massachusetts. Of these, 65 were executed (the last execution was in 1947). Of the remainder, 30 were commuted to life, 5 were sentenced to life by jury recommendation, and 1 committed suicide in prison. Of the 35 who received life sentences through commutation or jury recommendation, 25 are now (December 31, 1958) in prison or have died in prison, 10 were released by parole or were pardoned under parole conditions after serving an average of 22 years in prison. Of these 10, none has been convicted of any later crime—2 of the 10 were returned to prison for violation of parole by "indiscreet behavior." One was paroled and deported. None had a new conviction for any crime.

## Conduct of Life Prisoners in Abolition States

The advocates of the death penalty lay great stress on the imaginary viciousness of those who would remain behind bars if executions were discontinued. But authoritative opinions from abolition states do not support their view at all.

In 1955 Donald E. Currier, M.D., surgeon general of the Commonwealth of Massachusetts, sent a questionnaire to prison administrators in states where capital punishment had been abolished, asking the following questions:

1. Do you consider "lifers" a special morale problem in your correctional institution? If so, please describe.
2. Have any guards been murdered by "lifers" in your institution in recent years?
3. Have any guards been murdered by other prisoners?
4. Have persons other than guards been murdered by "lifers" in prison?
5. What has been the conduct of "lifers" who have been released from prison through pardon or otherwise?
6. In your opinion is capital crime more prevalent in your state as a result of the abolition of capital punishment?
7. In your opinion are the police in any greater danger in your state than in neighboring states which have retained capital punishment?

Replies were received from all abolition states (except Michigan). The excerpts cited below show unanimous agreement as to the safety with which lifers may be imprisoned and in many cases eventually released.

Harold V. Langlois, assistant director of correctional services for Rhode Island, replied:

> In my opinion [murder] is no more or less prevalent in the State of Rhode Island as a result of the abolition of capital punishment. I do not believe the presence of capital punishment in law serves as a deterrent to the crime of murder in the first degree. . . . I believe in Rhode Island, the police are not in any greater danger than the police in neighboring states which have retained capital punishment. I believe such a conclusion is absurd. . . . The conduct of "lifers" released from prison through pardon or parole has been generally very good to excellent. . . . So-called "lifers" are no more or no less a morale problem than any other prisoner serving a lengthy sentence. . . . A Rhode Island law provides that anyone serving a life sentence for the crime of murder committing a second murder while incarcerated shall be punished by hanging, upon conviction. This statute has never been invoked.

A. C. Gillette, acting director of corrections for Minnesota, said:

I will be interested in knowing if the State of Massachusetts moves in the direction of abolition of capital punishment, as it is my feeling that it meets no constructive end and is a definite handicap to effective law enforcement. . . . If you will refer to the national statistics on crime, you will note that Minnesota has a comparatively low rate of murder. There is no indication that the abolition of capital punishment resulted in an increased rate of murder. . . . The conduct of most lifers who have been released from prison through pardon or parole has been generally satisfactory and they have adjusted much more satisfactorily than other types of offenders. . . . I would like to point out that our experience has been that "it" would serve no useful purpose in solving our correctional problems in the State of Minnesota.

C. J. Myzaard, warden, North Dakota State Penitentiary, replied:

"Lifers" are not a special morale problem in the institution. No guard or any other persons have been murdered by lifers. . . . Conduct of lifers, upon release—satisfactory, one returned on burglary charge. . . . Capital crime is not more prevalent as a result of the abolition of capital punishment in North Dakota. The police are not in any greater danger in North Dakota than in neighboring states which have retained capital punishment.

Allan L. Robbins, warden, Maine State Prison, reported:

Lifers are not a special morale problem. No guards or other persons have been killed by lifers. Conduct of lifers who have been released—very good. No complaints whatsoever. Capital crime is not more prevalent in Maine as a result of the abolition of capital punishment. The police are not in any greater danger in Maine than in neighboring states which have retained capital punishment. . . . I do feel that capital punishment certainly has its advantages for killings in certain categories. Police guards and others in a law enforcement category should be protected in every way possible. If an inmate kills a guard or prison employee "or perhaps other prisoners" I believe he could well be exterminated.

John C. Burke, warden, Wisconsin State Prison, stated:

I have a notion that if we had capital punishment in this State it would be far more difficult to get a jury to vote a man guilty than it is now. When a jury finds a man guilty under the present set-up, they must be unconsciously aware of the fact that if by any chance of making a mistake in finding the man guilty and if he were committed to the prison for life, any mistakes made could be corrected in years to come. On the other hand, if we had capital punishment, they might be so reluctant in taking a man's life that they might hesitate in cases where there was just a speck of a question, to find the man guilty. . . . My notion is that the police in this State are not in any more danger than are the police in those states that don't have capital punishment. . . . I have a notion that in states where there is capital punishment, a man, seriously involved in a crime, might be more apt to try to kill a policeman so that he would not be available to testify against him. . . . I am certainly of the opinion that we do not have any more murders in Wisconsin than do other states that have capital punishment. I am pretty sure that the Uniform Crime Reports put out by the Federal Government indicate that those states that do not have capital punishment have a lot less murder than the others. . . . Lifers have never created any special morale problem in this institution. I would say that they have had a good effect on the morale of the institution because usually they have been the best behaved and have made the greatest effort to help themselves while in the institution. . . . I have been warden here since 1938 and no guard, other civilian employee or prisoner has been murdered by anyone. . . . The general impression I get from parole officers in the State is that generally speaking the lifers are some of their most successful parolees.

These opinions seem to be supported by such facts as are available. In 1955, before the Canadian Parliamentary Commission investigating the death penalty,[12] Professor Albert Morris, criminologist at Boston University, testified:

> In the United States . . . it is quite clear that . . . assaults with intent to kill . . . occur more frequently in prisons in states which have the death penalty than they do in those which do not. It is of some interest also to note that four out of six states which do (not) have capital punishment for murder were among those having no assaults with intention to kill.

## Ever-Present Danger of Executing the Innocent

Erle Stanley Gardner, famous attorney-author, wrote in Federal Probation in March 1959: "I have seen guilty persons who have been wrongfully acquitted. I have seen innocent persons who have been wrongfully convicted. . . ." Although this statement did not refer to any particular crime, it is true of murder as of other crimes. And somewhere Mr. Gardner is quoted as follows: " . . . when a prisoner protests his innocence to the end the probabilities are that he is, in fact, innocent."

The claim is frequently made that innocent persons are not executed, but no one denies that many innocent persons are sentenced to death. The assumption seems to be made that their innocence is always discovered by the courts or their sentences commuted by the governor. Nevertheless, this does not always happen and it is a fact that innocent people have been put to death. In a brief submitted by the Province of Saskatchewan to the Canadian Parliamentary Commission, 1955, this statement was made:

> Miscarriages of justice have occurred in Canada. . . . Ronald Powers, Paul Cachia, both were imprisoned many months (for robbery) before the error of the court was discovered. If a person had been killed in the course of the robberies, they may have been executed, although they had no connection with the offense (The authors of the brief added). . . . This would not have been the first time that innocent people have been executed.

It is, however, almost impossible to secure evidence of innocence *after* a person is put to death. Even a confession by someone else may not be acceptable as actual proof of innocence.

For instance, in England it is now generally believed, although it cannot be "proved," that Timothy John Evans was innocent when he was hanged in 1950 for murdering his child. His wife had been killed also. Evans first confessed to killing his wife, and then later denied it. He never admitted to killing his child. The chief witness against Evans was his neighbor, John R. Christie. Four years after the hanging of Evans, Christie confessed that he himself had murdered at least seven women whose bodies were found walled up in his home, among them Evans' wife and child. Christie was then hanged also. In reference to the death of Evans, Mr. Chuter Ede, former Home Secretary, said, "I hope no further Home Secretary will feel that although he did his best —in fact, he sent a man who was not guilty as charged to the gallows."[13]

Earlier, in England, Walter G. Rowland had been hanged in 1947, protesting his innocence, although another man, David John Ware, made three confessions of guilt. In 1951, Ware committed another murder, under much the same circumstances as the crime for which Rowland was hanged.[14]

Much less famous than these two English cases are several in this country which deserve closer attention. In Virginia, one Rogers was convicted and sentenced to death in 1943. He served 9 years before being given his freedom. The fight for his freedom was led by a New York newspaper editor. Governor Battle stated he was a "victim of a gross miscarriage of justice."[15]

In Massachussets, Santos Rodriguez, a penniless Puerto Rican bus boy, was freed after 39 months in prison for a murder he never committed. In 1954 he had been found guilty of second degree murder for killing a woman. In January 1957 another prisoner confessed his guilt in the murder. He had withheld his confession until after the death of his mother. Rodriguez was released and given $12,500 compensation.[16]

In Georgia, James Fulton Foster had been twice sentenced to death. A former policeman confessed he was guilty and Foster was freed on July 9, 1958. He had spent 26 months in a prison cell.[17]

In the U.S. Army, Private A. B. Ritchie had been convicted of murder by a court martial and was sentenced to hang July 1, 1945. Another man confessed guilt. Mrs. Ritchie reached President Harry S. Truman at a "home-coming" celebration in Independence, Missouri. Ritchie's death sentence was commuted and he was pardoned in 1947.[18]

In Texas, Anastarcio Vargas was sentenced to die in 1926. His head had been shaved for execution. A man who resembled Vargas confessed. The judge himself made an investigation which cleared Vargas. The death sentence was commuted to life. He was pardoned in 1930 and compensated by the State ($26,500).[19]

In Connecticut, Frank Smith had been in the death house 4 years. Eight times his date of execution was set. He had received reprieves from Governors Chester Bowles and John Lodge. He was finally saved June 7, 1954 when a police official offered new evidence. Smith's sentence was commuted to life by the State Board of Pardons two hours before the execution was to have taken place. The *Hartford Courant* carried a front page full account on June 8, 1954.

In Pennsylvania, David Almeida was granted a second trial after 6 years because the prosecutor had withheld evidence at the first trial. Almeida had had 30 execution dates! In the same State, Paul A. Pfeffer was serving a sentence of 20 years to life when John F. Roche, who had taken at least three other lives and who wanted to die, confessed his guilt.[20]

The New York *Journal-American* of July 24, 1961, reported that Pietro Matera had been released from New York Prisons after serving 30 years for murder. Originally sentenced to death, Governor Franklin Roosevelt commuted his sentence. Then, in the winter of 1960, the real culprit's wife, Adalgisa Lo Cascio, confessed on her deathbed that she had "fingered Matera to save her husand."

Massachusetts has had several dramatic capital cases in which grave doubt of guilt exists. The Sacco-Vanzetti case is the most famous. Most students of the case believe there is grave doubt of guilt. Efforts are still being made to unearth evidence. At the time, another prisoner's confession confirmed by a mass of corroboration might have exonerated the defendants, but the court refused to grant a new trial.[21]

Then there is the strange Cero-Gallo case. Cero Gangi, a young Italian seaman, had been found guilty of murder and sentenced to die in September 1928. His employer, Samuel Gallo, provided his own lawyer to defend Cero. On the night of the execution a witness identified Gallo as the murderer. Cero was reprieved. Gallo was then indicted. Both men were then tried together in an unprecedented capital trial. Cero was acquitted; Gallo was convicted. Finally, after the main witness had left the country and after still another trial, Gallo was also acquitted.[22]

The Berrett-Molway Taxi Cab case in Lynn, Massachusetts, involved two men who almost went to the electric chair for a crime they did not commit. Their case was tried in Superior Court of Salem in February 1934. Eight undisputed eye witnesses had identified the two defendants, Clement Molway and Louis Berrett, Boston taxi drivers, as the two men who murdered an employee of the Paramount Theatre in Lynn. Just before final arguments by counsel, Abraham Faber, who with the Millen brothers had been found guilty of the Needham Bank murders, confessed they had murdered the Paramount Theatre employee and that Berrett and Molway were entirely innocent. Berrett and Molway were exonerated and freed and granted compensation. The foreman of the jury, Hosea E. Bradstreet, said:

> Those witnesses were so positive in their identification that it was only natural that we should be misled. While I sat at the trial I somehow hated the thought of sending those two men to the electric chair; but we were sworn to perform our duty and we would have done it—to the best of our ability. I don't say we would have returned a guilty verdict—but it certainly didn't look like anything else for a time. This trial has taught me one thing. Before it I was a firm believer in capital punishment. I'm not now.[23]

The *Boston Post,* Monday, June 26, 1950, reported the following account of the hanging of an innocent man:

Jack O'Neil was hanged on Friday, January 7, 1898 for the murder of Hattie McCloud, at Buckland, near Shelburne Falls. O'Neil denied the killing and charged that he was the dupe of racial bigotry when this prejudice was still widespread. . . . He said calmly, as he went to his death, "I shall meet death like a man and I hope those who see me hanged will live to see the day when it is proved I am innocent—and it will be, some time."

This was the last *hanging* in Massachusetts. (Electric chair was installed in 1900.) A few months later a dying Shelburne Falls soldier, fighting the Spaniards in Cuba as a member of the old Sixth Massachusetts Militia confessed to the murder and cleared O'Neil.

Eddie Collins, an ace newspaper reporter, was correspondent in Cuba interviewing the soldier and arranged for a signed confession. He flashed the news to Dan W. Gallagher, of East Boston, ace reporter for the Boston Post who covered O'Neal's execution in Greenfield.

## Executing the Mentally Ill

Many persons are judged legally sane who are medically insane or mentally ill. Judge Evelle J. Younger, of the Los Angeles Municipal Court, said:

> A compelling reason which cries out for abolition of the death penalty is the new view furnished by "medical knowledge and experience" that a person may be declared legally sane even where the problem is one of mental illness or "diminished responsibility."[24]

The draftsmen of the Model Penal Code said:

> No problem in the drafting of a penal code presents larger intrinsic difficulty than that of determining when individuals whose conduct would otherwise be criminal ought to be exculpated on the ground that they are suffering from mental disease or defect when they acted as they did.[25]

Three recent Massachusetts cases will illustrate the truth of these two statements. Jack Chester, a mentally ill youth who killed his sweetheart, was sentenced to die in 1957. He had made several suicide attempts, had pleaded with the jury for death in the electric chair. Addressing the jury, he said, "It is my opinion that any decision other than guilty of murder in the first degree with no recommendation for clemency is a miscarriage of justice." When he was sentenced to die he thanked the judge. He refused to request commutation. Before the final execution date, September 15, 1957, further examination made by the Department of Mental Health, revealed that Chester had "suicidal tendencies" and could not "appropriately be executed." Commutation was about to be recommended by the Governor on Monday, December 1, but on November 29th Chester hanged himself with his sweater in his cell.[26]

In 1956, Kenneth Chapin, 18 years old, was sentenced to die for savagely slaying a teenage baby sitter and the boy in her charge. According to technical legal definitions the defendant was sane. Yet his act was the deed of a maniac. A reprieve came a few hours before execution. After further medical testimony the death sentence was commuted to life. Former Governor Christian A. Herter recommended commutation, stating:

> My own views are that society would not be benefited by the execution of Chapin because of his abnormal characteristics and questionable personality condition, as well as his youth and complete lack of prior criminality.

A letter published later by defense counsel and the Commissioner of Mental Health stated that the Chapin jury had not had a complete account of Chapin's mental state.[27]

In 1961, Tucker Harrison, a Negro and former waste collector in Springfield, Massachusetts, killed his estranged wife and was found legally sane and sentenced to die. He is an epileptic and was a chronic alcoholic. After shooting his wife he tried to kill himself. He managed to shoot away a large portion of the frontal lobe of his brain. The Supreme Judicial Court found no error in his trial and denied his appeal for a second trial. The Supreme Court decision states in part:

> We conclude that it was not error to decide that the defendant, notwithstanding his illnesses, weaknesses and injury, was sufficiently a human being to be brought to trial, with ability, although impaired, to cooperate in his own defense.[28]

On September 27, 1961, Harrison's death sentence was commuted to life imprisonment by Governor John Volpe and the Executive Council.

These last three cases are all too typical. A study of the dispositions of capital cases during 17 years in Massachusetts, 1925 to 1941 inclusive, revealed that out of 238 cases, 68 defendants were found insane and 2 committed suicide.

A sampling of cases from across the United States proves that this problem is a national one. In California, the *Sacramento Bee* and the *Oakland Tribune* reported on March 29, 1961 that Erwin Walker, 43, a former Army officer, "cop killer," had had his death sentence commuted to life without the possibility of parole by Governor Brown (after nearly 15 years in the shadow of death in the gas chamber). In 1949 the execution had been called off hardly 1 hour before it was scheduled. Walker has since been judged insane and is now confined in a state mental hospital. Clinton Duffy, recently retired member of the California Adult Authority and former warden at San Quentin who had seen at least 150 men go to their death, said Walker's case was the "worst ever." Walker attempted suicide the morning before he was to die. Dr. David Schmidt, chief psychiatrist at San Quentin, said Walker had lost his personality as a human being and "had almost become a vegetable."

In Lansdale, Pennsylvania, George L. Derbyshire, now legally sane, faced trial February 22, 1960 for strangling his wife 7 years ago. Most of the time since his crime Derbyshire had been in a state hospital for the criminally insane.[29]

In Kentucky, Henry R. Anderson was tried three times before a jury agreed on the death penalty. The cause of disagreement was whether Anderson knew what he was doing when he shot the doctor. The Assistant Attorney General told the Court of

Appeals that Anderson was a schizophrenic paranoid when he was tried, but that he was "not insane."[30]

In Iowa, Governor Herschel Loveless commuted to life imprisonment the death penalty for first degree murder imposed on Lee Hawkins. Hawkins is illiterate and there is reason to believe he may have misunderstood the statements he signed prior to the trial admitting his guilt.[31]

In Illinois, Charles Townsend, a Negro, was sentenced to die for a crime in 1953. The defense claimed that his confession was improperly obtained by police when he was under the influence of a "truth drug." Townsend said he committed the crimes to get money for narcotics. Townsend has undergone the tension of an execution date being set 14 times. The *Illinois Daily News* of April 4, 1961 reported that the defense attorney sought an early clemency hearing because of Townsend's "mental and physical deterioration."

In California, Governor Brown commuted Vernon Atchley's death sentence to life without possibility of parole because of new medical evidence.[32]

In Washington, D. C., James J. Clark twice was scheduled to face the electric chair for first degree murder, but was recently sentenced to the maximum 5 to 15 years for manslaughter. There was testimony at both trials that Clark was drunk, and expert witnesses said he had an "emotionally unstable personality" but that the crime was not a product of his mental condition.[33]

In Pennsylvania, Norman Moon, 25, was sentenced to die for shooting a judge in the courtroom. He attempted suicide as an officer arrested him. The Pittsburgh *Post-Gazette* of October 22, 1954 commented as follows:

> A three-man sanity commission, in accordance with the mental health act, has held that Moon "is not a mental defective" although he is a "proper subject for commitment to a mental hospital." His mental illness is that of dementia praecox of the paranoid type. The finding that Moon, for legal purposes, including electrocution, is sane while for most practical purposes he is off his rocker is bound to open further avenues for delay in pronouncement of the death sentence recommended by the jury last May 25.

William F. (Billy) Rupp was executed in California on November 7, 1958 for slaying a 15-year-old babysitter in 1952. He was a mental defective suffering from a schizoid type of mental disorder, but he "knew right from wrong"—according to some physicians, government witnesses. Another government witness disagreed, "He had a damaged brain, couldn't think for more than a few seconds, a minute and conceivably didn't know right from wrong on August 8th." Defense medical testimony claimed Billy "was legally and medically insane at the time of the crime." It took the jury 22 minutes to decide he was sane. By 1957 at least six of his jurors had signed petitions to spare his life.

Dr. Henry Sjaarjems, head of the electroencephalograph (brain testing) departments of three Los Angeles institutions and of Camarillo State Hospital, had tested Billy's brain when he was 14. The substance of his findings was that Billy's thought processes "diffused and degenerated" at 14, and could not have improved at 18.[34]

Austin H. MacCormick, at that time professor of criminology at the University of California, at Berkeley, had urged clergymen "as a Christian duty" " . . . and on the grounds of justice in its truest sense—to society as well as the individual"—to try to get the death sentence commuted. He wrote the following statement:

> Even if I believed in the death penalty, I would not believe it should be inflicted on this mentally defected young man, penniless and practically friendless whose own sister asks only that his sentence be commuted to life imprisonment without possibility of parole.[35]

## Only the Poor and Friendless Are Executed

It is difficult to find cases where persons of means or social position have been executed. Defendants indicted for capital offenses who are able to employ expert legal counsel throughout their trials are almost certain to avoid death penalties.[36] In the famous Finch-Tregoff case in California, there were three trials, two hung juries, and finally verdicts of guilty but *without* the death penalty. It is estimated that the cost of these trials was over $1 million. But in the trials of some defendants without funds, juries have deliberated for as little as 19 minutes, or an hour more or less, and then returned verdicts of guilty and death.[37]

Almost all of the persons eventually executed were represented by court-appointed counsel. Although many such attorneys are able and devoted, they are often severely hampered by the lack of funds needed for research and investigation on behalf of their clients. Lawrence Cowan, attorney, was appointed by the court to defend Louis Franklin Smith and John Allen, who were sentenced to die in California in March 1951. He was convinced the two men were not guilty. But he had spent $1,200 of his own money, and could not finance the cost of appealing to the United States Supreme Court.[38]

In Delaware all of the persons executed since 1902 were from the unskilled laboring class and poorly educated.[39] Every person executed in Oregon for the last 21 years has been defended by a court-appointed lawyer.[40] Yet many first-degree murderers escape the maximum penalty (see footnote 36).

Likewise, most of the defendants sentenced to die and those executed are from minority racial groups, especially Negroes. In Delaware, of the 25 persons executed, 17 were Negroes. During the years 1930 to 1959,[41] a total of 3,666 prisoners were put to death. Of these, 1,972 were Negroes, 1,653 were white, and 41 were from other groups.[42]

Fifty-seven prisoners were executed in 1960. Of these, 35 were Negroes and 22 were white. Of the 45 persons executed for the crime of murder, 26 were Negroes, 19 were white. The 8 persons executed for rape were all Negroes. On December 31, 1960 there were 210 prisoners awaiting death, of whom 110 were Negroes and 100 white.

In Illinois, Paul Crump, a Negro, now 30, was sentenced to die in 1953 for a holdup slaying in 1952. He had no attorney when he signed a confession. He has had 41 stays of execution. During his imprisonment Crump has written several novels.

Warden Jack Johnson says, "Today Crump is a model prisoner . . . and an example of rehabilitation as expounded by penologists." *The American,* February 23, 1961, quotes Warden Johnson's opinion that "rehabilitation is the most important factor in penology today. Punishment alone is not the answer. . . ."

## YOUTHFUL OFFENDERS SENTENCED AND EXECUTED

Sensational news stories, television, and radio programs are advertising most effectively, murder, guns, knives, and violent crimes daily. Some children, highly suggestible, are incited to murder and other crimes. Those from underprivileged and minority groups are the most likely to be condemned and to be executed.

In 1954, 10 "teenage" offenders were executed. They were all Negroes: 7 in Georgia, 2 in New York, and 1 in Florida. During the previous 4 years 9 "teenagers" were executed. Seven were Negroes, 2 were white.

In New York, Concepcion Correa, a 17-year-old Puerto Rican boy, was sentenced to die at Sing Sing on May 10, 1952—the youngest person ever condemned in New York County.[43] He and two others, age 17 and 22, were convicted of first degree murder for killing an 85-year-old woman while stealing $90. Death in the electric chair is mandatory since the jury did not recommend mercy. Sentencing of the other defendants was postponed when a witness claimed he had testified falsely. Maintaining his innocence, Correa refused to plead guilty and to accept a short reformatory sentence. He had been in this country 1½ years, his family was poor, his father was in Puerto Rico, and his mother was dead. He could not speak or understand English, and he remained entirely mute during the trial.

Paul Giacamazza, who had just turned 17, was put to death in Massachusetts in 1942, the youngest person to be executed in this State.[44] However, in another case involving a 17-year-old boy in Massachusetts, a judge took the initiative and accepted a plea of "guilty to second degree murder" on the ground that "no Massachusetts governor would ever allow so youthful an offender to be electrocuted."[45]

In 1949 in Germany, General Lucius Clay commuted to life the death sentence of a 17-year-old German boy convicted of killing two persons. General Clay said he could not bring himself "to approve the death sentence for a crime, no matter how heinous, committed by a young boy of 17 and a half."

An editorial in the Washington, D. C. *Daily News,* October 7, 1959, expressed the hope that a death sentence of a 14-year-old boy who had been sentenced to die in Canada would be commuted:

> The boy should be punished. We do not dispute that fact. But to take his life at such a tender age would only add tragedy to tragedy. . . . Justice is one thing but legal murder is another. To our way of thinking, hanging a 14-year-old boy is but legalized murder.

From Arkansas, on September 10, 1960, came news that a 14-year-old boy had killed two playmates and quoted him as saying (in explanation), "because I want to die. If I killed one they would just send me to reform schools again but if I killed them both they'll send me to the chair."[46]

In New York, Salvador Agron, a Puerto Rican, 16 years old at the time of the offense, was sentenced to die in December 1960 with a 17-year-old youth, Luis Antonio Hernandez. A new committee has been formed in their defense, of which Anna M. Kross, New York City Commissioner of Correction, is a member. There is no capital punishment in Puerto Rico. An offender under 18 would be looked upon as a juvenile. Mrs. Kross said that the Bar Association of Puerto Rico will enter a "friend-of-the-court" brief in behalf of the youths.[47]

## Reversals and False Confessions

The United States Supreme Court has been reversing a number of convictions because the confessions were obtained under duress. Recently the court ordered the release from prison or the retrial of Emil Rick on the grounds that the confession he made to the killing of a Chicago doctor 25 years ago was obtained by physical abuse.[48] How many defendants today are able to pay the costs involved in taking their cases to the United States Supreme Court?

False confessions by innocent people are not infrequent. *Coronet Magazine,* September 1957, states that 205 innocent people made false confessions of guilt in the Lindberg kidnap-murder 25 years ago. They state also that the Los Angeles police were harassed by countless "phony" confessions in the "Black Dahlia" case. In New Jersey, a 15-year-old schoolboy confessed that he had murdered his mother with his boy scout knife because she had interfered in his relations with a girl. He retracted this confession 4 hours later. The school authorities say that he is a "disturbed personality."[49]

An Associated Press dispatch published at Fort Wayne, Indiana, tells of a signed statement made by a 30-year-old farm hand in which he admitted three Fort Wayne sex killings in 1944 and 1945, two of which had been already confessed by another man who was under sentence of death. The man awaiting execution was Ralph Lobaugh, whose date of execution had been set but who was reprieved by Governor Henry F. Schricker.[50]

## Delays in Criminal Justice

The unnecessarily long duration of most murder trials is due almost solely to the presence of capital punishment.[51] A recent study by the American Bar Foundation, "Delays in the Execution of Death Sentences," by Donald M. McIntyre, shows that the federal court calendars are increasingly clogged with appeals of death sentences.[52] What this study does not describe is the frequent agonies through which the condemned person and his family must pass as he awaits the action of the courts. In Connecticut, for example, it was reported that "At least three men had been so close to the electric chair they could almost touch it. Their heads were shaved, their pants' legs slit, last meals eaten . . . when stays were granted."[53] Prisoners in other states have had similar experiences.

Since 1958, four trials have been unable to settle the fate of Silas Manning, 40-year-old Hopkinsville, Kentucky, Negro, twice condemned to die. A fifth trial has been set for next spring. The fourth jury was hopelessly deadlocked. It was understood that the jurors could not agree on the man's *punishment,* not his *guilt.*[54]

In Illinois a federal judge said "there must come a time when these cases must end," when he granted an eleventh stay of execution to Vincent Ciucci, who has maintained his innocence of triple murders in 1953. The *Daily News,* September 16, 1961, points out that this betters the record of Caryl Chessman, executed in California after eight reprieves and years of delay.

In California, Barbara Graham went to her death after a series of last-minute reprieves. She cried out, "Why do they torture me?" The grim succession of legal maneuvering she endured, as portrayed in the film, *I Want to Live,* "put the Chinese water torture to shame."[55]

While all praise is due our judicial system for the opportunities it affords condemned persons to have their sentences carefully appraised, the fact remains that capital punishment creates an insoluble dilemma—either we increase the risk of executing the innocent by speeding up the judicial process, or we increase the agonies of the condemned by stretching it out—and this can be removed only by abolition.

## Public Opposition to Executions Growing

The willingness with which state and federal courts hear appeals in capital cases suggests a growing reluctance among the judiciary of this country to permit executions to occur. Perhaps the best evidence of discontent with the inhumanities of the death penalty which I have tried to describe in this article is the almost unanimous opposition of religious groups within the last few years.[56] Typical of the views of American clergymen today is the statement of the subcommittee of the Massachusetts Investigating Commission of 1960, consisting of the Reverend Dana McLean Greeley, Rabbi Roland B. Gittelsohn, and the Right Reverend Monsignor Thomas J. Riley:

> The only moral ground on which the State could conceivably possess the right to destroy human life would be if this were indispensable for the protection or preservation of other lives. This places the burden of proof on those who believe that capital punishment exercises a deterrent effect on the potential criminal. Unless they can establish that the death does, in fact, protect other lives at the expense of one, there is no moral justification for the State to "take life."[57]

It should be noted, however, that Monsignor Riley dissented from the majority recommendation that capital punishment should be abolished.

It is not possible to indicate here the number of correctional officials who oppose the death penalty. Austin H. MacCormick, dean of American corrections, had this to say,[58] and it is characteristic of unnumbered wardens, penologists, and criminologists:

> I do not believe in capital punishment because it is an archaic and barbarous practice which has not only failed to accomplish the desired result but has actually had the opposite effect by making convictions on murder charges slower and more difficult. If capital punishment were more effective in curbing murder, I would probably still be opposed to it on the ground that it cheapens the very commodity which it seeks to protect and that capital punishment is itself nothing more than murder of the most cold-blooded and deliberate type.

## Conclusion

The foregoing data concerning persons facing execution are merely samples of the vast amount of information concerning capital punishment which should be analyzed and made available to the public. My own office is bursting with newspaper stories, magazine articles, reports, letters, and important historical information which require collating, cataloguing, and careful study. *The Worcester* (Mass.) *Telegram,* October 8, 1957, described our office, "modest, upstairs in a print shop at 14 Pearl Street, Brookline, Massachusetts, almost literally bursting with facts, pro and con, on capital punishment."

I have dealt with only a few phases of a large and complex problem. But even this brief and incomplete account given here shows the urgent need. Information, collected on a day-to-day basis, on all capital offenders, must be available to the authorities, who often are unprepared through their own ignorance of the facts to recommend commutation or clemency. Finally, information dealing with all phases of capital punishment, and especially with the human side of the injustices and inhumanities it involves, must be made more generally available to offset the hit-or-miss approach of the tabloids to this vital issue.

But even the brief and incomplete account given here shows the urgent need of some official central office of information which will place the study of capital punishment as it affects the administration of justice on a systematic basis. There is no such information center. Seeking reliable data concerning the operation of the death penalty in this country, the British Royal Commission, the Canadian Parliamentary Committee, and the various state investigating commissions, as well as governors, attorneys general, judges, counsel for the condemned, correctional officials, and the press have been forced to turn to this volunteer, unofficial office as the chief source of vitally needed information.

In the Department of Justice and in the law schools of the country, research departments on capital punishment are lacking.

Human lives are taken according to statute, while evidence produced through the century as to the necessity of capital penalties for public protection is not known by some prosecutors and lawmakers.

The news that Delaware has restored the death penalty over the veto of Governor Elbert N. Carvel (and has made whip-lashing mandatory for some felonies) comes as this paper is written. Perhaps this step would not have been taken if the true facts about capital punishment were publicized as widely as some sensational statements about capital punishment, usually incorrect. Progressive legislation has been vetoed in other states by the chief executives who apparently did not know that similar laws had operated successfully elsewhere.

On April 9, 1948 Governor Dewey vetoed a bill to liberalize New York's capital punishment statutes. The proposal would have mandated a judge to hand down a life imprisonment sentence in murder cases when a jury returns a guilty verdict with a recommendation for leniency.[59]

A few days later, Governor Robert F. Bradford vetoed a bill in Massachusetts which would have allowed juries to recommend life imprisonment instead of the death penalty. The veto was called "unfortunate" by Dean Erwin N. Griswold of the Harvard Law School,[60] who said the innovation proposed had long been in force in other states without the "dire consequences" which the Governor feared. Dean Griswold said the Governor might have made a different decision had there been a research division at the Harvard Law School to whom he might have referred such a question for its investigation and conclusions. The Dean said that such a research division "might well play a much larger part in connection with developments in the law of Massachusetts and likewise serve in improving the law in many other states in the country." It could also be used, he explained, "to ascertain facts in fields where lawyers now act on 'hunch and intuition.' . . ."

If a means can be found by our Federal Government to provide the facts desperately needed in the neglected area of capital punishment, the voices of the leaders of America will be heard over the decades in protest against the taking of life for civil crimes. These are voices of presidents, justices of the United States Supreme Court and of other courts, governors, and countless others.

One such voice is that of the late Professor August Vollmer, former chief of police at Berkeley, California, and former president of the International Association of Police Chiefs, who was perhaps this country's most distinguished law-enforcement official. In his address to the California Legislature on April 7, 1931, Chief Vollmer said in part: "As a police executive I am opposed to the death penalty for the very practical reason that it obstructs the effective enforcement of the law and more often protects the criminal than society. . . . If capital punishment has completely broken down; if it is an encouragement to crime rather than a deterrent as I believe this review of the case will demonstrate, then it is certainly time to face the facts and adopt a satisfactory substitute penalty. We can ill afford, with our appalling California murder toll, to sacrifice certainty and swiftness of punishment for spasmodic brutality."

## NOTES

1. Thorsten Sellin, "Capital Punishment," *Federal Probation,* September 1961, pp. 3–11.
2. James A. McCafferty, "Major Trends in the Use of Capital Punishment," *Federal Probation,* September 1961, pp. 15–21.
3. Ralph G. Murdy, "A Moderate View of Capital Punishment," *Federal Probation,* September 1961, pp. 11–15.

   Mr. Murdy's suggestion of "compromise" is not necessarily a solution. The Massachusetts Council for the Abolition of the Death Penalty campaigned 25 years on legislative proposals to modify the mandatory capital punishment law (finally enacted 1951) and for the appointment of an impartial investigating commission (enacted 1957). In 1959 the group led a powerfully backed public campaign for an abolition bill, favorably reported and amended by the Joint Judiciary Committee, the provisions of which are somewhat similar to Mr. Murdy's suggested compromise. In 1961 the abolition group again campaigned for a measure which would provide the penalty of life imprisonment unless the jury recommended death. All of these measures to modify the capital punishment statute or to study it have been opposed (almost solely) by the Massachusetts Chiefs of Police Association who conduct an opposition lobby.
4. *National Prisoner Statistics,* No. 20, *Executions, 1958,* Federal Bureau of Prisons, Washington, D. C., February 1959. For data on executions since 1958, see more recent issues of the annual "Executions" bulletin.
5. James Reinhardt, *The Murderous Trail of Charles Starkweather.* Springfield, Ill.: Charles Thomas Co., 1961.
6. "Delaware Abolishes Capital Punishment," *American Bar Association Journal,* November 1958, pp. 1053–1054.

7. Lewis E. Lawes, *Life and Death in Sing Sing*. New York: Garden City Publishing Co., 1928.
8. Official report to the Governor of Massachusetts, 1946.
9. "Abolish the Death Penalty," Massachusetts Council for the Abolition of the Death Penalty, 1928, p. 8.
10. Data taken from Massachusetts Senate Documents and Department of Correction Reports.
11. Massachusetts Legislature. Special Commission Appointed to Investigate the Advisability of Abolishing Capital Punishment. *Report and Recommendations.* Boston: Wright & Potter Printing Co., 1958, pp. 29–30.
12. Canada. Parliament. Joint Committee the Senate and House of Commons on Capital and Corporal Punishment and Lotteries. *Minutes of Proceedings and Evidence.* Ottawa: Edmund Cloutier, 1954–1955.
13. *Manchester Guardian,* February 17, 1955. For details on the Evans-Christie case, see Ludovic Kennedy, *Ten Rillington Place.* London: Victor Gollancz, Ltd., 1961.
14. Arthur Koestler, *Reflections on Hanging.* New York: The Macmillan Company, 1957.
15. Letter to Mrs. Herbert B. Ehrmann from Morton L. Wallerstein, March 22, 1957. For the court record, see 31 S.2d 576.
16. *Boston Globe,* April 10, 1957.
17. John Bartlow Martin, "The Question of Identity," *Saturday Evening Post,* August 13, 1960.
18. *Boston Traveler,* February 14, 1947.
19. "Brighter Days Loom," San Antonio (A.P.)—date missing.
20. *New York Herald Tribune* series, July 20, 1954, "The Ever-Present Possibility of Executing an Innocent Man."
21. For details see Herbert B. Ehrmann, of defense counsel, *The Untried Case.* New York: Vanguard Press, 1961.
22. Dr. Winfred Overholser, former commissioner, Department of Mental Diseases, Massachusetts, wrote an article on this case, printed in a leaflet by the American League to Abolish Capital Punishment.
23. *Boston Globe,* March 1, 1934.
24. *Christian Science Monitor,* August 13, 1955.
25. American Law Institute, Model Penal Code, Draft No. 4, p. 156, quoted in Commonwealth v. Chester, 150 N.E.2d 914.
26. "Killer Chester, Denied Death Chair He Sought, Ends Life," *Boston American,* November 28, 1958, p. 1.
27. *Boston Herald,* December 16, 1956.
28. *Springfield News,* March 27, 1961.
29. *North Pennsylvania Reporter,* February 22, 1960 (Lansdale, Pa.).
30. *Louisville Times,* June 16, 1961.
31. *Des Moines Register,* December 29, 1960.
32. *San Francisco Examiner,* August 23, 1961.
33. *Washington Daily News,* February 24, 1961.
34. *Sunday News,* New York, January 4, 1959.
35. *Register,* Santa Ana, California, May 18, 1955.
36. See John Bartlow Martin, "Who Killed Susan Hansen?" *Saturday Evening Post,* August 6, 1960; and John Mulligan, "Death, the Poor Man's Penalty," *The American Weekly,* May 15, 1960, p. 9.

37. *New York Journal-American,* February 14, 1960, and *New York Times,* March 28, 1961.
38. *San Francisco Chronicle,* March 5, 1955.
39. Statement of Attorney General J. D. Bove, Jr., April 26, 1960.
40. *Congressional Record,* July 25, 1958, testimony of Richard McGee.
41. *National Prisoner Statistics,* No. 23 and No. 26, *Executions,* 1959 and 1960. Federal Bureau of Prisons, Washington, D.C. See also Franklin Williams, "The Death Penalty and the Negro," *The Crisis,* October 1960; also Elmer Johnson, "Selective Factors in Capital Punishment," *Social Forces,* December 1957.
42. See also *New York Times,* October 8, 1961.
43. *New York Herald Tribune,* Saturday, April 3, 1954.
44. Details are in the files of the Massachusetts Council for the Abolition of the Death Penalty.
45. Herbert B. Ehrmann, "The Death Penalty and the Administration of Justice," Murder and the Penalty of Death, *The Annals,* November 1952, p. 79.
46. American League To Abolish Capital Punishment Bulletin, December 1960. *Capital Punishment,* Staff Research Report No. 46, Ohio Legislative Service Commission, January 1961, p. 49.
47. *New York Times,* March 26 and May 9, 1961.
48. *Civil Liberties,* September 1961, No. 191.
49. *Boston Herald,* January 4, 1958.
50. Fort Wayne, Indiana, August 22 (A.P., The year on the press clipping in our files is not legible).
51. See Commonwealth of Pennsylvania v. James Carter, Robert Lee Williams, George Lee Rivers, 152 A.2d 259 (1959).
52. American Bar Foundation, Research Memorandum Series, No. 24, December 1960.
53. "Should the State Kill," *Sunday Courant,* Hartford, Conn., February 27, 1955.
54. Kentucky *New Era.* Hopkinsville, Ky., November 8, 1961.
55. *New York Times,* November 19, 1958. See also Tabor Rawson, *I Want to Live!* New York: Signet Books, 1958.
56. Some of the rapidly growing number of religious groups on record as opposed to capital punishment are: American Baptist Convention: American Evangelical Lutheran Church: Augustana Evangelical Lutheran Church of North America: California-Nevada Conference of Methodists: Central Conference of American Rabbis: Christian Churches (Disciples of Christ) International Convention: Church of the Bretheran: Church Federation of Greater Chicago: Congregational Conference of Southern California and the Southwest: Connecticut Valley Presbytery: Connecticut Valley Quarterly Meeting of Friends (Quakers): Connecticut Universalist Convention: Greater Red Bank Area Council of Churches: Massachusetts Baptist Convention: Massachusetts Council of Churches: New York State Council of Churches: Northern California and Nevada Council of Churches: Protestant Episcopal Church in the United States of America: Protestant Episcopal Church, Diocese of Massachusetts: Southern California Council of Churches; Southern California-Arizona Conference of the Methodist Church; Union of American Hebrew Congregations: United Presbyterian Church in the United

States of America—General Assembly; United Synagogue of America: Universalist Church of America.

57. See *supra,* footnote 10.
58. Part of a statement prepared for presentation to the Massachusetts Legislative Hearing on February 11, 1937 (in a letter to the author of February 5, 1937).
59. *New York Times* (U.P.), April 9, 1948.
60. *Boston Evening Globe,* May 14, 1945.

# 14 *Let's Abolish Capital Punishment*

VICTOR H. EVJEN

In 1935 there were 199 executions in the United States, 23 in one state. In 1965, seven were escorted to their death. Since 1968 there have been no executions.

During the 1930's, the average number of executions was 167 a year compared with 72 a year in the 1950's and 27 in the first seven years of the 1960's.

This downward trend in executions is not explained by a drop in convictions for capital crimes (crimes for which the death penalty may be assessed). Rather, it indicates a general decline in the use of the death penalty by imposing, instead, life imprisonment or a definite term of years, or by commutation of a death sentence to a life term. About a fourth of those sentenced to death are actually executed. In other words, the death penalty seems to be on its way out.

Reprinted by permission by *Lutheran Women,* March 1968, Official Magazine of Lutheran Church Women. Revisions made with approval of the author.

Today, 13 states have abolished capital punishment (Alaska, Hawaii, Iowa, Maine, Michigan, Minnesota, New York, North Dakota, Oregon, Rhode Island, Vermont, West Virginia, Wisconsin). Of those states which have the death penalty, six have not used it in the last 10 years.

Although there are in this country 31 offenses for which the death penalty can be imposed, only seven of the offenses, since 1930, have resulted in executions.

The death penalty has been abolished in at least 35 countries. With the exception of France, Greece and Spain, all Western European countries have done away with the death penalty or have not used it in this century. Most Latin American countries have abolished capital punishment.

In 1963 the National Council on Crime and Delinquency voiced its opposition to the death penalty. Two years later the Department of Justice announced its position favoring abolition of capital punishment. In 1967, the American Correctional Association (an organization of prison administrators and professional personnel) recorded its oppostion to capital punishment, recommending that the death sentence be eliminated from the Federal Criminal Code and commending the efforts of the abolition committees in the several states.

Myrl E. Alexander, retired Director of the Federal Bureau of prisons says: "After 35 years in prison administration, I am fully convinced that execution of criminals is a vestige of those ancient and barbaric punishments which are grossly inconsistent with the growing knowledge of the human behavioral sciences."

Warden Clinton T. Duffy of San Quentin Prison (retired) calls capital punishment a "tragic failure."

## Why Oppose the Death Penalty?

1. *It is not a deterrent.* Those who favor capital punishment say it deters others from committing similar crimes. No valid research, however, proves that the abolition of capital punishment leads to an increase in homicides nor that retaining it actually

deters crime. The proclaimed deterrent effects of capital punishment are not supported by contemporary studies and systematic research.

There is no pronounced difference in the rate of murders and other crimes of violence between states which impose the death penalty and those bordering on them which do not. Many states and countries without capital punishment have an incidence of homicide below that of comparable states and countries touching their borders which have the death penalty. In the United States, only 10 persons per 1,000 who have committed first-degree murder pay the extreme penalty. This would hardly cause the penalty to serve as a deterrent.

Following its 4 year study of capital punishment, the British Royal Commission concluded in 1953 that "there is no clear evidence in any of the figures we have examined that the abolition of capital punishment has led to an increase in the homicide rate or that its re-introduction has led to a fall."

Professor Thorsten Sellin, one of the world's foremost criminologists, concludes that: "The death penalty has failed as a deterrent."

2. *Most persons commit murder without premeditation.* A high proportion of murders are committed impulsively, without forethought, and often in an irrational state of mind. The killings occur during quarrels when persons are so bewildered they cannot control what they say and do. A large proportion of homicides are committed by family members and friends and lovers of the victim. Most persons involved in homicides do not deliberate on the death of the victim or contemplate the consequences, and many do not intend the victim's death.

Warden Duffy states: "I have asked hundreds, yes thousands, of prisoners who have committed homicides whether or not they thought of the death penalty before the commission of the act. . . . I have to date not had one person say that he has ever thought of the death penalty prior to the commission of his crime."

3. *Many charged with crimes of violence suffer from undetected mental illness.* Crimes of violence frequently are committed by persons suffering from a serious mental disorder; they are

irresistably driven to their crimes. Their mental illness is not detected until violent acts occur. Some have been convicted and sentenced to death when they should have been declared incompetent to stand trial.

4. *There are gross inequities in application of the death penalty.* The death penalty imposes a discrimination against those in society who are most generally the victims of bigotry and prejudice. It does not mete out even-handed justice. Its application is uneven, unpredictable, and frequently unjust. Those who receive the death penalty are usually the disadvantaged members of society—the friendless, the uneducated, the mentally unstable and retarded, the poor and minority groups. More than half (53.5%) of those executed in the United States since 1930 were Negroes. Since Negroes make up far less than half of those charged with crimes punishable by death, this is hardly equality before the law.

"In the 12 years of my wardenship," said Warden Lewis E. Lawes of Sing Sing, "I have escorted 150 men and one woman to the death chamber and the electric chair. In age they ranged from 17 to 63. They came from all kinds of homes and environment. In one respect they were all alike. All were poor, and most of them friendless."

The poor cannot afford competent legal counsel or appeal their convictions. The affluent, the influential and those adequately represented in court are seldom executed. Those in organized crime seldom are brought to justice. When they are, they escape the death penalty.

Since 1930, 160 American servicemen have been executed, including 148 during the period 1942–1950. All were Army and Air Force personnel. The last execution in the Navy was in 1849, more than 125 years ago. Thus, the application of the death penalty may even be determined by the geographical area in which one lives or the branch of military service in which he serves. There are in the death row of some states persons awaiting execution for crimes identical in degree and extenuating circumstances to those for which prisoners in other states are serving life terms or less, with a possibility of parole.

5. *The innocent have been put to death.* Human judgment is not infallible. The death penalty poses the terrifying possibility of putting to death an innocent man. Criminologists and penologists refer to a number of instances where innocent persons have been executed. Convictions are obtained, at times, by forced confessions or other violations of due process of law. Execution is the only penalty which makes final and irrevocable any miscarriage of justice.

6. *Capital punishment obstructs justice.* Capital punishment is an obstruction to the swift and certain administration of criminal justice. Trials in capital crimes are lengthy, involved and costly. Trial and appellate courts are confronted with numerous post-trial applications, petitions and appeals which are time-consuming and expensive.

There also are delays from time of conviction to execution. In the last dozen years in California no one has been executed less than 8 months after being received in death row. One man spent more than 11 years in death row and finally was put to death. In one state, two men have been in the death house for nearly 14 years awaiting execution. Society is thus carrying out a deliberate infliction of the death penalty years after the occurrence of the offense.

7. *There is no basis to the savings-in-cost argument.* Execution, it is argued, would result in sizeable savings. To the contrary, life-term prisoners in many jurisdictions more than pay for the cost of their keep through productive labor in prison industries and other occupational assignments. Even if this were not so, society should be no more alarmed by the costs for the custody and care of life-term prisoners than that for the hopelessly insane who are in institutions for the remainder of their lives.

Cost is hardly grounds for taking a human life.

8. *Life termers rarely commit another homicide.* Those who favor the retention of the death penalty express concern about the recurrence of another homicide either in prison or following release to the outside community. This contention is not supported by the facts. Most of those convicted of homicide eventually return to society as law-abiding citizens and rarely commit

another homicide. Career prison wardens declare that society is amply protected by a sentence to life imprisonment.

"Prisoners serving life sentences for murder," Professor Sellin asserts, "do not constitute a special threat to safety of other prisoners or to the prison staff. They are, as a rule, among the best-behaved prisoners and if paroled, they are the least likely to violate parole by commission of a new crime. In a few cases where such a violation occurs, the crime usually is not a very serious one. A repeated homicide is almost unheard of."

A recent 10-year study of 342 persons committed in California for first-degree murder and paroled after serving a prison term averaging 12 years showed that 90 percent completed their parole without violation. Of those who did violate parole, only 2.9 percent committed acts of such seriousness that they had to be returned to prison.

9. *The death penalty is a crude and primitive form of retributive justice.* The death penalty is more an act of hate and vengeance than it is justice. Retribution cannot be considered a legitimate goal of criminal law. Yet simple retribution is one of the most appealing arguments for the retention of the death penalty.

A responsible society wants protection, not revenge. It does not need to avenge itself, nor should it want to do so. Punishment for punishment's sake is not justice and is repugnant to modern civilized man. The death penalty is not only unnecessary and futile, but is also barbaric and brutal. It has no place in a civilized society that does not require the taking of a human life for its safety and welfare. As one of the country's leading prison administrators has said: "Capital punishment is brutal, sordid, and savage—unworthy of a civilized people."

The progress of any civilization is measured by the reverence it accords to human life. "The mood and temper of the public with regard to the treatment of crime and criminals," the late Winston Churchill has said, "is one of the most unfailing tests of the civilization of a country."

Historically, the death penalty was imposed to seek vengeance. Vengeance and retribution were deemed sufficient reasons for taking a life. Life tends to be short and cheap in primitive societies. But a civilized country has greater respect for the worth, dignity and life of a human being and a deeper appreciation of human behavior and its motivations.

"Capital punishment is an archaic and ineffectual practice that is as evil as the crimes it is designed to punish," declares Austin H. MacCormick, America's leading penologist. "In the name of humanity and justice, civilized nations should take the forthright step of abolishing it."

# V Attack on the Death Penalty

One of the major attacks on the death penalty in this century has been the fight for repeal in Great Britain. The advance toward British abolition was first highlighted by the repeal in 1908 of the death sentence for children under the age of 16. It culminated in the passage of the Murder (Abolition of Death Penalty) Act of 1965, which provided for the abolition of capital punishment in Great Britain for a trial period of five years with continuance subject to the later affirmative vote by both Houses of Parliament.

The Murder Act, which would have expired on July 31, 1970, was brought before the House of Commons late in 1969. A majority favored the permanent abolition of the death penalty in Great Britain. The crucial vote was taken on December 16, 1969, and on the following day the House of Lords approved permanent abolition.

The reasons given for this decision were:

1. Capital punishment was not a deterrent. There was no

clear evidence based on statistics that homicide rose during the abolition period, 1965–69. Nor could it be proved that the death penalty was necessary to protect law enforcement officials.

2. Repeal of the death penalty had no relationship to the incidence of violent crime.

3. Great Britain has fewer murders than other civilized countries.

4. Innocent persons might be executed if capital punishment were reinstated.

5. The moral standard of the community is lowered by the use of the death penalty.

Some members of Parliament opposed permanent abolition but wanted to extend the experimental period. They offered three reasons:

1. There were instances where the murderer might commit another murder to prevent detection or arrest and, if caught, the convicted murderer would receive only a sentence to prison.

2. Lives would be saved and violence discouraged if capital punishment were restored.

3. Most of the British citizens were opposed to permanent repeal of the death sentence.[1]

The measured movement toward complete abolition of the death penalty in Great Britain has no real counterpart in the United States, since the matter is primarily a state concern. But there are four distinctive trends in the capital punishment issue.[2]

First, there has been no marked decline in the number of persons sentenced to death in the United States. The number has averaged about 100 a year since 1960. But with the drop-off of executions an incongruous situation has developed. There are now more than 620 persons under sentence of death . . . and the number continues to rise. One of the 620 was sentenced to death over 15 years ago. (The last execution in the United States as of this writing was on June 2, 1967 in the State of Colorado gas chamber. The execution of Luis Jose Monge for murder occurred three years, five months and 16 days after sentence had been pronounced.)

Second, there is a growing opposition by officials, both Federal and State, to the use of the death penalty. The opposition has included many governors, state's attorneys general, correctional administrators, wardens, and several religious denominations and professional organizations.

Third, there has been an increase in the number of appeals on behalf of condemned persons by court-appointed lawyers and large citizens groups, such as the American Civil Liberties Union and the NAACP Legal Defense and Educational Fund, Inc.

Many felt that the *Maxwell* v. *Bishop* case,[3] argued before the United States Supreme Court on April 27, 1970, would bring together all of the issues on capital punishment. Instead, the case of William L. Maxwell, a Hot Springs, Arkansas Negro, was sent back to the state trial court.

Maxwell was found guilty and sentenced to death in 1962 for raping a white woman. Maxwell sought a writ of habeas corpus in the United States District Court for the Eastern District of Arkansas. Among his claims was that both his conviction and punishment were unconstitutional. The jury in the Maxwell case, it was argued,[4] had determined the issue of guilt or innocence and also the punishment—life or death—in a single proceeding. Further, the Arkansas jury trial prevented Maxwell from furnishing information that could be used to weigh the possible mitigation of the punishment. In addition, the jury had no legal standards or guidelines by which to determine the sentence.

The unsigned per curiam decision the Supreme Court handed down on June 2, 1970, a few days before the close of the October Term 1969, put "a judicial freeze" or postponement of executions in the United States for as much as a year. The 6 to 1 *Maxwell* decision avoided the issues noted above, but instead noted that several persons had been barred from sitting on the jury because they had conscientious scruples against capital punishment. In the *Witherspoon* v. *Illinois* 1968 Supreme Court case,[5] it had been held that death sentences imposed by juries from which persons who object to capital punishment have been barred are unconstitutional; therefore, on the narrower ground, *Maxwell* was sent back to the state court for disposition.

The basic issues raised by the *Maxwell* case were argued on

November 9, 1970 in the appeals of two convicted murderers: Dennis C. McGautha of Los Angeles, who was convicted and sentenced to death for killing a shopkeeper in 1967, and a Toledo, Ohio man, James E. Crampton, convicted of shooting his wife to death in 1967.

On May 3, 1971, the United States Supreme Court upheld, 6 to 3, the unconstitutionality of capital punishment procedures in the States. The Supreme Court held:

> 1. In light of history, experience, and the limitations of human knowledge in establishing definitive standards, it is impossible to say that leaving to the untrammeled discretion of the jury the power to pronounce life or death in capital cases violates any provision of the Constitution.
>
> 2. The Constitution does not prohibit the States from considering the compassionate purposes of jury sentencing in capital cases are better served by having the issues of guilt and punishment resolved in a single trial than by focusing the jury's attention solely on punishment after guilt has been determined.[6]

News accounts following this decision noted a reluctance of State authorities to act until the Supreme Court rules on what they see as the central issue, the constitutionality of capital punishment itself. The ultimate question tends to be joined with the interpertation of the Eighth Amendment's prohibition against "cruel and unusual punishments."

A fourth trend in capital punishment discussions centers on our understanding of persons who commit homicides, together with an analysis of victims of such homicides. Intensive studies have been published by Marvin Wolfgang and Negley K. Teeters. Various monographs and articles by Thorsten Sellin are regarded as landmarks in capital punishment literature.[7]

These contributions, together with the annual summary of murders and non-negligent manslaughters appearing in the FBI's *Uniform Crime Reports,* and the annual statistics on capital punishment trends published by the United States Department of Justice, provide basic statistical information.

Current trends may indicate that we have at last come face to face with the realization that the death penalty, when not carried out, creates difficult conditions. We have delayed direct confrontation with capital punishment by executing fewer and fewer persons, while at the same time continuing to mete out the sentence.

We have arrived at a point in the history of the capital punishment controversy where we must either continue to use it on a selective basis (by selectivity, I mean for those individuals whose act's were so repulsive, so unbelievable, or so callous, that any thought of their possible release in the community has to be discounted) or call an outright moratorium, if not a repeal, to the use of the death penalty.

The two articles that follow show that the attack on the death penalty is far from over and that the issue is increasingly becoming a matter for the courts. Jack Greenberg and Jack Himmelstein, respectively Director-Counsel and Assistant Counsel for the NAACP Legal Defense and Educational Fund, Inc., served as attorneys for petitioner Maxwell in the case cited above. Sol Rubin, Counsel for the National Council on Crime and Delinquency, helped prepare the *amici curiae* brief for the NCCD on behalf of Maxwell.

These attorneys represent a growing list of members of the bar who seek a resolution of the capital punishment issue. But they cannot do it alone, according to Rubin, who warns that "abolitionists must continue to work for legislative abolition and, at the same time, utilize every possible legal device to prevent executions."

## NOTES

1. *Government and Administration, Survey Volumes,* Vol. 2 (Nov. 23, 1965) and Vol. 4 (Jan. 16, 1970), Her Majesty's Stationery Office, London.
2. Adapted from "Trends in Capital Punishment," by the author, which appeared in *Proceedings of the American Correctional Association, 1967.* Used with permission.
3. Maxwell v. Bishop, No. 13, October Term, 1969, Supreme Court Reports, June 1, 1970. Also see Maxwell v. Bishop, 257 F. Supp 710 (E.D. Ark. 1966); Maxwell v. Bishop, 398 F. 2d. 138 (8th. Cir. 1968).

4. Special appreciation is owed to Anthony G. Amsterdam who argued Maxwell's case before the U.S. Supreme Court. Mr. Amsterdam provided the author with a copy of the briefs submitted on Maxwell v. Bishop.
5. 391 U.S. 510 (1968).
6. For writings by these authors see Bibliography.
6. McGautha v. California, No. 203 and Crampton v. Ohio, No. 204, October Term, 1970, Supreme Court Reports, May 3, 1971. Syllabus.
7. For writings by these authors see Bibliography.

# 15 *Varieties of Attack on the Death Penalty*

JACK GREENBERG
JACK HIMMELSTEIN

The latest execution in the United States occurred on June 2, 1967. Since then, death sentences have been stayed as courts across the country consider a legal challenge to the constitutionality of the death penalty. This paper describes the distorting effect that capital punishment has had on the legal system and the discriminations in the way it has been administered—for example, in rape cases, it is applied almost exclusively to Negroes convicted of raping white women. The legal attack focuses on those procedural vices that reflect the arbitrariness and irrationality inherent in capital punishment. Courts are being called

Based on an address delivered by Jack Greenberg at the NAACP Legal Defense Fund National Conference on Capital Punishment, New York City, May 3, 1968.

From *Crime and Delinquency,* Vol. 15, No. 1, January 1969, National Council on Crime and Delinquency, pp. 112–120.

on to subject the death penalty to a reasoned examination and to test its validity against the commands of the Constitution, while the number of persons on the nation's death rows continues to grow past the 500 mark. This confrontation on the issue of capital punishment is part of the more general conflict taking place over how society may best cope with its problems without resort to violence.

Any organization that concerns itself with America's racial problems and their relation to the law soon confronts the grim fact of capital punishment. This has been the continuous experience of the Legal Defense Fund. Early cases in criminal law involving Negroes, such as the Scottsboro cases,[1] posed issues of right to counsel,[2] jury discrimination,[3] and forced confession,[4] among others. But lurking in the background of each case was the awareness that what was at stake was not merely justice, not just the legal standards that evolve out of new situations, not simply the number of individuals affected, but the irreversible fact of death.

## The Groveland Case

From 1950 to 1954 a great part of the time of the Legal Defense Fund staff was spent on the investigation, trial, appeals, and post-conviction proceedings[5] in the Groveland, Fla., case,[6] in which four Negroes were charged with the rape of a white woman. One of the four was killed, while asleep in a wood, by a sheriff's posse. Another received life imprisonment, most likely because he was only sixteen at the time of the crime or because the jury had misgivings about his guilt. The two other defendants were sentenced to death. After reversal of their convictions by the Supreme Court of the United States, one was killed by a sheriff on the way to the courthouse for the retrial, and the other was resentenced to death. After several more years of litigation, the prosecutor, asserting that he had serious doubts about the man's guilt, joined in the defendant's plea to the governor for commutation. The death penalty was commuted and, after approximately eighteen years of imprisonment, that defendant is now on parole. What is most significant, however, is that the sixteen-year-old refused to appeal his life sentence (which, in the case of his codefendants, was reversed by the U.S. Supreme Court[7]) for fear that on the second trial he might be sentenced to death. The death penalty had worked its injustice.

## Other Rape Cases

Another case we dealt with at that time was that of a Negro convicted of rape who was electrocuted even though his lawyer confessed publicly that at the start of the trial, he was not in possession of what was perhaps the most important fact in the case—that the victim was white.[8] In the early fifties, the courts were not as receptive as they are today to a variety of arguments, and it was often impossible to obtain a stay and a hearing before a defendant was executed. In the case of the Martinsville (Va.) Seven, seven Negroes, convicted of raping a white woman, were electrocuted.[9]

In such cases, the issue of the validity of capital punishment imposed discriminatorily was occasionally raised. The reply of the courts was, "How could one prove that race was a factor?" Each case, they said, is different; each jury is different. Some defendants have criminal records; some are more vicious; some have good lawyers and others have bad ones; some victims were innocent, and some may have invited the assault.[10] The courts were not impressed by the fact that, of 455 men executed since 1930 for rape, 405 (90 per cent) were Negroes.[11] In these and many other cases, therefore, we relied principally on other constitutional defenses, often with success. The issues of discrimination in selection of the jury, the right to counsel, illegal search and seizure, and coerced confession were taken to the Supreme Court many times. And many defendants had their convictions reversed.[12]

## Discrimination in Application of the Death Penalty

As the courts became more sensitive to the issue of racial discrimination as well as discrimination against the poor, we began to think of attacking capital punishment as such, and particularly racial discrimination in imposition of the capital penalty.

The race statistics for all capital crimes are somewhat less extreme than for rape cases, but they are significant. Of the nearly 4,000 persons executed since 1930, 55 percent were Negroes.[13] And, if we relate executions to poverty, we approach 100 per cent.

These facts were brought home vividly to us when, in connection with pending litigation in Florida, discussed below, we were authorized to interview the inmates of death row. Of the thirty-four condemned men interviewed whose state appeal had been denied at that time, all were indigent. Half were without counsel; most of the others were represented by volunteer counsel. The mean intelligence level was considerably below normal. The mean number of years of schooling (not necessarily grades attained) was eight. Most were unskilled farm or industrial laborers.[14]

These facts form the basis of one of our legal claims. We argue that the state is required to appoint counsel to represent these men even after their appeal to the state courts. Too often an illiterate man about to be executed attempts to write to appropriate courts and lawyers across the country to secure a stay of execution.

The case which triggered our campaign was *Hamilton v. Alabama.*[15] Hamilton, a Negro, entered the apartment of an elderly white woman near Birmingham, Ala., where he was arrested. Though there is considerable doubt about what actually happened, no claim was made at the trial that he had touched her. Nevertheless, he was sentenced to death for burglary with intent to commit rape. We took the case to the United States Supreme Court, maintaining that he had been denied counsel at his arraignment, and on this ground his conviction was reversed.[16] Hamilton's new trial, we felt, would be an appropriate case in which to raise two issues—(1) racial discrimination in the imposition of the death penalty and (2) cruel and unusual punishment, because capital punishment was grossly unfair when imposed in a case where no life had been taken and no bodily harm had been inflicted. At his second trial, however, Hamilton received a life term.

## PROVING RACIAL DISCRIMINATION

Soon thereafter, Justice Goldberg wrote a brief dissent from the denial of certiorari in *Rudolph v. Alabama,*[17] where a Negro had been sentenced to death for the rape of a white woman, questioning whether capital punishment where no life had been taken or endangered was not cruel and unusual punishment.[18]

To develop the claims of cruel and unusual punishment and the denial of equal protection, we began to search for statistics that might isolate the racial factor. Professors Anthony Amsterdam[19] and Marvin Wolfgang,[20] to whom we presented the problem, designed a study which inquired into every possible ground that a jury might take into account in deciding whether to impose life imprisonment or death for the crime of rape. These grounds included such things as the viciousness of the crime, the prior relationship between the defendant and the victim, the time of the attack, the place of the attack, the number of attackers, whether a simultaneous crime occurred, whether the defendant testified at the trial, and every other conceivable factor that might influence sentencing. A team of thirty-five law students searched the records of 2,500 cases and the results were subjected to rigorous statistical analysis.[21] The likelihood that any factor other than race accounted for the disproportionality in sentencing proved insignificant. Race alone stood out as the constant factor in distinguishing cases in which the death penalty was imposed from those in which some lesser penalty was chosen. If the defendant was Negro and the victim was white, the chance of a death penalty proved high; in all other rape cases, the chance of a death penalty was remote. The results of this study have been introduced in several cases,[22] and we are taking a petition this term to the Supreme Court of the United States.[23]

Once having raised these claims, however, it was not adequate to assert them on behalf of some defendants and ignore other defendants in the hope that they would receive the benefit of a new rule announced at a later date. And one cannot ignore the prejudices, not merely racial, that bring a jury to select this man and not another for death—indeed, to select any man for death for any crime. The attack quickly became one against capital punishment as such.

## The Legal Issues

It was not difficult to find solid legal arguments for an all-out attack on the death penalty. An institution as irrational and archaic as capital punishment is bound to be surrounded by procedure whose irrationality is readily assailable and whose only claim to validity is the length of time it has been used.

First, selecting a jury for a capital trial has often lasted several days. The prime reason was that all persons who had religious or moral scruples against the death penalty were systematically excluded from jury service. A capital jury was, therefore, made up entirely of that part of the population which approves of the death penalty as a sanction. This procedure was challenged as a denial of the defendant's right to a jury that is representative of a cross-section of the community and as a denial of a fair trial. The demand for a true cross-section is no theoretical abstraction. It insures the accused an equal opportunity to benefit from all the attitudes people may have so as to prevent any one group from dominating the delicate jury process.

On June 3, 1968, the Supreme Court of the United States reversed the death sentence of William C. Witherspoon, who, on his own and with the assistance of court-appointed attorneys, had been staying alive and challenging his death sentence in Illinois and federal courts for nine years. (Again, the need for all states to provide counsel for condemned men becomes obvious.) In *Witherspoon v. Illinois,*[24] the Court held that a sentence of death cannot be carried out if the jury which imposed or recommended it excluded persons who were generally opposed to the death penalty. That decision, however, left unresolved the question of whether a state could validly exclude a prospective juror who made clear (1) that his attitude was so fixed that he would automatically vote against the death penalty in every conceivable case or (2) that he would not be able to make an impartial decision on the defendant's guilt. Thus, states have continued to seek and secure death sentences by procedures designed to fall outside the condemnation of *Witherspoon.* And although *Witherspoon* would seem to invalidate the death sentences of many of the five hundred men on the nation's death rows, some state courts have given the Supreme Court's opinion a hostile reception.[25] By reading *Witherspoon* narrowly, limiting the interpretation to the particular facts of the Illinois case, these courts have affirmed death sentences imposed by death-qualified juries in other states. Thus, we are still litigating the issue of whether any form of moral or religious opposition to the death penalty can constitutionally disqualify a person from sitting on a jury which determines whether a man is fit to live, and particularly whether the exclusion of this segment of the population makes for a jury more prone to convict.

Second, in capital trials the jury decides punishment—whether or not death will be the penalty—in addition to its regular task of determining the issue of guilt. In making this decision between life and death, the jurors are left completely without guidance. They receive instruction that they must follow on every aspect of the case except the question of the death penalty; there they are told simply to do as they see fit. Such total discretion compels the kind of arbitrariness that is illustrated by the prevalence of racial discrimination in sentencing for rape. On appeal, courts cannot review such a decision in any meaningful way because the law has never established any set of criteria for the death penalty. This process of undefined responsibility carries all the way down to the execution. At some hangings, three men tripped releases, only one of which actually sprung the trap. That way, no one person could be identified as responsible; but the man was dead.

The vice of the jury's limitless discretion in sentencing is compounded by the fact that, in most states, the jury decides the issues of guilt and capital punishment at the same sitting.[26] In noncapital sentencing, the judge usually receives a presentence report and the defense can address the court on the issue. In capital cases, however, the defendant (unless he gives up his privilege against self-incrimination) cannot introduce evidence relevant to sentencing. In determining whether the defendant shall live or die, the jurors have only the evidence about the crime and their own standards about the death penalty.

Finally, the death penalty is challenged as cruel and unusual punishment within the prohibition of the Eighth Amendment. Among those who are condemned, many are winnowed out by postlitigation procedures, in courts and before the governors, based on legal issues, appeals of mercy, or evidence of insanity. Following this grisly lottery, a few are chosen to be executed. Death in such cases is truly "unusual," as it is cruel. The arbitrariness and the irrationality of the death penalty are thrown into sharp relief in a case currently being considered by the Supreme Court of the United States—a case in which the death penalty was imposed for the crime of robbery.[27]

These issues have been raised in differing forms for years by lawyers struggling to keep condemned men alive. But developments in the law have given new form and currency to the arguments. Developments in the social sciences have given a new evidentiary support. The temper of the times seems to be turning against capital punishment, with executions in the last seven years falling from 47 to 21 to 15 to 7 to 1 to 2 to 0.[28] Of course, the smaller the number, the greater the anomaly and the irony.

These arguments do not all necessarily mean, on their face, that capital punishment is unconstitutional. Instead, much of the attack is focused on the unfair and irrational procedures that inhere in the administration of the death penalty. But the result may well be the same. If rational decision-making processes are required, reason and responsibility will focus on an institution where reason does not exist and where responsibility has become diffuse.

## Collective Suits

These several assertions, while first made on behalf of Negroes in several of our cases, are equally applicable to all defendants.

In the first Legal Defense Fund collective suit, raising these claims common to all men under sentence of death, Tobias Simon, of Miami, Fla., went into the United States District Court in Jacksonville, claiming that constitutional rights were denied all those on Florida's death row. As a result, on April 13, 1967, the court granted a stay of all executions[29] so that none of the fifty condemned men could be executed while the several claims were being litigated. (During the gubernatorial campaign, Claude Kirk vowed that he would end the stays of execution given by his predecessor. After taking office, he visited death row to appraise the situation, shook the hands of the condemned men, and then sought to schedule the execution of fourteen during the spring.)

The scene then shifted to California, where Governor Brown's reluctance to execute had produced a backlog of about seventy condemned men at the change of administration. Following the inauguration of Ronald Reagan, Aaron Mitchell was executed on April 12, 1967, and eleven gassings were scheduled for the summer months. As the result of a Legal Defense Fund suit, a similar class stay was granted by the federal District Court on July 5, 1967.[30] Since then, in one of our cases, argued by lead counsel, Professor Anthony Amsterdam, claims have been brought before the Supreme Court of California (which similarly granted a class stay of all executions).[31] By the fall of 1968, Florida had fifty-four men on death row; California, eighty-three men and one woman.

In other states, where the number of condemned men is so much smaller, resort to class actions has been deemed inappropriate. But the same arguments have been and are being presented on behalf of the majority of the approximately five hundred inmates of the nation's death rows. Stays have always been secured.[32] There has been no execution in the United States since June 2, 1967, when a Colorado man was executed after refusing the assistance of counsel. (The phenomenon of "judicial suicide"—men who kill in order to be killed—is, incidentally, not uncommon, and it is an interesting commentary on the death penalty as a deterrent.) There is, thus, ample legal authority to prevent any executions before resolution of these issues, which have now been brought to the Supreme Court of the United States.[33]

## The Death Penalty

I have mentioned what we are doing as lawyers, but the consequences of capital punishment go beyond these limited legal arguments. The very existence of the death penalty distorts the legal system. Many men have been known to plead guilty to crimes they did not commit when the prosecutor threatened them with the death penalty if they pleaded not guilty. The Supreme Court of the United States recognized the coercive impact of capital punishment in *United States v. Jackson.*[34] There the Court struck down a provision of the federal kidnaping statute, which reserved the death penalty for those who pleaded not guilty and demanded trial by jury but authorized a maximum of life imprisonment for those who pleaded guilty or waived jury trial.[35] Also, as in the Groveland case,[36] men have often refused to appeal a conviction for which they were sentenced to life imprisonment for fear that a new trial would again present the possibility of the death penalty. The judicial process has also been distorted when judges, reluctant to send a man to his death, have strained a rule of law to save him. Finally, the mockery of a man executed and later found to be innocent is self-evident.

Today, deterrence is the only argument we hear in support of the death penalty, and there is simply no evidence that the threat of the death penalty is a better deterrent than the threat of imprisonment.[37] On this uncertainty, society sends men to death. Rather than providing the solution, the death penalty diverts attention from a reasoned approach to crime and contributes to the irrationality underlying most criminal behavior. For the death penalty is no less than a resort to and legitimization of extreme violence.

The battle over capital punishment may be seen as a microcosm of the conflict between those in authority who believe in violence as a means of coping with society's problems and those who oppose the use of violence. We have seen it in war. We have heard it in political promises to "get tough with crime in the streets." Reasonable force may sometimes be the only possible way to cope with violence. However, violent force, employed after the fact, legitimizes a method of coping with issues that is the antithesis of the right procedures of a just society. Capital punishment is the supreme example of this irrational response.

Either explicitly or implicitly, as Justice Cardozo said, the courts assert the moral sense of the times.[38] Things are in a state of uncertainty at the moment, with executions stayed all over the country while numerous courts consider the issues. As the reassessment continues, we think that consideration of these cases will persuade the courts, the legislatures, and the public that we owe ourselves a commitment to reason. We do not know how to solve all of society's ills, and particularly all of the problems of crime. But we do know that one way not to do it is to kill needlessly. If the goal of this litigation is achieved, we will have spared a few lives that, thereafter, will be spent in prisons. We will perhaps make it possible, in some cases, for men whose innocence is established years from now to go free. Most important of all, we may make a small contribution to advancing the day when man's problems are dealt with by reason and persuasion and not by brute force.

## NOTES

1. Powell v. Alabama, 287 U.S. 45 (1932).
2. E.g., Powell v. Alabama, *supra* note 1; Hamilton v. Alabama, 368 U.S. 52 (1961).

3. Patton v. Mississippi, 332 U.S. 463 (1947); Shepherd v. Florida, 341 U.S. 50 (1951).
4. Fikes v. Alabama, 352 U.S. 191 (1957).
5. Under the direction of Thurgood Marshall, chief counsel of the Legal Defense Fund from its formation in 1949 until his appointment in 1961 to the United States Court of Appeals for the Second Circuit.
6. Shepherd v. State, 46 So. 2d 880 (Fla. 1950), *rev'd*, Shepherd v. Florida, 341 U.S. 50 (1951), *appeal from second conviction*, Irvin v. State, 66 So. 2d 288 (Fla. 1953), *cert. denied*, 346 U.S. 927 (1954), *habeas denied*, Irvin v. Chapman, 75 So. 2d 591 (Fla. 1954), *cert. denied*, 348 U.S. 915 (1955).
7. See *supra* note 6.
8. Jones v. State, 209 Ga. 685, 75 S.E.2d 429 (1953); *habeas denied* 210 Ga. 262, 79 S.E. 2d 1 (1953), *cert. denied*, 347 U.S. 956 (1954).
9. Hampton v. Commonwealth, 190 Va. 531, 58 S.E.2d 288 (1950), *cert. denied*, 339 U.S. 989 (1950).
10. Hampton v. Commonwealth, *supra* note 9; see also Florida *ex rel.* Copeland v. Mayo, 87 So. 2d 501 (Fla. 1956); Thomas v. State, 92 So. 2d 621 (Fla. 1957), *cert. denied*, 354 U.S. 925 (1957); Florida *ex rel.* Thomas v. Culver, 253 F.2d 507 (5th Cir. 1958); Maxwell v. Stephens, 229 F. Supp. 205 (1964), *aff'd*, 348 F.2d 325 (8th Cir. 1965), *cert. denied*, 382 U.S. 944 (1965) (see notes 21 and 23 *infra*).
11. Bureau of Prisons, United States Department of Justice, *National Prisoner Statistics, Executions*, 1930–67, No. 42, June 1968, at 10–11.
12. E.g., *supra* notes 2–4.
13. *National Prisoner Statistics, supra* note 11, at 11–12.
14. Petitioners Report on Prisoner Interviews and Memorandum in Support of Maintaining Class Action, Adderly v. Wainwright, No. 67-298-Civ.-J. (M.D. Fla.).
15. Hamilton v. State, 270 Ala. 184, 116 So. 2d 906 (1960), *cert. denied*, 363 U.S. 852 (1960); see also note 16 *infra*.
16. Hamilton v. Alabama, 368 U.S. 52 (1961).
17. 375 U.S. 889 (1963).
18. "The following questions, *inter alia*, seem relevant and worthy of argument and consideration:

"1. In light of the trend both in this country and throughout the world against punishing rape by death, does the imposition of the death penalty by those States which retain it for rape violate 'evolving standards of decency that mark the progress of [our] maturing society,' or 'standards of decency more or less universally accepted'?

"2. Is the taking of human life to protect a value other than human life consistent with the constitutional proscription against 'punishments which by their excessive . . . severity are greatly disproportioned to the offenses charged'?

"3. Can the permissible aims of punishment (e.g., deterrence, isolation, rehabilitation) be achieved as effectively by punishing rape less severely than by death—e.g., by life imprisonment; if so, does the imposition of the death penalty for rape constitute 'unnecessary cruelty'?" 375 U.S. 889.

19. Professor of law and co-director of the Center for Studies in Criminology and Criminal Law, University of Pennsylvania.
20. Chairman of the Department of Sociology and co-director of the Center for Studies in Criminology and Criminal Law, University of Pennsylvania.
21. A description of the Georgia aspect of the study appears in the opinion of the Court of Appeals for the Fifth Circuit in Matter of Sims and Abrams, 389 F.2d 148 (5th Cir. 1967), and its South Carolina counterpart described in the memorandum order of the Court of Appeals for the Fourth Circuit in Moorer v. South Carolina, 368 F.2d 458 (4th Cir. 1966); see also for Arkansas, Maxwell v. Bishop, 257 F. Supp. 710 (E.D. Ark. 1966); Maxwell v. Bishop, 398 F.2d 138 (8th Cir. 1968).
22. Aaron v. Simpson, Civ. No. 2170-N (N.D. Ala.); Alabama v. Wheeler Billingsley, Jr., Etowah County Cir. Ct., No. 1159; Alabama v. Robert Butler, Etowah County Cir. Ct., No. 1160; Alabama v. Liddell, Etowah County Cir. Ct., No. 1161; Alabama v. Robert Swain, 7th Div. No. 796; Craig v. Wainwright, No. 66-595-Civ.-J. (M.D. Fla.); Drumwright and Gilley v. Wainwright, No. 67-110-Orl. Civ. (M.D. Fla.); Arkwright v. Kelly, No. 5283, Super. Ct., Tatnall County, Ga.; Williams v. Kelly, No. 5284, Super. Ct., Tatnall County, Ga. See also cases cited *supra* note 21.
23. Maxwell v. Bishop, O.T. 1968, No. 622.
24. 391 U.S. 510 (1968).
25. See Forcella v. New Jersey, 52 N.J. 263, 245 A.2d 181 (1968), *petition for cert. pending,* Misc. No. 947 (O.T. 1968), see *infra* note 33; Pittman v. State, Tex. Crim. App. No. 41393 (decided July 29, 1968); Bell v. Patterson, —— F.2d ——, 10096 (Oct. 18, 1968).
26. California, Connecticut, New York, Pennsylvania, and Texas now provide for bifurcated trials (separate hearings on guilt and punishment).
27. Boykin v. Alabama, O.T. 1968, No. 642, *cert. granted* Oct. 14, 1968.
28. *National Prisoner Statistics, supra* note 11, p. 8.
29. Adderly v. Wainwright, M.D. Fla. No. 67-298-Civ.-J.
30. Hill v. Nelson, Cal., No. 47318 (Order of July 5, 1967).
31. Application of Anderson, Cal. Sup. Ct., Crim. No. 11572; Application of Saterfield, Cal. Sup. Ct., Crim. No. 11573, order of Nov. 14, 1967. See transcript of oral argument, March 28, 1967, on file with the Supreme Court of California. On Nov. 18, 1968, the Supreme Court of California reversed the death sentences of petitioners Anderson and Saterfield on *Witherspoon* grounds; it rejected the constitutional challenge to the death penalty as administered in California (Justices Tobriner, Traynor, and Peters dissenting); and it held that counsel would be appointed at the post-appeal stage.
32. Stays of execution of condemned men have been issued by numerous state and federal courts in post-conviction proceedings raising *inter alia* the capital punishment issues together with, in some cases, the contention of racial discrimination in capital sentencing. *E.g.,* Spencer v. Beto, 5th Cr. No. 25548, order of Nov. 16, 1967 (death penalty later reversed on *Witherspoon* grounds, 398 F.2d 500 [5th Cir. 1968]); Brent v. White, 5th Cir. No. 25496, order of Nov. 28, 1967 (remanded for exhaustion of state remedies), 398

F.2d 503 (5th Cir. 1968); Shinall v. Breazeale, 5th Cir., No. 25807, order of Feb. 21, 1968; Bell v. Patterson, No. 67-C-458, order of Sept. 14, 1967 (U.S.D.C., D. Colo.), *death sentence affirmed,* Bell v. Patterson, 402 F.2d 394 (10th Cir. Oct. 18, 1968); Segura v. Patterson, No. 67-C-497, order of Oct. 13, 1967 (U.S.D.C., D. Colo.), *death sentence affirmed,* Segura v. Patterson, 402 F.2d 249 (10th Cir. Oct. 1, 1968), Brown v. Lane, No. 4129, order of Dec. 29, 1967 (U.S.D.C., N.D. Ind.); Childs v. Turner, No. 2663, order of May 12, 1967. (U.S.D.C., W.D.N.C.); Chevallier v. Beto, No. 68-H-57, order of Jan. 24, 1968 (U.S.D.C., S.D. Tex.); Arkwright v. Kelly, *supra* note 22, order of Dec. 1, 1967; Williams v. Kelly, *supra* note 22, order of Dec. 1, 1967, State v. Davis, Indictment No. 185-J-62, order of March 5, 1968 (Union Cty. Ct., N.J.).

33. The issues are now pending before the Court in petitions for writ of certiorari in Forcella v. New Jersey, O.T. 1968, Misc. No. 947, presenting the several capital punishment issues; Maxwell v. Bishop, O.T. 1968, No. 622, presenting *inter alia* the issue of racial discrimination in capital sentencing for rape; and Boykin v. Alabama, *supra* note 27, in which certiorari has been granted.
34. 390 U.S. 570 (1968).
35. Forcella v. New Jersey, *supra* note 33, includes a challenge to the New Jersey procedure, common to other states, which, in capital crimes, provides for a maximum of life imprisonment to one sentenced pursuant to a guilty plea.
36. See *supra* note 6.
37. See, e.g., Sellin, *The Death Penalty* (1959), published as an appendix to *Model Penal Code* (Tent. Draft No. 9, May 8, 1959).
38. Cardozo, *The Nature of the Judicial Process* (1921).

# 16

# *The Supreme Court, Cruel and Unusual Punishment, and the Death Penalty*

SOL RUBIN

The history of the Eighth Amendment (prohibiting cruel and unusual punishment) as interpreted by the Supreme Court of the United States is bleak. For all practical purposes, the Court's rulings have rendered the Eighth Amendment a dead letter.

This generalization is true of the application of the Eighth Amendment to the death penalty as well as to other punishments. Every form of execution—whether by the electric chair, hanging, shooting, gas, or whatever the legislatures have devised—has been accepted as valid by the Supreme Court. It has sim-

Adapted from a paper given at the Congress of Correction, Miami, Fla., Aug. 22, 1967.

From *Crime and Delinquency*, Vol. 15, No. 1, January 1969, National Council on Crime and Delinquency, pp. 121–131.

ply failed to take account of the cruelty involved in these various methods of execution.

Even today, when the sentiment of the country has become evident in the steady reduction of executions, the Court is unlikely to apply the Eighth Amendment to strike down the death penalty. Abolitionists must continue to work for legislative abolition and, at the same time, utilize every possible legal device to prevent executions.

Will the Eighth Amendment to the United States Constitution, which prohibits cruel and unusual punishment, be applied to strike down the death penalty? The question is one part of the more general issue, the application of the Eighth Amendment to punishments in general. I will first outline the history of the broader question, from which I conclude that the Supreme Court of the United States has failed to apply the Eighth Amendment —indeed, has refused to allow it to be applied—to punishment of criminals. Its failure to apply the Eighth Amendment to the death penalty is consistent with this general attitude.

## The Supreme Court and the Eighth Amendment

The Eighth Amendment states: "Excessive bail shall not be required, nor excessive fines imposed, nor cruel and unusual punishments inflicted." What do the words "cruel and unusual" mean? Do they have the meaning here that they have in ordinary usage? Some have argued that the only punishments forbidden are those that were deemed barbarous when the Constitution was adopted, but this static interpretation was authoritatively rejected in the leading case of *Weems v. United States,* in which the Supreme Court said: "Time works changes, brings into existence new conditions and purposes. Therefore a principle to be vital must be capable of wider application than the mischief which gave it birth. . . . In the application of a constitution . . . our contemplation cannot be only of what has been but of what may be."[1] The Court referred to the physical cruelty of chains, to the prolonged period of imprisonment (a minimum of twelve years under the statute), and to the imposition of "painful as well as hard labor" rather than merely "hard labor."[2]

Although chains, extremely long terms of imprisonment, painful labor, and other cruelties are far from unknown in the United States, the prohibition of cruel and unusual punishment is rarely applied by any court and, as astonishing as it may seem, not a single kind of physical punishment has ever been condemned by the Supreme Court. Aside from the *Weems* case, which is quite out of the stream of its other holdings, the high court has refused to condemn corporal punishment.

It is true that in *Weems* the Court condemned the chaining, along with other punishments, of a prisoner, but this was in a foreign land, the Philippines, and the statute passed on was a Filipino law. On the United States mainland the worst kind of brutal abuse of prisoners (including chaining) has occurred and still occurs, but the Supreme Court has not found any occasion to condemn these punishments under the Eighth Amendment.

Although corporal punishment has been abolished by legislation as a punishment in all states except one, it is still held to be constitutional.[3]

The Supreme Court has also refused to condemn sterilization, the most likely candidate for condemnation, reminiscent as it is of the mutilations that were the original cause of the prohibition. Twice the Court refused to condemn sterilization of criminals as cruel and unusual punishment, though in one instance it found another—but less appropriate—way to prevent application of the statute.

In the first case, in 1942, the Supreme Court had an opportunity to strike down an Oklahoma statute providing that a habitual criminal—one convicted of a felony three times—could be rendered "sexually sterile." The main argument on behalf of the prisoner was that the statute authorized cruel and unusual punishment. The Court did not adopt that argument. Instead, it cited certain inconsistencies in the statute—for example, that it was applicable to larcenies but not to embezzlement—and held it invalid under the equal protection clause of the Fourteenth Amendment.[4]

The Court was asked to rule on sterilization again in 1965, this time in California, where judges impose sterilization as a condition of probation. (The doubly doubtful procedure raises not only the question of cruel and unusual punishment, but also the question of specific authorization by the legislature for a punishment of such gravity. The California statutes say nothing about imposing sterilization as a condition of probation.) A dishwasher named Andrada had submitted to sterilization in lieu of a jail commitment for non-support of his minor children. He later asked the state court to allow him to have the operation undone. The state court refused. Andrada sought review in the United States Supreme Court, which refused to review his case and wrote no opinion.[5]

Other courts, including a federal Court of Appeals, have attempted at times to apply the Eighth Amendment. In the most important of these cases—more significant than the *Weems* case—the Supreme Court slapped down the Court of Appeals for applying the Eighth Amendment to brutal treatment in prison. This was the case of *Dye v. Johnson,* decided in 1949, involving the plea of an escaped prisoner who protested his return to a prison in which he had already experienced serious brutality and presented evidence that the same awaited him upon his return. Obedient to the history of the Eighth Amendment, the District Court refused to free him. The Circuit Court reversed the decision and ordered the prisoner freed.[6] Citing the Eighth Amendment and *Johnson v. Dye,* another federal court freed another prisoner.[7] Revival of the Eighth Amendment seemed in store. But the Supreme Court, typically refusing to examine whether the punishment to which the prisoner had been subjected was, in fact, cruel and unusual, reversed the Circuit Court on the ground that the prisoner had not exhausted his state remedies.[8]

The ground of reversal is subject to criticism on its own procedural terms,[9] but the more pointed comment on the Supreme Court reversal came in a later case when the Court reiterated its view, again ordering the return of an escapee to prison. In a dissenting opinion Justice Douglas said: "If the allegations of the petition are true, the Negro must suffer torture and mutilation, or risk death itself, to get relief in Alabama. . . . I rebel at the thought that any human being, Negro or white, should be forced to run a gauntlet of blood and terror in order to get his constitutional rights. . . . The enlightened view is indeed the other way."[10]

So much for physical punishments. How does the Supreme Court view other kinds of punishment? It has not condemned any other kind of punishment under the Eighth Amendment. In one opinion it declared that denationalization was a new and cruel punishment and seemingly forbade it as a sentence for any crime,[11] but on the same day it handed down another opinion that held quite differently.[12] Then, some years later, it reversed the latter opinion, holding that the government could not deprive a citizen of his citizenship for voting in a foreign state, and it based its decision on the Fourteenth Amendment, not the Eighth.[13]

Another kind of condemnable noncorporal punishment akin to denationalization is the loss of civil rights upon conviction. An old Michigan case declared that preventing a druggist who violated a liquor sale statute from conducting his business for five years after conviction constituted cruel and unusual punishment.[14] The Michigan Supreme Court said: "It is safe to say that throughout the United States any fine or forfeiture is unusual which forfeits any civil rights. Dueling and conviction on an impeachment are the only two things in most states which involve civil incapacities of a public nature, and both of these are provided for by the Constitution. Disability to transact business is almost or quite unheard of in this country."

In 1888, perhaps, but not today. It is a great pity that a decision such as the one quoted above is currently "quite unheard of" in this country, since the civil disabilities consequent upon conviction or imprisonment are obstacles to rehabilitation and are no additional protection to the public.[15] The principle of the case is simply a relic, at least outside the State of Michigan.

When a doctor's license to practice medicine was suspended because he was convicted of failing to produce documents subpoenaed by a congressional committee, the Supreme Court upheld the suspension.[16]

*Robinson v. California*,[17] handed down in 1962, held that a drug addict, being sick, could not be deemed a criminal on that ground alone. To declare a sick person a criminal, the Court said, constitutes cruel and unusual punishment. It was not a question of the measure of punishment. "Even one day in prison," said the Court, "would be a cruel and unusual punishment for the 'crime' of having a common cold."

The real meaning of the case is revealed in that passage. The true holding is *not* application of the Eighth Amendment to punishment of a criminal, but rather the quite elementary rule that there can be no crime without a criminal act and without a criminal intent. In cases that followed it, dealing with the issue of the public drunkenness of chronic alcoholics, other courts reversed convictions without indulging in this distortion even while they cited the *Robinson* decision.

When the United States Court of Appeals in the Fourth Circuit held that a conviction for public intoxication of a man with two hundred similar convictions was improper, on the ground that a person who is powerless to stop his drinking does not commit a crime by appearing intoxicated in public, it did not rely on "cruel and unusual punishment." It said that the conduct was "neither activated by an evil intent nor accompanied with a consciousness of wrongdoing, indispensable ingredients of a crime."[18]

The United States Court of Appeals for the District of Columbia Circuit also held that chronic alcoholism was a defense against the charge of public intoxication: "An essential element of criminality, where personal conduct is involved, is lacking . . . the criminal mind. . . . One who is a chronic alcoholic cannot have the *means rea* necessary to be held responsible criminally for being drunk in public."[19]

Then the Supreme Court itself dealt with the chronic alcoholism issue.[20] It had held drug addiction to be a disease but refused to hold that chronic alcoholism is a disease, and hence upheld a conviction for public drunkenness despite the fact that the defendant had constantly been in and out of jail on this charge. The case is inconsistent with *Robinson* in regard to both its definition of illness and its view of civil commitment. In both cases the Court indulged in dicta—in *Robinson,* declaring that states could civilly commit drug addicts; in *Powell,* frowning upon "therapeutic civil commitment" of chronic alcoholics. The dissenting opinion in *Powell* argued for the cruel-and-unusual-punishment principle of *Robinson;* the majority rejected that argument on the ground that, unlike Robinson, Powell did have *mens rea,* the capacity and intent to commit a criminal act, and that, again unlike Robinson, Powell committed an act. Both rejections are sound, but suddenly the "cruel and unusual" ground for the holding is forgotten and the ruling is on the grounds (which I submit are correct) on which the Court of Appeals acted. *Robinson* is important because, rightly or wrongly, it has revived interest in the Eighth Amendment. *Robinson,* however, does *not* stand for application of the Eighth Amendment to strike down cruel and unusual punishment for a criminal act.

## THE SUPREME COURT AND THE DEATH PENALTY

The statutes provide various methods for carrying out the death penalty. About half the death-penalty states today use electrocution; eleven states use lethal gas; eight use hanging; and Utah offers the condemned person a choice between hanging and shooting. The last legal burning in the United States was in 1825, in South Carolina. All of the methods in use since the nation was founded have been upheld by the courts.[21]

It has been said that two specific criteria are applied under the Eighth Amendment: (1) Is the punishment repugnant to the conscience of civilized men? (2) Is the punishment out of all proportion to the offense or otherwise cruel? In a country where taking a life feloniously is considered the gravest crime, taking a life as a punishment is not considered cruel, whether the execution is carried out by shooting, hanging, electrocution, or any other device the states have chosen. The legislatures in thirteen states have determined that the penalty is not suitable for our civilization, and at least one was led to abolish capital punishment because of the cruelties of a hanging.[22] The courts, however, led by the United States Supreme Court, have refused to acknowledge that execution is a cruel punishment. Their words reveal that they are governed by precedent rather than reason.

The Supreme Court has not recently examined the death penalty to see whether it is at variance with the times and the popular temper. There are signs that it is. The test is not satisfactory if it merely asserts that the legislatures have declared themselves, for then the constitutional provision would be a futility; and it does not consist of taking a poll, official or unofficial.

One can point to the steady decline if the application of the death penalty in the United States (one execution in 1966, two in 1967, and none in 1968); to the difficulty in filling death case juries[23]; and to the obvious shame that accompanies application of the death penalty, as shown not only by the abandonment of public executions, but also by concealment of the identity of the persons who perform the act of execution in private.[24]

Several years ago, a commentator on the history of the Supreme Court and the death penalty said: "Careful review of the opinions and close analysis of the language of the decisions support the view that the constitutionality of capital punishment depends on questions of judically noticeable fact. The evidence, responding to the language and opinions of the judges, has not heretofore been presented in any of our courts."[25] This is a polite way of saying that the courts have never even examined the question of whether the death penalty is cruel.

Regarding a case in which a man survived electrocution, through a fault in the equipment, and then was subjected to it a second time, the Supreme Court said: "The cruelty against which the Constitution protects a convicted man in cruelty inherent in the method of punishment, not the necessary suffering involved in any method humanely employed to extinguish life humanely."[26]

The Court used the word "humanely" twice, emphasizing that a successful execution is humane. But it has not examined the evidence. Eighty years ago a New York governor who sought and obtained passage of a bill to substitute electrocution for hanging[27] said: "The present mode of executing criminals by hanging has come down to us from the dark ages, and it may well be questioned whether the science of the present day cannot provide a means of taking the life of such as are condemned to die in a less barbarous manner." Despite these words, which the Supreme Court quoted two years later in a case testing electrocution (a means that the Court supported),[28] it upheld hanging,[29] as it still upholds the other forms of execution.

The Court has not considered the mental cruelty imposed not only on the one who is being executed but also on many other persons who are under sentence of death but will not be executed because their innocence will be opportunely established or legal error will be proved or executive clemency will be exercised. Generally reprieves are granted only minutes before an execution is scheduled to occur;[30] similarly, and apparently as a regular practice, commutations are granted only shortly before the scheduled time of execution.

The Court did say, in 1889: "When a prisoner sentenced by a court to death is confined in the penitentiary awaiting the execution of the sentence, one of the most horrible feelings to which he can be subjected during that time is the uncertainty during the whole of it, which may exist for a period of four weeks, as to the precise time when his execution shall take place."[31] But it drew only the conclusion that the death penalty is lawful. It might now re-examine the question of psychological cruelty by pondering *Musselwhite v. State,*[32] a 1952 case in which the Supreme Court of Mississippi stayed an execution indefinitely and said: "There is agreement among the examining physicians that at the time of the hearing the petitioner had lost awareness of his precarious situation. . . . If he were taken to the electric chair, he would not quail or take account of its significance. There is reaction neither to audible nor physical stimuli. He takes no nourishment voluntarily. . . . We accept therefore the finding that the petitioner is insane and that such insanity has befallen him since his conviction nearly two years ago. . . . We declare immunity to any clamor of vengeance or to the moving recitals of a brutal murder heretofore adjudged and condemned. We are content to stand upon ground higher than the common urge of outraged reprisal which revives the *lex talionis,* demanding a life for a life."

It is true that the evidence here was considered in the context of the rule that an insane person may not be executed; but it is equally significant in demonstrating the general psychological effects on persons sentenced to death. A 1962 article entitled "Reaction to Extreme Stress: Impending Death by Execution,"[33] by Dr. Harvey Bluestone and Carl L. McGahee, also illustrates this point. The prisoners studied (with perhaps one exception) exhibited a variety of destructive symptoms, including psychopathy, delusions, obsessions, and withdrawal.

There is no dearth of evidence of the physical cruelty of the execution.

Alabama uses the electric chair. The following descriptions of an execution there were written by a newspaper reporter from accounts given her by two prison officers. One of them had witnessed about twenty executions; the other had witnessed eight:

> The final switch is thrown and the electricity strikes the body, which stiffens violently.
>
> The clenched fists whiten and turn slowly upward as the current builds up to a maximum of 2,500 volts. This is a reflex action. A blister begins to rise on the lower left leg beneath the electrode.
>
> The noise is loud. The dying man fights the straps with amazing strength. Usually, some smoke rises up from the chair.
>
> "It is a most violent death but it's over in 40 seconds," said Traywick.[34]

Rex Thomas, Associated Press writer here, has probably witnessed more electrocutions than anyone in Alabama. He describes unforgettable death chamber scenes:

> Years ago, a Negro boy and his brother were sentenced to die one week apart. After the first was electrocuted, his brother was

so emotionally upset that during the death walk, he broke away from guards and lunged into the electric chair. Thomas commented, "The boy just couldn't wait to meet his maker."

Thomas has seen bodies catch on fire in the chair, filling the death chamber with smoke and the smell of burning human flesh.

"That's something you just don't forget," he said.

The body will burn if it requires a second or third jolt or if the condemned perspires excessively.

One guard said the worst part of an electrocution is removing the hood from the head of a man who is badly burned.

Ordinarily, however, the body requires only one jolt of electricity and does not burn, or burns only slightly where the electrodes are attached to the head and lower left leg.

The jolt caused a man's eyeball to fall from its socket in one case.

Another time the waist strap broke while a big, powerful Negro was being electrocuted. "He darn near came out of that chair," said Thomas.

The black hood has been known to drop down, revealing the face of the dying man.

False starts are uncommon but have occurred.

"One of the worst cases I've ever seen," said officer Alford "was a Negro from Troy convicted of murder. He fought us all the way to the death chamber. Several of us had to overpower him to get him strapped in the chair."

Guards have been known to "go all to pieces" during episodes such as these. "Some just can't take it." "Their nerves just don't hold up."

"The guards are always nervous before and during an electrocution," said Alford. "In my opinion it's something you never become accustomed to. It's the most gruesome job I've come in contact with during my 35 years with the department."[35]

Another recent witness of execution by gas writes a "letter to the editor":

Sir:
As one of 17 reporters who watched while Luis Jose Monge [June 9] choked to death in the Colorado gas chamber, I take issue with your statement that "five seconds after a pound of cyanide eggs had been dropped into the vat of acid beneath his chair, he was unconscious."

The public likes to believe that unconsciousness is almost instantaneous, but the facts belie this. According to the official execution log, unconsciousness came more than five minutes after the cyanide splashed down into the sulfuric acid. And to those of us who watched, this five minute interlude seemed interminable. Even after unconsciousness is declared officially, the prisoner's body continues to fight for life. He coughs and groans. The lips make little pouting motions resembling the motions made by a goldfish in his bowl. The head strains backward and then slowly sinks down to the chest. And, in Monge's case, the arms, although tightly bound to the chair, strained at the straps, and the hands clawed tortuously, as if the prisoner were struggling for air.

Any account that leads readers to believe that death comes quickly, painlessly, almost pleasantly, is less than accurate. Send your reporter to cover a legal asphyxiation sometime.

Cary P. Stiff II[36]

## The Current Situation

Several cases are probably en route to the Supreme Court, challenging the death penalty on several grounds, principally the Fourteenth Amendment's protection against unequal treatment (the evidence being that a great disproportion exists between Negroes and whites executed) and the Eighth Amendment's protection against cruel and unusual punishment.

Some renewed hope for application of the Eighth Amendment to capital punishment is based on recent application of the Amendment to noncapital cases by several state and federal courts, whose decisions required prison administrators to cease certain practices.[37]

The greatest hope derives from the unprecedented reduction in executions in the last few years and from interest in several legislatures. The death penalty is being subjected to the most powerful public attack it has ever had in this country. This is an election return of a kind, and the Supreme Court does "follow the election returns"; indeed, the Eighth Amendment requires it to do so—that is, to consider whether a punishment is condemned by the general sentiment of the population. Even the requirement of "exhaustion of state remedies" has been weakened.[38]

But if the Supreme Court follows some of the election returns all of the time, and all of the election returns some of the time, it does not follow all of the election returns all of the time. It has a sentiment of its own, and it may be able to resist the current attack on the death penalty, which is, after all, defended by some. The Supreme Court can say, with considerable truth, that the legislatures have not spoken out very strongly; for the most part, abolition has been effected by judges and juries, citizen committee pressures, legal action, and other elusive measures.

Furthermore, the Court can alleviate the immediate situation by reversing a few sentences of execution under the Fourteenth Amendment, requiring equality of treatment. It may decide that execution for a crime less than murder—rape, for example—is excessive, although not long ago it rejected that argument.[39] The Court may well use such alternatives, fearing that its application of the Eighth Amendment to the death penalty would be much stronger—as it would be—than its citation of the Eighth Amendment in *Robinson*.

Since the Court is more amendable to the Fourteenth Amendment than to the Eighth, I hope another argument will be made. An inherent vice of the death penalty is that it renders due process of law inoperable. When the condemned man is executed, errors in the proceedings are placed beyond the reach of later decisions that would provide new grounds for examining whether the proceedings leading to the execution contained error.

The recent Supreme Court decision in *Witherspoon,* reversing a jury-imposed death sentence, held that the jury, from which were excluded veniremen who indicated they were opposed to the death penalty, was not representative of the community.[40] This new doctrine, the Court has held, is retroactive; it applies to those now in death rows all over the country. But it also means that, among those who have been executed, there surely must be many whose cases would have had to be reopened—if they were alive. Their execution deprived them of due process of law.

Furthermore, a dissenting opinion held that the majority did not go far enough. Said Justice Douglas: "I see no constitutional basis for excluding those who are so opposed to capital punishment that they would never inflict it as punishment." Suppose that juries conforming to the *Witherspoon* decision but not adopting Justice Douglas' view decree more executions—and then afterward the Court does adopt that view? Due process too late is due process denied.

Other instances are the decisions of the Court invalidating the death penalty provisions of the "Lindbergh" kidnaping law and the Federal Bank Robbery Act. But six men have been executed under the kidnaping law. Surely they were deprived of due process—and every man executed is deprived of due process of law, since he cannot be given the benefit of new holdings or of the finding of new facts that might be sufficient to reopen his case.

I wish I could be confident that the outcome would be the application of the Eighth Amendment to the death penalty, which should be abolished because it is not only cruel but also useless and harmful. But, aware of the Court's bleak history of avoidance of application of the Amendment, I do not have that confidence.

Yet that assessment does not constitute pessimism about the future of the death penalty in the United States. Turn for analogy to the history of the burning of witches. It was not the Establishment that put an end to witch-burning but the new philosophical climate of rationalism. The laws for the burning of witches were repealed only some time after the burning of witches had stopped.[41]

This means that abolitionists have to work harder than ever to use every possible means of legal procedure and education for preventing every single death sentence from being carried out and, at the same time, strive for legislative abolition of the death penalty in every jurisdiction.

## NOTES

1. 217 U.S. 349 (1909).
2. The crime for which Weems, a minor port official, had been convicted was a violation of the penal code of the Philippine Islands: he had made false entries of port duties involving payment of 616 pesos.

3. State v. Cannon, 190 A.2d 514 (Del. 1963).
4. Skinner v. Oklahoma *ex rel.* Williamson, 316 U.S. 535 (1941).
5. *In re* Andrada, 280 U.S. 953 (1965).
6. Johnson v. Dye, 175 F.2d 250, 256 (C.A. 1949), 59 *Yale L.J.* 800 (1950).
7. Harper v. Wall, 85, F. Supp. 783 (D.C.N.J. 1949).
8. Dye v. Johnson, 338 U.S. 864, 70 Sup. Ct. 146, *rehearing denied,* 388 U.S. 896, 70 Sup. Ct. 238.
9. Levin, *Habeas Corpus in Extradition Proceedings Involving Escaped Convicts,* 40 *J. Crim. L., C. & P.S.* 484 (1949): "The consideration is one of comity between the federal and state governments," hence requirement of exhaustion of remedies could be waived by the federal courts "whenever necessary to prevent an unjust and illegal deprivation of human liberty," citing Wade v. Mayo, 334 U.S. 672, 681 (1948). It also cites the Civil Rights Act as a basis for protecting such a prisoner. See also, Comment, 74 *Yale L.J.* 78 (1964); Frank, *The U.S. Supreme Court 1949–50,* 18 *U. Chi. L. Rev.* 1, 39–40 (1950).
10. Sweeney v. Woodall, 344 U.S. 86 (1952).
11. Trop v. Dulles, 356 U.S. 86 (1957), 5–4 decision.
12. Perez v. Brownell, 356 U.S. 44 (1957), 5–4 decision.
13. Afroyim v. Rusk, 87 Sup. Ct. 1660 (1967).
14. People *ex rel.* Robinson v. Haug, 68 Mich. 549, 37 N.W. 21 (1888).
15. Rubin, *Law of Criminal Correction ch.* 17, 620–644.
16. Barsky v. Board of Regents, 347 U.S. 442 (1953).
17. 370 U.S. 660, 8 L. Ed. 758, 82 Sup. Ct. 1417 (1962).
18. Driver v. Hinnant, 356 F.2d 761 (1966).
19. Easter v. District of Columbia, 361 F.2d 50 (1966).
20. Powell v. Texas, 88 Sup. Ct. 2145 (1968).
21. Shooting—Wilkerson v. Utah, 99 U.S. 130, 25 L. Ed. 345 (1878); 30 A.L.R. 1457, 35 L.R.A. 575; hanging—*Ex parte* Medley, 134 U.S. 160, 10 Sup. Ct. 384, 33 L. Ed. 835 (1889); Dutton v. State, 123 Md. 373, 91 Atl. 417 (1914); lethal gas—State v. Gee Jon, 46 Nev. 418, 211 Pac. 676, 30 A.L.R. 1443 (1923), 217 Pac. 587, 30 A.L.R. 1443 (1923) on rehearing; electrocution—McElvaine v. Brush, 142 U.S. 155, 12 Sup. Ct. 156, 35 L. Ed. 971 (1891); *In re* Kemmler, 136 U.S. 436, 10 Sup. Ct. 930, 34 L. Ed. 519 (1890); Storti v. Mass., 183 U.S. 138, 22 Sup. Ct. 72, 46 L. Ed. 120 (1901); State v. Burdette, 135 W. Va. 312, 63 S.E.2d 69 (1950); People v. Daugherty, 40 Cal. 2d 876, 256 P.2d 911 (1953), *cert. denied,* 346 U.S. 827, 74 Sup. Ct. 47, 98 L. Ed. 352, *rehearing denied,* 346 U.S. 880, 74 Sup. Ct. 120, 98 L. Ed. 387.
22. A scandal was caused when an unauthorized reporter witnessed a hanging—of a man who to the end claimed innocence—in which the rope was too long, and the victim had to be held up while the sheriff and deputies pulled on the rope. Death came by strangulation after fourteen and a half minutes (*St. Paul Dispatch,* Feb. 13, 1906). The report praised the demeanor of the condemned; the headline read—"Displayed His Nerve to the Very Last." As for the crowd, the reporter wrote: "The spectators who saw the execution were in haste to make their departure after it was over. 'Yes, I saw it,' said one. 'But, ugh, I never want to see another one.' It is safe to say that the feature of a crowded execution was eliminated by Sheriff

Miesen; but, if the number of persons who left the jail at its close are any index of the number who saw it, it is certain that the six persons designated in the law as the number the sheriff may personally invite was unmercifully stretched. People of a morbid turn, attracted by the hangings, began to gather around. The three sides of the building were lined by them. All were eager to catch a glimpse of the condemned man as he walked from his cell to the waiting elevator that was to lower him to the basement, where death awaited him."

The next day the press reported the governor's outrage at the sheriff's behavior in admitting twenty-five or thirty people, and particularly at the admission of reporters. The death penalty was abolished in 1911.

23. Lindley R. McClelland, a member of the Pennsylvania bar, writing in the March 1959 issue of the *Pennsylvania Bar Association Quarterly,* reports the case of one Miner Davis, tried for murder in Erie in 1958. The prosecuting attorney and defense counsel "examined 142 prospective jurors on their voir dire, before we were able to accept 12 jurors and 2 alternate jurors. . . . Why? The answer, in large part, is that the prospective jurors had conscientious scruples against bringing in a penalty of death. . . . [Defense counsel] continually asked them, 'Granted the death penalty is revolting in most cases, couldn't you bring in such a verdict against a professional killer, a hired assassin or the brutal murderer of a little child?" Many of the jurors said no. As this example indicates, the gulf between the community and the death-qualified jury grows as the populace becomes more infected with modern notions of criminality and the purpose of punishment." Oberer, "Does Disqualification of Jurors for Scruples against Capital Punishment Constitute Denial of Fair Trial on Issue of Guilt?" 39 *Texas L. Rev.* 545, 555, 556 (1961).
24. On the gradual elimination of public executions in the United States, see Hartung, "Trends in the Use of Capital Punishment," *Annals,* Nov. 1952, p. 10.
25. Gottlieb, "Testing the Death Penalty," 34 *So. Cal. L. Rev.* 268, 270 (1961).
26. Louisiana *ex rel.* Francis v. Resweber, 329 U.S. 459, 67 Sup. Ct. 374, 91 L. Ed. 422 (1947), *rehearing denied,* 330 U.S. 853, 67 Sup. Ct. 673, 91 L. Ed. 1295.
27. *Laws of 1888,* ch. 489.
28. *In re* Kemmler, 136 U.S. 436, 10 Sup. Ct. 930, 34 L. Ed. 519 (1890).
29. *Ex Parte* Medley, 134 U.S. 160, 10 Sup. Ct. 384, 33 L. Ed. 835 (1889).
30. A man sentenced in Texas to die for the rape-murder of a three-year-old was reprieved less than three hours before he was to die, upon the confession of another man to the crime (*New York Post,* Feb. 5, 1958); John Resko (see his book, *Reprieve,* 1956) was given a reprieve twenty minutes before his scheduled execution. But Burton W. Abbott was executed in California on March 15, 1957, two minutes before the governor's reprieve was telephoned to the warden (*New York Times,* March 16, 1957).
31. *Ex parte* Medley, *supra* note 29.
32. 215 Miss. 363, 60 So. 2d 807.
33. *American Journal of Psychiatry,* Nov. 1962.

34. Danielle Harris in the *Montgomery Advertiser,* Oct. 23, 1961.
35. *Id.,* Oct. 25, 1961.
36. *Time,* June 23, 1967.
37. Jordan v. Fitzharris, 257 F. Supp. 674 (1966); Talley v. Stephens, 247 F. Supp. 683 (1965); Johnson v. Avery, 252 F. Supp. 783 (1966); Mahoney v. State, 392 P.2d 279 (Idaho 1964); the cases are discussed in Rubin, "Developments in Correctional Law," 13 *Crime & Delin.* 356 (1967).
38. Particularly since Fay v. Hoia, 372 U.S. 391 (1963) ruled that the requirement that state remedies be exhausted referred to remedies available at the time the petition is filed; and that a state prisoner's failure in the past to pursue a remedy which is not presently available could not bar federal habeas corpus relief unless the federal district judge found a "deliberate bypass" of the prior state remedy.
39. Rudolph v. Alabama 375 U.S. 889, 84 Sup. Ct. 155 (1963), *cert. denied.*
40. Witherspoon v. Illinois, 88 Sup. Ct. 1770 (1968).
41. Lecky, *History of the Rise and Influence of the Spirit of Rationalism in Europe,* 134 (1955). On the general process, ch. 1, "The Declining Sense of the Miraculous: On Magic and Witchcraft."

# *For Further Reading*

## Articles


Adamo, S. J. "It's Time to Outlaw Capital Punishment," *U.S. Catholic,* 31 (May 1965), pp. 19–20.

Bedau, H. A. "Capital Punishment in Oregon, 1903–64," *Oregon Law Review,* 35 (May 1963), pp. 410–419.

——— "Death Sentences in New Jersey, 1907–1960," *Rutgers Law Review,* 19 (1965), pp. 1–64.

Beichman, A. "The First Electrocution," *Commentary,* (December 1965), pp. 1–39.

"Capital Punishment," *Existential Psychiatry,* 1 (Spring 1966), pp. 7–20.

Coakley, F. J. "Capital Punishment," *American Criminal Law Quarterly,* (May 1963) pp. 27–48.


This is a selected list of publications of the 1960s and the year 1970. Excludes reference to articles appearing in this book.

"Death Penalty," *Crime and Delinquency,* (January 1969). (Entire issue devoted to capital punishment. Includes bibliography.)

"Executive Clemency in Capital Cases," *New York University Law Review,* (January 1964) pp. 136–92.

Hook, S. "The Death Sentence," *The New Leader,* 44 (April 3, 1961), pp. 18–20.

Lassers, W. J. "Proof of Guilt in Capital Cases—An Unscience," *Journal of Criminal Law, Criminology and Police Science,* (September 1967) pp. 310–316.

McCafferty, J. A. "The Death Sentence and Then What?", *Crime and Delinquency* (October 1961), pp. 363–372.

———— "Major Trends in the Use of Capital Punishment," *Federal Probation,* (September 1961) pp. 15–21. Also, *Criminal Law Quarterly,* (February 1963) pp. 9–22.

Mattick, H. W. "The Unexamined Death" (2nd Ed.), Chicago: John Howard Association, 1966, pp. 1–46.

Murdy, R. G. "A Moderate View of Capital Punishment," *Federal Probation,* (September 1961) pp. 11–15.

National Council on Crime and Delinquency, Board of Trustees. "Policy Statement on Capital Punishment," *Crime and Delinquency,* (April 1964) pp. 105–109.

Oberer, W. E. "Does Disqualification of Jurors for Scruples Against Capital Punishment Constitute Denial of Fair Trial on Issue of Guilt?", *Texas Law Review,* (May 1961) pp. 545–567.

Partington, D. H. "The Incidence of the Death Penalty for Rape in Virginia," *Washington and Lee Law Review,* (Spring 1965) pp. 43–75.

*Police Chief.* International Association of Chiefs of Police, June 1960. (Several articles on capital punishment.)

Ringold, S. M. "The Dynamics of Executive Clemency," *American Bar Association Journal,* (March 1966) pp. 240–243.

Robin, G. D. "The Executioner: His Place in English Society," *British Journal of Sociology,* (September 1964) pp. 234–253.

Sellin, T. "Capital Punishment," *Federal Probation,* (September 1961) pp. 3–11.

Thomas, T. "This Life We Take" (4th Rev.), San Francisco: Friends Committee on Legislation, (February 1970) pp. 1–34.

Wolfgang, M. E. (ed.) "Patterns of Violence," *The Annals,* 364 (March 1966).

Wolfgang, M. E., A. Kelly, and H. C. Nolde. "Comparison of the Executed and the Commuted Among Admissions to Death Row," *Journal of Criminal Law, Criminology and Police Science,* (September 1962) pp. 301–311.

Zeisel, H. "Some Data on Juror Attitudes Toward Capital Punishment," Center for Studies in Criminal Justice, The University of Chicago Law School, (1968) pp. 1–51.

## Books

Bedau, H. A. 1967. *The Death Penalty in America, An Anthology* (Rev. Ed.). Garden City, N. Y.: Doubleday & Co. (Anchor Books). (Includes extensive bibliography.)

Block, E. B. 1962. *And May God Have Mercy . . . The Case Against Capital Punishment.* San Francisco: Fearon Publishers. (Includes bibliography.)

Camus, A. 1961. *Resistance, Rebellion and Death.* New York: Alfred A. Knopf.

Christoph, J. B. 1962. *Capital Punishment and British Politics; The British Movement to Abolish the Death Penalty, 1945–57.* Chicago: The University of Chicago Press.

Cohen, B. L. 1970. *Law Without Order.* New York: Arlington House Publishers.

DiSalle, M. V., with L. G. Blochman. 1965. *The Power of Life or Death.* New York: Random House.

Duffy, C. T. 1962. *88 Men and 2 Women.* Garden City, N. Y.: Doubleday & Co.

Eshelman, B. E. 1962. *Death Row Chaplain.* Englewood Cliffs, N. J.: Prentice-Hall.

Ingram, T. R. (Ed.) 1963. *Essays on Death Penalty.* Houston, St. Thomas Press.

Joyce, J. A. 1961. *Capital Punishment: A World View.* New York: Thomas Nelson & Sons.

Machlin, M. and W. R. Woodfield. 1961. *Ninth Life.* New York: G. P. Putnam's Sons.

McGehee, E. G. and W. H. Hildebrand (Eds.) 1964. *The Death Penalty: A Literary and Historical Approach.* Boston: D.C. Heath and Co.

Prettyman, B., Jr. 1961. *Death and the Supreme Court.* New York: Harcourt, Brace and World.

Sellin T. 1967. *Capital Punishment.* New York: Harper & Row, Publishers (Contains topical bibliography.)

Smith, E. 1968. *Brief Against Death.* New York: Alfred A. Knopf.

Teeters, N. K. 1963. *Scaffold and Chair: A Compilation of Their Use in Pennsylvania, 1682–1962.* Philadelphia: Pennsylvania Prison Society.

Teeters, N. K., with J. H. Hedblom. 1967. *Hang by the Neck.* Springfield, Ill.: Charles C. Thomas, Publisher.

Tuttle, E. 1961. *The Crusade Against Capital Punishment in Great Britain.* Chicago: Quadrangle Books.

## Offical Reports

*Capital Punishment, 1962.* 1967. New York: United Nations Department of Economic and Social Affairs.

*Capital Punishment Developments, 1961–65.* 1967. New York: United Nations Department of Economic and Social Affairs.

*Capital Punishment: Material Relating to Its Purpose and Value.* June 1965. Ottawa: Queen's Printer.

Commission to Study Capital Punishment. October 1964. *Report.* Trenton, N.J.

Committee on Capital Punishment. 1962. *Report to the Legislative Council of Maryland.* Baltimore.

Committee on the Judiciary, House of Representatives, 86th Cong., 2nd Sess. 1960. *Abolition of Capital Punishment, Hearings . . . on H. R. 870 to Abolish the Death Penalty . . ., 1960* Serial No. 21 Washington, D.C.: U.S. Government Printing Office.

DeMarcus, J.P. 1965. *Capital Punishment.* Inf. Bull. No. 40 Frankfort: Kentucky Legislative Research Commission.

General Assembly of Pennsylvania. 1961. *Report of the Joint Legislative Committee on Capital Punishment.* Harrisburg.

Gibson, E., and S. Klein. 1969. *Murder—1957 to 1968.* Home Office Research Study No. 3. London: Her Majesty's Stationery Office.

Ohio Legislative Service Commission. January 1961. *Capital Punishment.* Staff Research Report No. 46. Columbus.

*National Prisoner Statistics "Executions."* Annual. Washington, D.C.: United States Department of Justice, Bureau of Prisons.

*Parliamentary Debates* (Hansard). 1969. House of Commons, Vol. 793. Nos. 35, 36 and 37 (December 15–17, 1969). House of Lords, Vol. 306. Nos. 25 and 26 (December 17, 1969). London: Her Majesty's Stationery Office.

Special Commission for the Study of Abolition of Death Penalty in Capital Cases, 1965. *Report, 1963–65.* Tallahassee, Fla.

State Temporary Commission on Revision of the Penal Law and Criminal Code. 1965. *Special Report on Capital Punishment.* Albany, N.Y.

Vialet, J. 1966. *Capital Punishment: Pro and Con Arguments.* Washington, D.C.: Library of Congress Legislative Reference Service, HV 8694. Ed-153.

## For Other Bibliographies Refer to:

"Bibliography on Capital Punishment," United States Department of Justice, Bureau of Prisons, Washington, D.C. 20537.

"Capital Punishment: A Selected Bibliography," September 1966, with Addenda, 1969. Friends Committee on Legislation, 2160 Lake Street, San Francisco, Calif. 94121.

"Selected International Bibliography on Capital Punishment," March 1968. The Center for Studies in Criminal Justice, The Law School, The University of Chicago, Chicago, Illinois 60637.

# *Name Index**

Adams, J. Frank, 135
Agron, Salvador, 208
Akman, Dogan, 60
Alexander, Myrl E., 219
Allen, Edward J. 86, 117–28, 157
Allen, John, 206
Almeida, David, 199
Amsterdam, Anthony G., 239
Aquinas, Thomas, 136
Atchley, Vernon, 204

Barry, John, 90
Barshay, Hyman, 131
Barzun, Jacques, 85, 89–101
Bates, Sanford, 141
Beccaria, Cesare, 13, 166
Bedau, Hugo Adam, 5
Bennett, James V., 85, 140–56, 190
Bernstein, Charles, 86, 141
Black, Hugo L., 76
Blackstone, William, 9, 10, 11, 20
Bluestone, Harvey, 254
Bowles, Chester, 199
Bradford, Robert F., 213
Bradford, William, 27
Brennan, W. J., Jr., 79
Brown, Arthur Ross, 86, 140
Brown, Edmund G., 204, 239
Brownell, Herbert, 152
Burke, John C., 196
Burney, Charles, 97
Bye, Raymond, 33

Calvert, Roy, 16
Capote, Truman, 150
Cardozo, Benjamin N., 241
Carvel, Elbert N., 212
Chafee, Zechariah, 192
Chapin, Kenneth, 202
Chebatoris, Anthony, 143
Chessman, Caryl, 26, 125
Chester, Jack, 201
Christie, John, 198
Churchill, Winston, 140
Ciucci, Vincent, 210
Clark, James J., 204
Clark, Ramsey, 109, 176–80
Clay, Lucius, 208
Cobin, Herbert L., 190
Cory, Giles, 20
Correa, Concepcion, 207

*Reference to cases will be found in notes following each chapter.

Cowan, Lawrence, 206
Crampton, James E., 228
Cranson, John R., 133
Crump, Paul, 206
Currier, Donald E., 193
Cvek, George, 93

Dann, Robert H., 59
Darrow, Clarence, 179
Derbyshire, George L., 203
Dewey, John, 213
Diodotus, 171
Douglas, William O., 79, 249, 257, 258
Duffy, Clinton, 203, 219

Ede, Chuter, 198
Edison, Thomas, 22
Ehrmann, Sara R., 159, 187–217
Eisenhower, Dwight D., 155
Elliot, Robert G., 22
Ely, Joseph B., 192
Evans, Timothy, 198
Evjen, Victor H., 159, 218–30

Ferrers, Earl of, 147
Finch-Tregoff case, 205
Foster, James F., 198
Franklin, Benjamin, 13, 25

Gardner, Erle Stanley, 197
George II, 8
George III, 8
Gerstein, Richard E., 85, 129–39, 157
Gillette, A. C., 195
Gittelsohn, Roland, 13, 211
Giacammazza, Paul, 207
Gold, Harry, 154
Goldberg, Arthur J., 79, 235
Gollancz, Victor, 90
Gowers, Ernest, 131
Graham, Barbara, 210
Greeley, Dana McClean, 211
Greeley, Horace, 14
Greenberg, Jack, 229, 231–44
Greenglass, David and Ruth, 153
Greenlease, Bobby, 147
Grimstone, Robert, 150
Griswold, Erwin N., 213
Groveland case, 232, 240

Hale, Leslie, 97
Hall, Carl Austin, 86, 147
Hammack, William, 142
Hawkins, Lee, 204
Harris, Phoebe, 9
Harrison, Tucker, 202
Heady, Bonnie Brown, 86, 147
Henry VIII, 146, 166
Herter, Christian A., 202
Himmelstein, Jack, 229, 231–44
Hochkammer, William O., Jr., 63, 65–84
Hogan, Frank S., 133–34
Hoover, J. Edgar, 150, 155, 156

Jackson, Robert H., 145, 183
Jefferson, Thomas, 21
Johnson, Jack, 207
Johnston, James, 144
Jon, Gee, 22
Joyce, James A., 90

Kaufman, Irving, 152
Kemmler, William, 22
Kent, Elroy, 32
Kirk, Claude, 239
Koestler, Arthur, 10, 90, 137
Kross, Anna, 208

Langlois, Harold V., 194
Lafayette, Marquis de, 178
Lawes, Lewis E. 16, 144, 191, 221
Livingston, Edward, 14
Lodge, John, 199
Loveless, Herschel, 204

MacCormick, Austin H., 205, 211, 224
Maxwell, William L., 227
McCafferty, James A. 39, 44, 187
McGahee, Carl L., 254
McGautha, Dennis C., 228
McGee, Richard A., 157, 161–75
McGrath, J. Howard, 153
McKinley, William, 18
Madison, James, 21
Manning, Silas, 210
Martinsville Seven, 233
Matera, Pietro, 199
Mitchell, Aaron, 239
Monge, Luis Jose 226, 255
Moon, Norman, 204
Morris, Albert, 196
Myzaard, C. J., 195

Nash, Stephan, 170, 172

Panzran, Carl, 148
Patrick, Clarence H., 6, 39
Pfeffer, Paul A., 199

Raleigh, Walter, 9
Reagan, Ronald, 239
Reckless, Walter C., 6, 38–62
Rick, Emil, 209
Riley, Thomas J., 211
Ritchie, A. B., 199
Robbins, Allan L., 195
Roche, John F., 199
Rockefeller, Nelson, 32
Rockefeller, Winthrop, 1
Rodriguez, Santos, 198
Rolph, C. H., 90
Roosevelt, Franklin D., 86, 199
Rosenberg, Julius and Ethel, 26, 87, 151
Rovere, Richard H., 137
Rowland, Walter G., 198
Rubin, Sol., 229, 245–61
Rush, Benjamin, 13, 14, 25, 27
Rupp, William F., 205
Ryan, John, 143

Sacco and Vanzetti, 159, 199
Salmond, John, 130
Schmidt, David, 203
Sellin, Thorsten, 39, 55, 58, 59, 111–13, 163, 177, 187
Shaw, Bernard, 176
Sheppard, Samuel H., Jr., 99
Shrickey, Henry F., 209
Simon, Tobias, 239
Sjaarjems, Henry, 205
Smith, Frank, 199
Smith, Louis F., 206
Speck, Richard, 151
Starkweather, Charles, 189
Stratchey, Lytton, 146
Stroud, Robert, 87, 149

Teeters, Negley, 228
Tesla, Niccola, 22
Thomas, Rex, 254
Townsend, Charles, 204
Truman, Harry S., 86, 87, 199

van den Haag, Ernest, 85, 86, 102–16
Vargas, Anastarcio, 199
Volpe, John, 203
Vollmer, August, 213

Walker, Erwin, 203
Ware, David J., 198
Webster, Daniel, 138
Wilson, Woodrow, 148
Witherspoon, William C., 236
Wolfgang, Marvin, 228
White, Byron, R., 77

Younger, Evelle, J., 201

# Subject Index


Abolition of death penalty, 18
Abolitionists, 14, 17, 28, 30, 100
Abolition movement 13–15, 19, 33
Abolition states, 18, 44, 60
Acquittal, 200
Air Force, U.S. 221
Alabama, 88, 254
Alaska, 50
American colonies, 5, 7, 11
American Bar Foundation, 178, 209
American Civil Liberties Union, 227
American Correctional Association, 219
American Institute of Public Opinion, 134
American League to Abolish Capital Punishment, 16, 188
Anti-gallows movement, 14–15
Appeals, 53
Arizona, 15, 50, 188
Arkansas, 1, 208, 227
Army, U.S., 221
  espionage, 151
Assassination, 18, 19
Assault, 54, 56, 57, 60, 179, 194–197

Basic issues, 63
Benefit of clergy, 10
"Black Dahlia" case, 209
"Bloody Code, The," 10
British Medical Association, 23
Brutality, 21, 120
Burning at the stake, 9, 20, 251

California, 31, 117, 125, 126, 127, 188, 239
Canada, 60, 197, 208
Canadian Parliamentary Commission, 197, 212
Capital crimes, 11, 12, 19
Capital punishment
  abolition states, 18, 48–49
  administering, 22, 23, 25, 183
  alternatives, 23, 174, 179
  arguments against, 66, 91, 117, 123, 157–230
  arguments for, 66, 85–156, 162, 226
  awaiting, 52, 234, 239
  before, during and after abolition, 56
  collective suits, 239
  cost, 71, 156, 168, 222
  delay, 165, 183, 209–10

as deterrent to crime, 53, 59, 60, 66–68, 102–16, 118, 130, 149, 163
discrimination, 68, 120, 145, 159, 205–07, 235–36
vs. imprisonment, 98
issues, 63–84
mandatory, 45
opponents, 161–224
poverty, 108
philosophy, 137
protection, 69, 136
reabolition states, 18
restoration states, 18
safety, 138
self-defense, 136
supporters, 85–155
trend, 8, 42, 50–52
use, 134
*see also* Execution
Cero–Gallo case, 200
Colorado, 15, 18, 50, 73, 226, 240, 255
Commutation, 53, 60, 191, 193
Compensation, 198, 199
Confession, 197–99, 209, 223
Connecticut, 18, 199
"Corruption of blood," 8
Counsel, 206, 234
Countries with death penalty, 33, 41
Countries without death penalty, 39–40
Crime rate, 108–09
Criminal law, purpose of, 172
Cruel and unusual punishment, 21, 22, 150, 228, 246–51
*see also* U.S. Constitution

*Death Penalty in America, The,* 5
Death penalty. *See* Capital punishment; Execution
*De facto* abolition, 38
Degrees of murder, 27
*De jure* abolition, 38
Delaware, 17, 18, 50, 127, 190, 206
Delay, 165, 183, 209–10
District of Columbia, 31, 39

Electrocution, 21, 23, 156, 254–55
England, 7, 16
Error, 70, 168–69, 197–201
Execution
age of condemned, 43, 207–08
effect on public, 9
homicide before and after, 58
indignity, 23
method, 21, 25, 43, 130, 146–47, 156, 166
number executed, 26, 51, 52
offense, type of, 206
possible error, 70, 168–69, 197–201
privacy of, 26
provisions, 46–47
public, 25, 43
race, 53, 68, 179, 188, 206
sex, 51, 68
time interval for, 52, 124, 183
warrant for, 47
*see also* Capital punishment
Executive clemency, 183
Federal Bureau of Investigation, 228
Federal Kidnapping Act, 17, 75, 76, 209, 240, 258
*Federal Probation,* 159, 187
Finch–Tregoff case, 205
Florida, 129, 188, 239

Gallup Poll, 23, 73, 182
Gas, lethal, 22, 23, 147, 255
Georgia, 31, 188, 198
Great Britain, 92, 131, 145, 182, 225–26
*Hanged by the Neck,* 90
Hanging, 8, 21, 25
Hawaii, 50
Homicide Act, 16
Homicide rates, 53, 54, 57

*I Want to Live,* 210
Illinois, 17, 31
Imprisonment, 96, 98, 168
*In Cold Blood,* 150
Indiana, 209
Inequities, 221
Information, need for, 188
Injustice, 221
Innocent, execution of, 70, 168, 197, 200, 222
Insanity, 47, 71, 94
Iowa, 15, 50, 125
Issues, 63

Judges, 121
*Judicature,* 185
Justice, obstruction of, 222
Juveniles, 207–08

Kansas, 15, 50, 125
Kentucky, 25

Legal issues, 74, 236–38
*Lex Talionis,* 254
Life imprisonment, 70, 73, 123, 191, 193, 194–97, 222
Lindbergh Kidnapping Law. *See* Federal Kidnapping Act
Louisiana, 14, 31
Lynching, 15

Maine, 14, 15, 50, 125, 127
Maryland, 31
Massachusetts, 11, 12, 14, 31, 159, 191, 192
Massachusetts Council to Abolish the Death Penalty, 188
Massachusetts Investigating Commission of 1960, 211
*Mens rea,* 29, 250
Mental cruelty, 253
Mentally ill, 71, 150, 201
Method of execution, 20, 25, 43, 130, 146, 147, 156, 166
Michigan, 50, 127, 249
Minnesota, 15, 50, 125
Mississippi, 188
Missouri, 15, 50, 125
Model Penal Code, 201
Mosiac Code, 11
Murder
  defined, 27, 29
  degrees of, 27
  rates, 125
Murder Act of 1965, 225
Murderers, 179

NAACP Legal Defense and Educational Fund, Inc., 229, 232
National Commission on Reform of Federal Criminal Laws, 158
National Prisoner Statistics, 51
Navy, U.S., 221
Nebraska, 125, 189
"Neck verse," 10
Negroes, 25, 145
Nevada, 17, 22
New Hampshire, 126
New Jersey, 14, 25, 31, 209
New Mexico, 31
New York, 14, 17, 21, 24, 31, 50, 70, 188
North Carolina, 11, 12, 31
North Dakota, 15, 50, 113, 126, 127

Offenses, capital, 8, 12, 19, 41, 45, 233
Ohio, 14, 28, 188
Oklahoma, 247
Old Testament, 186
*On Crimes and Punishments,* 13
Oregon, 15, 17, 50, 72, 125

Pardon, 193
Parole of lifers, 70, 192, 193, 223
*Peine forte et dure,* 20
Pennsylvania, 11, 12, 14, 25, 28, 29, 31, 199
Philadelphia, 32
Police killings, 59, 127
President's Commission on Law Enforcement and Administration of Justice, 145, 178
Press, 50
Pressing to death, 20
Prison killings, 59
Prisoners, 97
Prison assaults, 59, 194–97
Private execution, 24, 26
Premeditation, 220
Protection, 69, 136, 164
Public executions, 25, 43
Publicity, 50, 125
Public opinion, 72, 74, 78, 210–11
Puerto Rico, 207, 208
Punishment. See Capital punishment

Racial discrimination, 221, 233–36
Rape cases, 234, 235, 239
Reform movement, 13–17
Research, need for, 212–13
Rehabilitation, 74
Retentionists, 23
Retribution, 73, 162, 223
Reversals, 208
Robbery, 258
Roper Poll, 73

Royal Commission on Capital Punishment, 16, 23, 29, 131, 132, 134, 212
Royal prerogative of mercy, 10
Salem witchcraft trials, 20
San Quentin, 26, 144, 203, 219
Savings-in-cost, 222
Search and seizure, 235
Self-defense, 136
Sentence to death, 9, 47
Sex–homicide relationship, 135
Shooting, execution by, 251
Sing Sing Prison, 16, 98, 155, 156
Slaves, execution of, 21
Society of Friends, 17
South Carolina, 251
South Dakota, 15, 50, 113, 126
Special provisions on death sentence, 46–47
Sterilization, 247
Suicide, 202, 240

Tennessee, 15, 50, 125, 126
Texas, 188, 199
Theocratic criminal code, 11
Traitors, 9, 146, 155
Trials
  counsel for defendants, 206, 233, 234
  expense, 206
  jury, 30, 31, 121, 136, 150, 206, 233, 237
Truman, Harry S., 86, 87, 199

*Uniform Crime Reports*, 55, 228
United Nations, 16, 177
United States
  Bureau of Prisons, 39, 156, 188, 190
  Department of Justice, 212, 228
United States Constitution
  Bill of Rights, 21
  Fifth Amendment, 75
  Sixth Amendment, 75, 76
  Eighth Amendment, 21, 74, 75, 79, 228, 245–51, 256
  Fourteenth Amendment, 76, 249, 257
United States Supreme Court, 78, 185, 206, 208, 227, 228, 240, 245, 256–57
Utah, 188, 251

Vermont, 32, 33, 50
Victims, 53, 135
Vengeance, 223
Violence, 176, 186
Virginia, 28, 188, 198

Washington State, 15, 50, 125
West Virginia, 50, 188
William Penn's Great Act, 12
Witchcraft and hersey, 20
Women, 51